# Roman... & Melody

## Essays for Music Lovers

by

George Colerick, BA BSc (Econ)

Published by
JUVENTUS
LONDON

First published in 1995 by JUVENTUS, 81 Lumley Courtyard,
Holbein Place, London SW1 8LU

British Library Cataloguing-in-Publication Data

A catalogue record for this book
is available from the British Library

ISBN 0 9524964 2 9

Typeset by York House Typographic
Printed and bound by Biddles Ltd, Guildford

# Contents

# List of Illustrations

# Acknowledgements

I should like to thank the following who have provided information or material necessary for the satisfactory completion of this book:

Mrs Ursula Vaughan Williams, for permission to quote her husband's writings, and a choice of appealing photographs; herself, Marilyn Hill Smith and Maria Alexander, for valuably informative interviews; Professor James Lockhart, for his professional interest and advice; the Metropol theatre company, Friedrichstrasse, Berlin for the stage photographs and archival material; the Society of Authors on behalf of the Bernard Shaw Estate, for permission to quote the great man; Mr Henry Pleasants, for the use of his fine translation of Eduard Hanslick's writings; Le Musee national d'art moderne, Paris, for permission to use the Bakst sketch on the front cover; Henschel Verlag, Weidingerstrasse, Berlin, for the Paul Lincke illustration.

# Foreword

Books on music specially for the enlightened lay music lover are not easy to find. Too often musical history books or books about music are aimed well above the heads of many students of the arts or the general public who attend concerts and opera performances and who listen avidly to serious music broadcasts on radio and television. This book by George Colerick seems to me to fill a much needed gap in the literature. It is well-written, knowledgeable without being dryly academic, and straight-forward without being condescending or popular. I have read it, enjoyed it and learned a number of things for the first time. The book deserves success: it is extremely informative for the interested music-lover – a plain man's guide to music. I can recommend it whole-heartedly.

Professor James Lockhart,
Director of Opera,
London Royal Schools' Vocal Faculty
(Royal Academy of Music and Royal College of Music)

# Preface

I hope these essays, and numerous brief references in the notes at the end of the book, will also be of value to readers who like to pluck unfamiliar tunes from their local music libraries. As many people are intrigued by the relations between music and mathematics, an Appendix is included with some basic explanation and data.

The book is dedicated to friends in Berlin, Helsinki and London who have helped and encouraged me in this venture.

G.C.

Ralph Vaughan Williams, 1952, at Mont St Michel.

# 1   *Classical and Romantic Composers*

Who knows the names of our modern composers? There are obviously many of them but with few exceptions, how many merit attention? They are just taken for granted, and when we mention we have been to a concert, we are as likely to be asked 'who was performing?' as 'what did you see?' for we live in (what is said to be) the age of the performer; but there have been others.

Around 1990, three famous composers died within a few months: Aaron Copland, whose music seems to evoke America's vast open spaces: Leonard Bernstein of *West Side Story*: and Irving Berlin, the untrained musician who wrote so many good tunes. Will they be the last to be remembered for their immediately enjoyable melodies? Nowadays, we have to think hard before mentioning a great living composer, 'popular' or 'serious', whose songs can be enjoyably sung, if only in our baths.

Those three men, all Jewish, were among a number who made a relatively late contribution from the New World to the great Romantic tradition that goes back to the 1820s, from Chopin, Liszt, Wagner, Verdi, Tchaikovsky and Mahler to Puccini, Ravel and other 20th century masters. With the continuing growth in communications, that music from the past will be familiar to a much greater audience in the 21st century, sometimes spuriously on television. Even advertisers and organisers of international sports events have discovered that 'classical music' is quite the most exciting and ear-catching, and with modern recording techniques, we shall have chance to hear the unfamiliar works of great composers and of their lesser-known contemporaries.

These men had unusual lives, often the stuff of real drama, and seemingly more relevant to their creative work than that of composers in other times. They had been poets, composing in response to an inner necessity rather than to the specific requirements of wealthy patrons. This often meant poverty and lack of full recognition in their own life-time. Each had a very distinctive musical personality, and unlike most composers of previous centuries, needed to be listened to in silence.

Music before that had always been composed for a specific social purpose: for pomp and circumstance, for church or the theatre, for courtly or popular dances, for playing in the homes of the aristocracy, or for going into battle. Because it was functional, much of that music, as happens today, was of mediocre quality to be quickly dispensed with. The most clear case of over-production, but on a very high level, was the work of J. S. Bach whose unique intellectual gifts impelled him to compose additional works many of which have been lost or never performed. In the 18th century, music was not taken too seriously; did Joseph Haydn introduce an orchestral crash into his *Surprise* Symphony to stop the chatter or awake the sleepers?

Bach was an exception in many ways, coming towards the end of the great polyphonic era, when two or more melodies could be played simultaneously, and he adapted the style ideally for religious worship. He excelled as well in polyphony's highly disciplined form, the fugue.

From the mid-18th century, the style became 'classical' and homophonic, that is, one melody was dominant, but supported by chords with notes said to be in concord, in a 'desirable' state of harmony.[1] 'Classical' includes the period of Mozart and Haydn, the great neo-classical styles in the arts, when composition was carried-out in accordance with established and unchallengable rules of excellence. Melodies were symmetrical and clearly-defined, with reassuring harmonies and often with pronounced, stable rhythms.

Creating within clearly marked boundaries was not a tyranny, but a prescription which leads to mastery of an art. Haydn perhaps measured his compositions like a tailor measured a suit and comfortably produced some 200 symphonies and quartets, applying to each first movement the so-called 'sonata form', the definitive model which was a great feature of the classical period's contribution to music's heritage.

Although Mozart could take all the rules in his stride, he was 'modern' enough to upset his religious paymasters and cause the 'enlightened' Emperor Joseph II to complain that his music contained too many notes. Yet one has to be very confident before claiming the ability to distinguish all Mozart's works from Haydn's.

The existence of a strict logic did not make the classical period dull; relaxing or breaking rules creates a sense of drama or shock, and original minds know when to do so to the greatest effect. On the other hand, in our own times, it must be extraordinarily difficult to make anything but a brief, superficial impression because rules governing the arts have been largely abandoned. Are we living in a state of creative decadence?

Sonata and symphonic form remains a perfectly rational option for those who are unfashionable enough to write symphonies two centuries later: main subject, contrasting subject, development or argument, climax and conclusion: rather like writing an essay. Yet the classical rules went much further than that and did confine composers to some degree, such as in the range of emotions expressed.

The order of things was to be breached after 1800, most of all, and from necessity, on the part of Beethoven. The emotional intensity of his work increasingly demanded more complex harmonies, more rapid key changes, terse phrases, longer symphonic developments and altogether larger forms. From the classical 25 minutes, his symphonies began to extend to 45, then finally in the *Choral* ninth to 75. Orchestras eventually expanded almost proportionally.

Historical data can be very obliging, and Beethoven's dates (1770–1827) could mark him as the last of the classical and the first of the Romantic composers. In England, we might choose to date Romanticism from just after 1800 – the lyrical poems of Wordsworth and Coleridge – but in Europe, 1815 is a convenient year. The impetus of the French Revolution was finally checked, Napoleon and his neo-classical art fashions were ousted, political reaction was rampant, and young writers could remove themselves from the harsh industrialising world into the realm of pure imagination. The French poet, Victor Hugo, was soon to pronounce that Romanticism was Liberalism applied to the arts. The first generation of Romantic composers were emerging – Weber, Schubert – and the later ones would be addressing increasingly a large, newer audience, the middle class.

Conveniently but not always accurately, we call those composers who received their education before 1800 'classical', most of those who were born after 1880 'modern' and those in-between 'Romantic'. It may seem quaint to regard Bartok and Stravinsky (born 1881–82) as modern, but even today their rhythms and harmonies sound fresh and exceptionally exciting.

Schubert was another exception, a Viennese amateur who happened to be a genius, poverty-stricken, writing for himself and his friends. He was influenced by the popular styles of his native Austria, set lyric poetry to music, then in the sufferings of his final illnesses, produced more elaborate works, some left unpublished for others to discover, before dying at the tragic age of 31. Weber and Rossini became the most important figures of their time, for the future of German and Italian opera respectively. Weber died prematurely but Rossini, late-classical in melodic style, retired early from composing operas in 1829, partly because he was disconcerted by competition from the new upsurge of what we would call Romanticism.

In other directions, composers of great vision and intensity of expression were to become known during or after the 1830s. Some of the greatest, Berlioz and Brahms, considered themselves classicists in spirit, and most would embrace the classical forms, all the same modifying them for their own needs. Those that succeeded developed easily recognisable musical personalities, with very wide, enduring appeal.

Typical Romantic melody began to distinguish itself from the classical models, and the evolving shapes can be traced as a major aspect of music's more recent history. This has also retained an influence into our own times and popular music will continue to feed off it into the future. In that direction, a composer that can pour old wine into new bottles successfully might make a fortune, perhaps gain a knighthood and even have a street named after him in . . . Vienna.

For most of us today, Romanticism's greatest attraction lies in its melodic inspiration and the range of emotions it evokes. Sophisticated harmonies are a special feature of modern European music, and involve it in the expression of an unprecedented range of human emotions. It is also increasingly attractive to non-European societies who may have their own fine musical traditions based on melody and rhythm rather than harmony.

Romanticism from the start found greater richness through its harmonic experimentation. It also involved itself positively with many aspects of human affairs, and is of lasting interest in its original social context, as well as for our times.

## 2   *The Nature of Romantic Melody*

The compositions of Beethoven's final period were so advanced as to be widely misunderstood in the 1820s when they were written, but were to be of great significance for the future of music. The young Franz Liszt was within a few years earning a reputation for interpreting Beethoven's piano sonatas as well as promoting works by his young contemporaries, a practice he continued with some altruism throughout his active life. He did not habitually thrust his own works onto captive audiences; yet he was also composing very innovatively.

He played the piano in a distinctive bravura style, expansive or intimate, tender, personal well beyond the limits of classical restraint, music sounding as if it came from a new world of feeling.

After 1830, the new generation of composers were responding to a wide range of fresh inspirations. There had been a steadily increasing interest in the melodies and rhythms of folk song, exploited in the work of Chopin and Schumann. The influence of *bel canto*, extending and decorating the melodic line for its intrinsic beauty, had been displayed in Italian opera, notably those of Bellini, and can be heard in Chopin's piano music.

These composers were generally very sensitive to developments in the other arts, especially lyric poetry and Romantic drama of the period. There was much enthusiasm for the stark emotions of Shakespeare's plays which clearly had ignored the conventions of classical drama. Berlioz would have sacrificed much in his life to express this perfectly in music; in various musical forms, he was inspired by *King Lear*, *Hamlet*, *Cleopatra*, *Romeo and Juliet*, and the writings of Byron.

It became fashionable to invoke mysticism, rather than the conventional religions. Magic and the underworld were prominent for several decades, especially in opera and the symphonic poem. The irrational was always influential in Romantic art. The *Wolf's Glen* music from Weber's *Freischütz*, even totally removed from its dramatic context, is still very frightening to many children.

The history of Romanticism in music is concerned with the freer use of forms, and of harmonies, 'discords', and chromaticism, with an increasing tendency for melody to stray from its key-note without however entirely losing its centre of gravity.[1] In the half-century from Brahms to Rachmaninov, the long-flowing Romantic melody achieved unique popularity, right up to our own times. The harmonies were becoming richer, especially using chords of the warm, middle pitches of instruments, so creating the characteristically Romantic orchestral sound.

Traditionally, and in the classical period, a melody had been concise, easily defined and closed, that is, it reached a clear ending on its tonic (key-note), with a pleasing cadence. *Non più andrai*, the best-known aria from the *Marriage of Figaro*, has a model symmetry which gives it special appeal even among Mozart's wealth of fine tunes. It is also the slow ceremonial march of the Grenadier Guards. The trio in his 39th Symphony has a similarly cheerful spirit.

On the other hand, the opening of Mozart's 40th Symphony must have sounded very disturbing in the year 1788 and leaves us wondering how his style would have developed melodically if he had not died so soon afterwards. The theme stays clear of its keynote, does not have a formal ending, always pulling back to the start. Its unusual melodic line anticipates developments in Romanticism. A great theme, it has some affinity with the opening of his Fourth String Quartet which has an even more troubled feeling in its chromaticism. Both are in Mozart's 'tragic' key of G minor.

Employing short phrases, which expand or join-up with others, using soft, emotive discords and 'popular' rhythms: these and other techniques were by the middle of the 19th century being practised. Franz Liszt and Frederic Chopin made very emotive use of the piano to experiment with harmonies and to establish new shapes of melody. These included themes, open and extendable, with a capacity for growth, sweeping arpeggios (chords spread out as on a harp), musical sighs, hypnotic effect in note repetition, and leaping melodic lines. The equivalent dramatic declamation, transferred to piano or other instruments became characteristic of early Romanticism; instrumental recitative was to cause heart flutters in thousands of drawing-rooms in every European country.

Liszt's best-known piece, *Liebestraum* (Love's Dream) number 3, relates to sensual love and has a warmth half way to sheer abandonment which makes it a model of Romantic sentiment. It started life as a song, then appeared in its piano transcription, an unusually striking melody both intimate and dramatic. In its shape, it mirrors the feelings of the poet, occasionally finding the repose of its keynote but drifting away, caught-up in the anxieties of the lover, and moments of isolation. There are contrasting rhythms and tension between the left- and right-hand parts.

The first *Liebestraum* has some resemblance, being a fine example of *bel canto*, more tranquil as suits its theme of spiritual love, but not destined for equal fame. Such sounds would have been inconceivable at the time of Liszt's birth in 1811.

Partly in order to give more freedom in the use and combination of themes for expanding on a poetic idea, Liszt invented the symphonic poem. The story, the program, becomes sufficient reason at any time to introduce a new musical idea, without the formal conventions of the symphony. Liszt completed twelve of these, including *Les Préludes*, with its balancing of two rhetorical themes. The symphonic poem, or tone poem, became one of the century's most important formal innovations in the hands of Smetana, Franck, Dvorak, Tchaikovsky and Richard Strauss.

In Chopin, the emotive appeal is often enhanced by the intimate association of melody and harmony, and in Berlioz additionally with striking contrasts in the sounds of instruments, the tone colours. He came to be fully appreciated only in the 20th century where, for example in the work of Ravel and Sibelius, instrumental and orchestral timbre are of the greatest importance.

In the classical period, polyphony was down but not out, and in the 19th century it would play an increasing role in new compositional techniques. It was to be used with startling originality by many, as well as in respect to J.S. Bach, such as in the finale of the 4th Symphony by Brahms.

Wagner was Liszt's exact contemporary and friend, sharing many ideals. He aimed to reform and perfect the style of Romantic opera; his *Fliegende Holländer* (Flying Dutchman), as early as 1845, had dramatic arias and stirring recitative as well as new richness in characterisation and atmospheric colour.

He moved forward from Liszt's notions of thematic development, intending to dispense with operatic conventions whilst merging action, dialogue and aria into a symphonic unity. This was to create virtually a new art form, music drama, with continuous melody, embodied in his *Ring* cycle of four separately performed works. In this way, Wagner's progress became a watershed in the second half of the 19th century, leading to late-Romanticism, with its radical symphonic developments.

The new music made greater demands on the listener and the enthusiasm for Wagner's music reached levels of fanaticism. Increasingly among the late-Romantics, melodies were less clearly defined, but the resulting flow could raise dramatic tension over longer periods, using unfamiliar harmonies, 'discords'. After Verdi's achievements, Italian opera looked for new ways forward in the 'verismo' (realism) of the 1890 and after, and Richard Strauss' music dramas, *Salome* and *Elektra*, were even more radical. For these garishly violent stories, he aimed to increase suspense to unprecedented levels, and was accused by some of taking music beyond passion into neurosis. Arriving at these extremes of expression, he recognised the possibility of composing outside the tonal (key) system, but feared it as a precipice and quickly retreated. After that, he sought a softer Romanticism, and composed some of this century's most glowing melodies. Strangely, though he was born in 1864, it was not very controversial that he was described in the 'Sunday Times' (1994) as 'one of the few popular 20th century composers.' One could say the same for Puccini.

From the late 19th century onwards, it became normal practice in Britain's schools to teach the *tonic-solfa* system, the now familiar diatonic scales (major and minor) on which most music from classical to modern popular is based. This helped the listener to appreciate the more complex forms of sound, and that playing a note out of key either means a move to another one, or creates a feeling of suspense. This effect had been exploited by Liszt and others who experimented with intervening notes, forms of chromaticism. The trend increased over the decades, to reach a peak in Wagner's *Tristan & Isolde*, where uncertainty about key, the tonality, plays a part in expressing the extreme tensions and conflicts of the human experience.

In these conditions, music is less obviously 'tuneful'; instead of dramatic key changes, there may be subtle movements, generating a different kind of emotional response.

By the turn of the century, interest in pre-classical music, also modal and 'non-European' pentatonic scales[2] was widespread. Debussy's opera *Pelléas et Mélisande* (1902) used the 'drifting' whole-tone scale, which to some listeners proved wondrously hypnotic whilst being incomprehensible to others. It certainly distanced him from *do-re-mi*, the tonic system, and therefore from the recent past and Romanticism.

German folk music, which had influenced directly many of the generation after Liszt, used the familiar major and minor scales. Folk idioms in countries further south and east sounded quite different, many using modal and other scales. The emerging schools of nationalist composers were inclined to resist the strong German influence and experiment with the sounds they had known from childhood, but in the works of Dvorak, Grieg and many others, nationalism was applied as a stylistic offshoot of Romanticism and there was no conflict.

The music revolution came in the first decades of the 20th century, from composers who ventured outside the accepted melodic, tonal and harmonic systems. Their work made the final break with Romanticism.

# 3  G. B. Shaw as London Music Critic

George Bernard Shaw, or G.B.S as he liked to sign himself, on being asked what kind of music he liked, might have improvised variations on the theme of 'good' music. Today such an answer would be likely to create confusion or be considered provocative, because fashionable wisdom tells us that all values are relative. That is one reason I particularly enjoy Shaw's musical writings; as he said, the critic who is modest is lost.

Shaw's life spanned those years when an exceptional developing musical culture was reaching-out to vast audiences for the first, and perhaps unchallenged for the last time. Only 20 years old in 1876, when he was first appointed music critic in London, he had a remarkable maturity of judgment, the enthusiasm to address a wide readership, and perhaps to influence change. My special interest in approaching the 2,500 pages or more of his collected musical writings was to observe his reactions to the wealth of new material appearing for about 20 years, until he could no longer specialise in music.

With the lack of recording and the limited opportunities for witnessing music performances in those times, there was always a backlog for the critic to make-up, such as waiting half a century to hear an important composition. One of Shaw's provocatively engaging commentaries followed a rare visit to Paris in 1890 when, he reports, he found fresh cultural evidence concerning the need for a Channel Tunnel:

> The Paris Opera . . . is about 20 years behind Covent Garden; and Covent Garden, as everyone knows, is thirty years behind time, even New York leaving it nowhere.

He is particularly severe on Saint-Saens' grand opera, *Ascanio*:

> There is not an original phrase in it from beginning to end. The tragic scenes are second-hand Verdi; the love scenes are second-hand Gounod; the 'historic' scenes are second-hand

Meyerbeer. A duller pot-boiler I would not desire to hear anywhere.

Posterity it seems might not consider such words too harsh, but he is not even impressed by the love-song, *Mon coeur s'ouvre a ta voix* (Softly awakes my heart), from *Samson & Dalilah*, even though it is so well known as an expression of the archetypal *femme fatale*. Apart from that work, Saint Saens' operas are not widely performed now, though Shaw would probably have enjoyed light, amusing operas such as the *Princesse jaune* if Saint-Saens had been inclined to keep them under wraps in his desire to be considered very 'serious'. He is now mainly remembered as an infant prodigy who did not fulfil his early promise but whose most durable compositions are infused with Gallic wit and refinement.

Shaw had been brought-up in an intensely musical Dublin home, and as a boy he could sing many of the great classics from end to end. He was very well equipped for the post as music critic, which became an important step on the life-long pursuit of delivering entertaining monologues to his readers. The vast bulk of his music writings was completed by the time he had written four distinguished plays and was setting-off on a close commitment to the stage. Musical references are prominent in many of his fictitious works.

His dramatic sensibility powerfully influences his preferences in music, and his comments on opera, music drama and operetta generally carry more weight than those on the 'abstract' forms, such as symphonies and chamber music where his criticisms may lack precision. Though he has sometimes shown a tendency to over-intellectualise, or play-down the human factor, such as in politics, I find no suggestion of this in his musical comments.

In 1876, publicly sponsored music activities were in short supply; there was only one full-time concert hall in central London and opera was fashionably disregarded unless it followed the Italian models and employed that language. With a clear conception of what we should expect in art and entertainment, Shaw attacks with relish the money motive, and the inefficiency and snobbishness which afflicted much Victorian music-making.

I suspect there was a singing teacher in Shaw trying to get out; he was most severe on those who give faulty interpretations of the respected masters. At Drury Lane (1894), his writing accuses Katharina Klafsky of perverting the aim of a great work by converting Isolde's sacred joy over Tristan's death into excessive grief. Even Adelina Patti could have been nearer to the real Isolde than that, though she would have stopped the drama several times for encores, perhaps introducing *The last rose of summer* into the garden scene.

Patti had habitually played roles like a *spoilt child with an adorable voice*. Shaw heard her when her bird-like quality was in decline; as she was not interested in maturing as a dramatic soprano, her fine operatic career was restricted in years. Yet she frequently gave concerts with a wide repertoire, and Shaw could admire her adapting as a superb mezzo, especially singing ballads.

■  ■  ■

Shaw underlined the shortcomings of private sponsorship in the arts, advocating communal enterprise on a generous scale, which fitted his other role as an amateur, campaigning socialist; could not the churches, though not necessarily Westminster Abbey, welcome the poor for alcohol-free dances?

That historical curiosity, the Crystal Palace, was for decades London's greatest musical venue, even though so far out of town, with audiences up to the 80,000s, about ten times the Albert Hall's capacity to-day. It was nearer than any other building to having a permanent orchestra in the 19th century, and soon after its establishment in 1854 had become the most progressive institution for great music. It was there that encyclopaedist George Grove pioneered concert program notes whose wordy seriousness Shaw sometimes laughed at, as when a certain Mr Barrett had chosen to elaborate on Berlioz' admirably succinct write-up for his *Symphonie fantastique*.

It is regrettable that Shaw wrote no memorable account of an event in that building which was burnt-down a half-century later, but he was less concerned with atmosphere than ideas. Many would have found certain occasions very moving, and the following comment hardly conveys the spirit of a crowded event with Gounod's choral music:

The chords of the violins pulsating above the veiled melody of the horns, answered by the clear and brilliant notes of the trumpets in the gallery, transported us all into cloudland.

Now that we have moved into a world where noise has become the most extensive of all personal harassments, we are the more intrigued by Shaw's catalogue of street instruments once available to torture citizens in the 1880s, and bands which, at best, were the only source of musical enlightenment to the poorer classes. Shaw observes that the Germans had imposed an evening time limit even on pianos being audible from the street.

One hundred years later, he would applaud the ways in which opera generally has cleaned-up its act, such as in the much improved acting and athleticism of its singers. As a vegetarian, he had been an early protester that obesity, damaging to opera's stage effectiveness, was inexcusable, except in specific medical cases.

His span as a regular commentator covered slightly more than a period which enabled him to observe Richard Wagner, of the *tense, neuralgic glare*, conducting a scarcely coordinated band of some 170 at the Albert Hall in 1877, to Mahler's performing *Siegfried* in 1892.

He appears not to have travelled much out of London, but his occasional journeys abroad produce some readable impromptus. He spoke of that famous Passion Play, even now still performed 4-yearly at Oberammagau in southern Germany, with praise for its nativity drama and the inspired *tableaux vivants*, but not for the music.

Norwegian Ole Bull wrote and played music in Paganini fashion, and comes in for special praise because he was an honest man, well paid for his great skills, hero-worshipped but fleeced by countless fraudsters whom we might now call agents. He beguiled the sophisticated with his native idiom, and arranged the folk songs of lands he visited so that they did not sound hackneyed.

Shaw's short list of music's immortals would raise no surprise today. Beethoven is described as *the first man who used music with absolute integrity as the expression of his own emotional life*, and only Beethoven and Wagner among the great were receiving anything approaching the respect he believed they deserved in England. J.S. Bach was growing in wide esteem but Mozart was widely regarded as a composer without any depth, whilst Handel's incomparable oratorios, commemorated in the regular Crystal Palace festivals, should inspire intending composers. Shaw was not a generous man, which might have made him a better critic, and his trenchant views backed by a command of musical theory which he uses sparingly help to explain why he is so frequently quoted a century later.

Of the remainder of the composer fraternity, Verdi and Berlioz seem to come off best and the reputations of several early Romantics he wants to reduce slightly. Younger composers can rarely draw comfort from his reviews, and he is perhaps over-concerned with questions of alleged plagiarising. Yet he pursued his musical ideals with a commendable single-mindedness, and as a reformer, he cannot be blamed for colouring the extent of his crusading:

> I was born into evil days, when *Les Huguenots* was considered a sublime creation, and the *Magic Flute* a damned pantomime (as they say nowadays of its legitimate successor, *Das Rheingold*) and when the Ninth Symphony was regarded as a too long and perversely ugly and difficult concert piece . . . (written 1893).

This and Wagner's *Ring des Nibelungen* are works which inspired in Shaw feelings which came nearest to religious devotion. For the centenary of Mozart's death, there is a reflection on the father, Leopold Mozart's, harmful influence; his pressure would have led the boy to a barren formalism, except that Mozart discovered within himself the poetic and dramatic powers which enabled him to break the barriers. Shaw is grateful to German conductor Hans Richter for having re-introduced London to Mozart's neglected 39th Symphony.

*Cosi fan tutte* is *a silly intrigue* but there is praise for what are considered Mozart's lesser works, such as *Der Schauspieldirektor* (The Impresario). This contains lively theatrical parodies, and according to Shaw, all the arias are 'masterpieces', whilst its quartet would be suitable as the finale of a full-scale opera.

As an agnostic, he is grateful that Mozart's *Requiem* transports us away from death into the pure realm of music and a

movement not composed though inspired by Mozart, the
*Benedictus*, is given special praise. Since Beethoven, 'thinking'
composers, such as Schumann, have dropped the Bible and
the liturgy to devote themselves to secular poetry whilst Berlioz successfully used the form of the *Requiem* without religious
intent.

In 1927, on Beethoven's centenary, Shaw reminds us that
18th century music was a dance, a pleasant, symmetrical
pattern of steps and sounds:

> *Only a whirling dervish could dance a Mozart symphony*, but
> Beethoven *threw over pattern designing as an end in itself*. The
> *Eroica Symphony* starts with some patterns, but tremendously
> energised, then they are torn-up in the middle of move-
> ments. He *goes raving mad, hurling out terrible chords in which all
> the notes of the scale are sounded simultaneously, just because he
> feels like that* . . .

After Beethoven, the course of musical history is more
controversial. In an unsigned obituary for the 'Pall Mall
Gazette' (2 August 1886), Shaw equivocates about Liszt's
genius, as well he might concerning a man who covered such a
vast range of public musical activities over 65 years. He falls
back on Wagner's admiration for Liszt as a great conductor,
and interpreter of Beethoven's sonatas, but *who did not commit
himself on the subject of the* Dante Symphony *or* Mazeppa

Yet Mr Shaw committed himself on these two works elsewhere, and in unflattering terms, concluding that, as a composer, Liszt was like a child indulging in noise, speed and
irritating excesses:

> Liszt's range is very narrow as compared with that of Berlioz
> . . . He never surprises you as Berlioz does, by producing
> several different effects from the same instruments. He
> outdoes Berlioz in bidding for the diabolical; but he quite
> misses the strange nightmare sensation, the smell of brim-
> stone, as Schumann called it, which characterised Berlioz'
> exploits in the infernal field.

Liszt lacked Berlioz' musical fertility, but even his failures
deserve attention, being challenging in a broad sense.

Shaw could not appreciate the dramatic fantasies which
inspired Liszt's 'program' works. I suspect he might have been

more impressed by three trombones and a tuba at the gates of Hell if he had believed in Hell.

Shaw was, like the title of one of his books, *The Perfect Wagnerite*; he asserted the importance of philosophy and politics in art and music. That was by way of contradicting in 1899 the view of the distinguished music writer, Ernest Newman, who found the characters of Wagner's *Ring* cycle *dull abstractions drawn from anarchistic and socialist handbooks.*

Shaw underlines the importance of *Das Rheingold*, the least considered of the four parts of the *Ring*, and the most intensely political, with its gods, giants and dwarfs symbolising class war. An affection for its *Leitmotive*[1] is revealed, for example in relation to the visual beauty of the drama:

> The orchestra breaks into the pretty theme when the sun rays strike down through the water and light up the glittering treasure.

To-day, Wagner's *Kaisermarsch* (Imperial March) is much less heard in Britain than in the times of Shaw who expresses a high opinion of it, as most worthy of honouring the accomplishment of German unity in the year of its composition, 1871. Yet that most familiar fast march, from *Tannhäuser*, earns Shaw's accusation, that it was stolen from Weber's *Freischütz*. (Is this not a harsh judgment? Composers often use similar motives but infuse a different spirit).

We might value his account (Bayreuth, 1894) of Richard Strauss' successful conducting of *Tannhäuser's* final act, in which Shaw considers Wagner found enough inspiration to save this rather patchy work. Yet he regrets Strauss' remarkably slow rendering of the first two acts.

The first half of Wagner's career was devoted to creating music relevant to its dramatic action; then he proceeded to write poems, later giving them intense musical expression. Composing hundreds of Leitmotive, musical themes which represent specific ideas and persons, was essential to this aim. The synthesis of music, poetry, drama and the visual arts would be his new form, music drama.

The concept of program music is very important for Shaw's aesthetic. 'Program' relates not merely to music depicting a story, such as in Berlioz and Richard Strauss who also used designated motifs, but broadly as the dramatisation of human emotions.

Shaw asserts that the intoxicating success of the final part of the *Ring* cycle, *Götterdämmerung*, cannot conceal Wagner's political abandonment of the *Ring's* great plan, and, as if the heart had been taken out of his work, he finds the music less moving than in the previous three parts. Wagner had completed the written text (1853) in the aftermath of his revolutionary activities in the Dresden of 1848. Under the influence of socialism, Wagner had predicated that wealth, the gold stolen from the Rhinemaidens, could only be possessed by those that rejected love; humans were not present at the start of the drama (*Rheingold*, first performed 1869), but as it unfolds, they were to be the redeemers in the persons of Siegfried and Brunnhilde.

The music of the final part, with the defeat of Siegfried in *Götterdämmerung*, dates from 1876. By then, the hopes of 1848 had been dashed; Bakunin and the anarchists were seen as hopeless failures, the Paris Commune had been crushed in 1871, Karl Marx had nothing but his theories and political success was registered in the cynical policies of a Bismarck who loathed socialism. *How after the Kaisermarsch could Wagner go back to his idealisation of Siegfried*, even though the *Ring*, like the Communist Manifesto, might be *an inspired guess at the historic laws and predestined end of our capitalist-theocratic epoch*?

Wagner had come upon the theme of Christian revelation and his new protagonist was to be Parsifal, *a fool armed, not with a sword but with a spear which he held only on condition that he did not use it.*

Though Shaw has given an impressive Marxist interpretation of the *Ring*, he concedes that Wagner's beliefs may lack consistency, especially because the artistic impulse is foremost. Perhaps we should not concern ourselves with politics in *Parsifal*, which has so many other facets. Yet it seems that this apparent ideological switch might have limited Shaw's enjoyment of such a contemplative work:

To enjoy *Parsifal*, one must be either a fanatic or a philosopher. To enjoy *Tristan* it is only necessary to have had one serious love affair . . . its second act is an ocean of sentiment, immensely German, and yet universal in its appeal to human sympathy.

Shaw always had an inclination to send cryptic postcards. Around 1884, he surely received one or more in his own style reminding him that Brahms was the great master of absolute music.

Shaw had been exasperated at Brahms' venture into program music with his *Requiem*, resulting in a critical article (in 'The World') which also seems an opportunity to berate Brahms' British 'disciples', Charles Stanford and Hubert Parry, for their determination to compose so many oratorios. Was Shaw indulging in the ideological Brahms-Wagner war which had spread beyond Germany's frontiers, but which leaves modern observers perplexed?

Shaw states that Brahms has enormous musical power but, unlike Wagner, is neither a great thinker nor poet; he is a *sentimental voluptuary with a wonderful ear*. Elsewhere, Shaw finds his Clarinet Quintet 'verbose', the Fourth Symphony 'pretentious' and the First Piano Concerto *a desperate hash of bits and scraps*. There are suggestions that Brahms can be academic and boring, and should have concentrated on his strength as a miniaturist. Some forty years later, in 1936, Shaw confessed he had been wrong about Brahms, having failed to appreciate the idiosyncracies of a great man. He hoped with this confession to serve as a warning to other critics.

Shaw was one of many intellectuals who had difficulty in externalising their emotions, and partly for this reason were specially drawn to Wagner. In what seems to have been a blind spot, Shaw might in some ways have been too similar to Brahms to enjoy his music to the full. Yet he had written most promisingly about Brahms' opus 25 and 60 Piano Quartets on hearing them in 1877, as a very young man, perhaps before the Wagner spell was fully effective.

Though Dvorak's popularity in Britain today depends on other works, he is given short shrift by Shaw for having indulged in oratorio with *weird chords on muted cornets*. He finds the opus 70 Symphony, now renumbered as the seventh, distinctly 'northern' in feeling, but seems not to detect

Brahms's inspiration. The *Dumky Trio* Shaw deplores as dab-
bling in folk dance, not to be commended in its 'Slavonic',
'Hungarian' or other manifestations.

Most remarkably, he places Hermann Goetz in the forefront
of German composers, a great 'harmonist', with his Symphony
in F being judged vastly superior to those of Mendelssohn,
Schubert and Schumann. I do not recall Goetz's music being
played even on radio, and he barely appears in the British
catalogue of available recordings. We can now scarcely comment on a composer who incidentally died at the age of 36 but
may be remembered for a version of Shakespeare's *Taming of
the Shrew*, which Shaw considered the third greatest comic
opera of the 19th century.

As an example of public policy, he praises German municipal enterprise when he discovers cheap tickets for the Frank-
furt-am-Main opera. He even uses the German term
'Volkstheater', a people's theatre, to indicate what we need but
do not have. The Germans are said to produce the finest
conductors:

> The German musician gets soaked in music from his child-
> hood . . . the masterpieces of Beethoven and the music-
> dramas of Wagner; whilst the musical Englishman can only
> thump-out 'arrangements' on a cheap piano.

He can save-up for a once or twice yearly visit to a big city to
hear a symphony conducted by a German expert or an English
novice . . . or hear Gounod's *Faust*.

Shaw admires Bayreuth's *scrupulous artistic morality* and
stage-craft but not its musical sensibility, so hopes that
Wagner's widow will import any lead singers to make up for
some deficiencies, notably some observed in an 1896 *Siegfried*.
Visiting the town, he even complains about the minimum
admission charge of £1. Along with the 2nd class return fare of
£6.50p. from England, that makes the long, tiring journey
questionable for many. He considers that London may well be
capable of superior productions; he understands that the
fulfilment of Wagner's ideals, in particular the staging, will
always be a major problem.

The legend which absorbs Shaw most is *Faust*. He notes that
Gounod has converted Valentin, Margarite's unrequited
lover, (beautifully sung by the young Jean de Reszke) into an

heroic dreamer, and Faust into a weak sentimentalist; but the fine contrasting effect and characterisation of the cynical Mephistopheles with *fascinating* music, such as his serenade, ensures the opera's lasting success. Shaw greatly enjoys Berlioz' picturesque treatment of the *Damnation of Faust*, especially that terrible gallop to hell, the *Rákóczi March*, the supernatural dances, the students' *Amen* parody and the pathos of the love music.

Far less known to us are the *Scenes from Goethe's Faust*, in Schumann's concert version, an exceptional work which also pays some regard to the philosophical aspects. Shaw recalls indignantly that the finale of this was once performed alone in London on the grounds that the first two parts were unworthy. He praises the music of the second part, such as in the scene when Faust is dazzled by the rising sun. It is concerned with Faust's spiritual struggle, and his assertions of freedom and the *life force*[2]. These are the notions which inspired Schumann – primarily a lyric composer – to his most effective dramatising. Shaw grants Schumann one special gift: a strong feeling for harmony as a means of emotional expression. Conversely, on hearing his 4th Symphony, he considers it a failure, particularly its instrumentation, despite a promising opening.

As is the case today, one hundred years ago, the Royal College of Music would play interesting if under-performed operas, and Shaw was pleased to observe 34 females among the strings in an orchestra of 80: more beauty than on the stage. Elsewhere, he predicts that women will be competing effectively with men when they discover that composing is easier than writing. Dame Ethel Smyth comes to mind, but she had not reached full maturity when he was mentioning her compositions.

Schumann's *Genoveva* was the opera to which this College occasion had been dedicated. Shaw considers that it suffered from a foolish plot, frivolous music for a witch and a lack of any musical characterisation. The best music accompanied Genoveva when she was alone in her room. So much for Schumann and drama, but the students had done a very creditable job musically.

Schubert and Schumann are given due respect for their lyrical qualities but Schubert's 'Great C major' Symphony is said to have too many crescendos; and the generally admired String

Quintet has unsuitably long developments. Shaw believed that
Schubert was disadvantaged as a symphonist by attachment to
the ballad idiom.

Less talented than Schubert but more interesting might be
the 'Westphalian' Karl Loewe; Shaw even gives his dates
(1796–1869) and particularly commends to the British a song
about a bell-ringer's daughter which should soar like a Flemish
carillon.

■ ■ ■

Shaw was often critical of many favourites among British
audiences, not least Mendelssohn, not for lack of talent –
beautifully revealed in his *Midsummer Night's Dream* music –
but for indulging in sterile forms such as the fugue. His
oratorio *St Paul* had romanticised the Bible but omitted the
philosophy; Gounod took similar liberties with the Bible as he
had done previously with Goethe's *Faust*. Their works enor-
mously influenced English choral composition and the cult of
oratorios, which had become stereotyped. Of *Redemption* he
might be thought heartless for writing:

> I cannot stand listening to a band practising the chromatic
> scale in slow time for nearly three hours even when it is
> harmonised by Gounod.

Gounod's *Mors et Vita* was of similar proportions to *Redemption*, a great spiritual experience to many Victorian listeners,
but it may now be seen in its massive earnestness as a curiosity
which challenges the patience of modern man. Yet Shaw had
grudgingly accepted its mastery as a composition with the
qualification that it represented *a poetic child's conception of the
music of angels . . . men grapple with the problems of life and death in
another fashion*.

He had pointed-out that it had no more than four leading
motifs, insufficient to be sustained over three hours.

He praised the oratorio *Athalie* as one of Mendelssohn's
finest works, delicate but not suited to the massive treatment
for which Crystal Palace concerts were famed. A chorus of
2,500 he considered superfluous, especially as large numbers
of sopranos are nervous of any note above high F.

Italian opera is selectively criticised and with a confidence
based upon Shaw's close acquaintance with many scores. The
word 'star' was probably first used in its theatrical sense

around the time that Shaw was born, but the most blatant showing-off dated back to the Italian *castrati* of the 18th century when opera had been corrupted to the point of almost ceasing to be a serious art form. By 1850, excellent opera composers had emerged in numbers but decades later, Shaw was seeing fashionable English society still being seduced by meretricious fare and patronising many inferior works provided they were performed in Italian.

Where were the men who would transform the scene in London, giving the people opera in English as part of a national music revival? The tradition of showmanship meant that composers were too inclined to write for the spectacular extremes of the human voice instead of concentrating on the important middle registers and being kind to singers, as was Richard Wagner. He considers that even Verdi could be criticised here and that his middle-period works could be tiring for singers because of the concentration on a narrow melodic interval, the sixth. Yet because the bass voice is not so spectacular, he provided it with specially interesting material, such as that for the hired killer Sparafucile in *Rigoletto*.

Rossini deserved better than his Italian paymasters and composed only as well as was expected of him, which was why *William Tell*, written for the Paris Opera, was his masterpiece. Rossini once confessed to Wagner: *I could have achieved something if I had been German, because I had talent.*

In the 1990s, one may listen with wonder to the sound of Bellini's unique melodic gift as perfected in his last three operas, but perhaps Shaw had a surfeit of beautiful songs. If the music of Rossini's *Italiana in Algeri* seems more appropriate to a girl's finishing school than a harem, that does not interfere with my pleasure. Yet Shaw held out strongly for Wagner's view of dramatic relevance. He also deplored the tearful quality of Italian singing, including most of their famous executants in the criticism of 'bawling'. Partly for that reason, though he welcomes Verdi's final opera, *Falstaff*, he was not prepared to go to Milan for the experience. He might prefer an English production with an international cast, because he was confident it could achieve a superlative performance, even compared with Bayreuth.

When in 1901, Shaw offers us *a word about Verdi* ('Anglo-Saxon Review'), he gives us 4,500 of the best. He finds not the slightest evidence that Wagner had any influence on Verdi's greatest works. The extraordinary popularity of *Trovatore* is explained by its immense appeal to the senses, *its tragic power, impetuous vigour, and a sweet and intense pathos that never loses its dignity.*

Regardless, or because of its preposterous features, it should be played to its full solemnity or not at all. Years later, as the rich flow of inspiration slowed down, Verdi could compensate through his skills, insight and humour. Shaw perceived that Falstaff is an improvement on the Shakespeare original; but describes *Otello* as a play written by Shakespeare *in the style of Italian opera . . . its characters are monsters. Desdemona is a prima donna, with handkerchief, confidante and vocal solo all complete; Otello's transports are conveyed by magnificent but senseless music; the plot is pure farce.*

In Verdi's *Ballo in Maschera*, how could Shaw fail to praise the radiance of Oscar's music, and his lively exchanges with the King, giving perfect relief from the main plot? In 1888, Shaw said he found Ballo *melodramatic, old fashioned* and having too many *cavatinas*. He also criticised that King-Oscar scene at the end of Act I as being in the style of Offenbach. Only the scene in which the conspirators expose the King's presumed mistress earns his praise.

He does not approve the tendency to ridicule Italian operatic quartets of conflicting emotions, such as in Arthur Sullivan's parodies. He points out that quartets were a well established tradition even before Rossini. Verdi's innovation was to replace the conventional, separate *cabaletto* by

a simpler *cavatina* form with an integral *codetta*, combined fearlessly with popular dance and ballad forms, producing the popular, concise, powerful and dramatic solos such as found in *Trovatore*. Its *Di quella pira* is a *common bolero*, but with fine singing, that does not matter.

Henrik Ibsen had established himself internationally with his new, naturalistic conception of drama, by the time Shaw was a young man. Shaw was immensely influenced in his maturing years by this conception of the theatre of ideas, and the use of realistic dialogue. Even though Ibsen's *Per Gynt* was an exception, a masterpiece in the form of a fantasy, Shaw

would not have selected Eduard Grieg as its perfect interpreter. As an example, he refers to the death of Per's mother
when Per tells a story *to beguile the worn-out old woman painlessly
from this world*. Grieg cannot reach this poetry, but relates to the
earlier moments when the mother lay alone; yet the *Death of
Aase* was very moving as music. Shaw's faint praise of Grieg
places him not far above 'salon music', though the term is not
used.

Shaw's inclination towards realism on the stage should have
predisposed him towards the vigorous new movement of the
1890s, Italian *verismo*. He approved Puccini's early *Manon
Lescaut* as an important step forwards, particularly the 'Germanic' features: a symphonic approach, musical linking of episodes and the occasional *Leitmotif*. Puccini is inclined to the
startling chord of the 13th[3].

Unfortunately there is no record of Shaw's reaction to *Tosca*,
though years previously he had condemned the original play
by Sardou. *Cavalleria rusticana* has the continuous and passionate melody to be expected after Wagner, with poignant discords additionally of the 9th, and 11th; a *verismo* mannerism is
employing several snatches of melody, then breaking each one
off on a dramatic pretext. Shaw does not think that, in the case
of the youthful, phenomenally successful Mascagni, Verdi's
true heir has necessarily arrived. The cherry tree duet from
his next opera, *Amico Fritz*, is praised and it seems that Shaw
was once more seduced by Calvé's performance (May 1892),
this time in a more idyllic role. Shaw might seem to be
prepared for the subsequent but sad eclipse of Mascagni, who,
it may be argued, still deserves consideration for seeking new
paths rather than merely repeating the style of the renowned
*Cavalleria*.

One may still find people who affectionately remember the
Carl Rosa opera when it was the foremost, sometimes only
travelling company in England. Shaw is sympathetic to its
conscientious efforts with limited and overworked resources.
Yet it was likely, as in 1890, to overreach itself by attempting
such a precise work, dramatically and musically, as *L'Étoile du
Nord*, (The North Star).

It seems that Shaw was intrigued by its composer, Jakob
Meyerbeer, decades before that man's use of gigantic stage

effects would likely have acted as an influence on early Hollywood spectaculars, notably those of film pioneer, D. W. Grif-
fith. Though Shaw thought that showmanship could divert
Meyerbeer from the finest of purposes, he recognised a
genuine creative vision which was being severely mutilated
and misrepresented in nearly all productions. Whole acts
disappeared even if only to permit the audience to catch the
last public transport home. Yet because of Meyerbeer's exalted
19th century reputation, Shaw turns iconoclast:

> In *Les Huguenots* . . . he set forth the Reformation as a strife
> between a *Rataplan* chorus[4] and an *Ave Maria* . . . *Le Pro-
> phète*, meant to be luridly historical, is the oddest medley of
> drinking songs, tinder box trios, sleigh rides and skating
> quadrilles . . . even John of Leyden is . . . a hero without
> having anything heroic to do, and of having finally to
> degrade himself by shouting a vile drinking-song amid a
> pack of absurd nautch-girls.

Shaw concurs with the view that the librettist Eugene Scribe,
so closely associated with French Romantic opera from the
1830s, was not much more than a hack.

Throughout the late 20th century, Meyerbeer has been
known mainly in Britain by the exuberant march and extrovert ballet music from *Le Prophète*. In a late statement, (1947),
Shaw berates the BBC for ignoring the composer; and he calls
*Les Huguenots* . . . *a really great opera in its class*. As we now take a
fresh glance at Meyerbeer in opera houses, we might recall
Shaw's words of 1877:

> . . . striking individuality, his inexhaustible variety, and the
> piquant contrasts which prevent his longest operas, when
> justly performed, from flagging.

Whilst Verdi, Berlioz and Meyerbeer can offer excellent
models for grand opera, Shaw also welcomes a 'lighter' range
of works, including comic opera, provided the music is worthy
of intelligent, entertaining libretti. Sadly, these do not appear
to be plentiful, but he singles out Cornelius's *Barber of Baghdad*,
especially because he approves of comic opera which satirises
other operatic styles. He commends from its second act the
quintet and opening trio, but considers the patter songs too
heavy, not near enough to Rossini's.

There is praise for a dramatisation of a Zola novel, *Le Rêve*, by a young Frenchman, Louis Bruneau. Shaw presents him as one of the new kind of musician who does not compose apart from drama; they have been liberated from *pattern-making* by Wagner.ᵣThis is a jibe at Joseph Haydn and lesser men of an earlier age.

Tchaikovsky's *Eugene Onegin* is noted for its fine letter and duel scenes but Flotow's once fashionable *Marta* is judged as dull and too long. More importantly, at Covent Garden, perhaps because distracted by the inadequacy of the leading soprano, he seems blind to the possibility that *Mireille*, inspired by the music of the south of France, might be Gounod's finest opera.

If *Mignon* no longer enjoys its earlier popularity, the same Abroise Thomas' *Hamlet* is even less familiar in our times[5] Shaw went against popular opinion in 1890 by declaring it too far from the original to merit the title, and foolish largely because of its libretto; English people could not be expected to accept this language from Hamlet:

Such crime, good mother, were as bad
As kill a king and marry with his brother

Though Emma Calvé was one of several women for whom Shaw had a stage infatuation, therefore hardly trusting his own judgments, he criticises her famous Carmen for denying any nobility in the character, and in a melodramatic performance, disregarding the musical requirements.

Shaw finally has to approve a living French composer when he sees Massenet's *Manon* in 1885, noting his sensibility and a talent in writing for crowd scenes. In *Werther*'s four acts, *the lovelorn tenor only has two active moments*: stealing a kiss and killing himself, so that Massenet's ability to sustain the interest was remarkable. By then, Shaw saw him as an important new voice in opera, avoiding the pitfalls of the Parisian traditions. He was also quite independent, unlike many, of Wagner's influence.

In 1894, Shaw was overwhelmed by a Covent Garden production of *La Navarraise*, with noise levels exceeding even those he had so much enjoyed in Massenet's other works. Mme. Calvé had been *a living volcano* through mortification, despair, fury, terror and finally maniacal laughter, to death.

He had been waiting years for such an experience, and wants more. In this he is at one with London's opera-goers: the blood and thunder as presented by Massenet wins through; Shaw enthusiastically accepts the new realism, French style.

This conversion comes three years after Shaw said of French music:

> . . . colder and less humorous talents waste themselves on bogus classicism, and the lighter-hearted throw away all self-respect and take to what polite policemen call gaiety . . . Paris allowed Offenbach and Lecocq to play the fool with their art.

The comment is by way of praising Messager's *Basoche*, fresh, and ingenious, *high comedy . . . amusing without being slangy or vulgar*. It is tragic that this fine work cannot save Richard Carte's brave attempt to establish a permanent opera house in London, with one production playing nightly for weeks or months. Shaw here may have seized onto a point which a century later is generally accepted; no matter how popular, any opera needs, commercially and artistically, to be part of a repertoire.

He complains of having one evening a choice of five new 'comic operas' in London, but not one symphony, especially as none of the operas deserves much attention. They are mainly imitations of Lecocq who, given Don Giovanni's seduction song, *Ci darem la mano*, would have simply composed the first and fourth lines, then repeated them without altering a note. That had been tolerable in 1873, and Sullivan did likewise in the opening sailors' chorus from *HMS Pinafore*, making the tunes popular and easy to learn. In 1893, that technique was *vieux jeu*, old hat, thanks in part to Wagner.

At issue here is more precisely the decline – Messager excepted – not of opera but operetta or opera buffa, from the wit and verve of the classical originals, such as the *Grand Duchess of Gerolstein*, through the more sentimental Parisian offerings of Lecocq, to the pallid English successors.

Shaw analyses and differentiates reactions to fashion in the theatre. A genre may be deserted rapidly by the disciminating, then by those that can be persuaded through commercial 'puffs' or are just curious about a novelty; but there remains a mob that worships something for a million times its real value, and enjoys itself more as the entertainment becomes familiar, obvious and vulgar.

It was regrettable that because of the language problem, Shaw missed much of the fun when seeing Millöcker's *Poor Jonathan* in Munich, but he appreciated a more luxurious version in London, with comedian Harry Monkhouse portraying a man whose poverty induces his employer to hand-over all his property. Shaw seems surprised at the amount of music – large Viennese quantities composed for such a cheerful work. He thinks there could be a very popular demand for such stage works in London, given the low Munich entrance prices.

By 1910, many critics were declaring London's fashionable musical comedies as vastly inferior to Strauss and Millöcker. (Of course, but not so 'corrupting'?). Shaw defends Viennese operetta: *The public corrupts the artist, not the artist the public.*

He says this cryptically in an otherwise colourless statement to Vienna's 'Die Zeit'. I suspect he was hiding something from the Germans: that the romance and licentiousness of operetta had for him immense vicarious appeal. Elsewhere, he has a joke at his own expense:

> Offenbach's music is wicked, abandoned stuff; every accent of it is a snap of the fingers in the face of moral responsibility; every ripple and sparkle on its surface twits me for my teetotalism.

He pays the Viennese waltz a compliment which seems equally valid one hundred years later; that Waldteufel's are rich with associations:

> . . . the bloom of youth and the taste of love.

He does not spend too much time on the Russians, whose musical development largely independent of the Western European traditions had not excited his curiosity, yet he recognises the skill of Tchaikovsky who can overwhelm his emotions, not his reason:

> He has a Byronic power of being tragic, momentous, romantic about nothing,

as in the *Pathetic Symphony*. His 4th Symphony wins Shaw's approval, being free from the 'feminacy' of most modern

Romantics, yet he thinks Tchaikovsky tends to stick to the same key slightly longer than is justified, though on the other hand he suspects those composers who modulate very often of trying to cover-up their lack of inventiveness.

In July-August 1914, Shaw went to war with Ernest Newman, his last musical *cause célèbre*, in defence of Richard Strauss' later work, particularly the *Josefslegende*. Newman had declared that the post-Wagnerian vein was exhausted, and Richard Strauss with it; there were condescending remarks about *Rosenkavalier*, *Elektra* and *Ariadne auf Naxos* having whole sections which display genius. Newman deplored much ugliness in the music of *Elektra* and the concentration on madness. Shaw's indignant response was to place Strauss among the greatest.

Most revealing in this argument is Shaw's scepticism towards the kind of 'modern' music which Newman is assumed to champion: Debussy, Stravinsky, Scriabin and the atonalist Schoenberg. (Elsewhere, he asserted that Elgar: *could turn out Debussy and Stravinsky music by the thousand bars for fun in his spare time.*)

Shaw comes down heavily on the side of beautiful diatonic melody; he was part of a generation which could hardly have done otherwise.

■   ■   ■

Up to the turn of the century, Shaw could not find a living British composer of genius in the fields of orchestral and chamber music. He would have to wait until Elgar's First Symphony was heard in 1909 to reverse his pronouncement two decades earlier that the symphony was 'dead'. We can even infer from his writings that since Beethoven, the symphony had generally not progressed, except that Wagner had incorporated its essentials into his final dramatic works.

He believed the cults of Mendelssohn, favoured by Queen and Court downwards, and Brahms, considered a paragon in academic circles, had hindered the development of creative genius in Britain. If, for example, we hear Stanford's *Irish Symphony* today, despite some folk material, it sounds quite Germanic, with a mid-19th century, sometimes Schumannesque flavour, so that Shaw's adverse criticisms are not surprising. In a well-known article titled *Going Fantee*, he mockingly presents a conflict between the *aboriginal Celt and the Professor* in Stanford's symphony.

Shaw argues that great folk songs have achieved their highest form and require no further development, so that Liszt, Brahms, Dvorak and many others should not have indulged in such ventures. In this manner, he dispenses with the great fusion of Romanticism and nationalism which was underway during his youthful years.

Irish composers and dramatists had been very prominent in the London scene, but he makes nothing special of this. Consistent with his political philosophy, he tends to joke about 'national' matters, such as his country's folk music, regretting its characteristic sadness; the English, at least, avoided that feeling in theirs.

Contemporaneous opera seems to have embraced some very insubstantial music, whereas many libretti often had the heaviness of Victorian melodrama. This style for example must have put Frederic Cowen at a disadvantage in his opera concerning the virtuous *Pauline*:

> Villain (to the newly-wedded Pauline): *I'll taste these lips ere I depart; resistance is in vain.*
> She: *Fierce indignation fills my heart. Base coward, wretch, refrain.*
> He: *I shall not be by insult awed – no help is near.*
> She: *O, for a husband's arm.*
> Husband: *Pauline, thy Claude is here.*

Shaw does not quote this, but it helps to explain his irritation. Yet the libretto had been based on Bulwer-Lytton's *Lady of Lyons* (1838), according to Shaw a successful play of 'enduring' quality. The composer is allegedly unable to give the music any dramatic relevance and should keep to composing ballads.

Even the 789th performance of *Dorothy* could not detain him until the end. It is a chance for him to commiserate with the cast suffering over long periods for a relatively unworthy operatic cause. He concedes that *Dorothy* had enormous success in the provinces, but he does not mention that his sister Lucy on tour had taken the soprano lead.

The girl Dorothy was presented as an innocent, in keeping with what was to be expected from an English heroine, unlike her Continental counterparts, rather absurdly when singing the conventional *Come, fill up your glass to the brim*. The music by Alfred Cellier is 'pretty' but the source material 'stupid'; yet Shaw prefers Cellier's music to that of his (then) popular French counterpart, Planquette, who composed *Les cloches de Corneville*.

Shaw enjoyed a performance of a Gilbert work, *The Mountebanks*, with Cellier's music. Sullivan had quarrelled with Gilbert after refusing to work on this play and we are left with some curiosity about a composer good enough to have taken-over from Sullivan but who can now scarcely be found on any recordings.

One who may now benefit from the proliferation of C.D. is Goring Thomas, who wrote the opera *Esmeralda*, on Hugo's familiar *Notre Dame* story. Shaw was exasperated that this English work had to be performed in French, – for London – but thought it more interesting than Gounod's *Roméo et Juliette*, a remarkable comment considering his admiration for the music accompanying Juliette's sleep.

Shaw details the plot of Thomas's *Nadeshda* (1885), a blood-spilling drama of feudal Russia, seemingly to prove that British opera had not moved beyond the cliché and melodrama of the mid-century offerings. It enjoyed passing success, perhaps deserved in the case of the second act finale, but Shaw detected in both operas French, mainly Gounod's influence. Thomas may have used more technique than Donizetti, but could not adequately represent humans musically or make subtle distinctions between moods . . . a modern opera composer should be an observer of men and manners, especially with Berlioz and Wagner as guide.

A curiosity from an older, fairly prolific composer, George Macfarren, can still be heard. It is the overture to *Chevvy Chase*, and possesses an unusually wild feeling associated with hunting music. Shaw had once enjoyed it and probably knew that Wagner liked conducting it, so he travelled as far as Shoreditch for a revival in 1889, perhaps the only one, of Macfarren's *Robin Hood*. He could find nothing favourable to say about opera or performance and was specially disappointed because the worthy aim had been to offer cheap entertainment of quality in a less fashionable district.

He speaks well about a now-forgotten opera and composer Isadore de Lara's respectful treatment of an episode in Buddha's life, *The Light of Asia*. It included a mystical, voluptuous song, *Loosen thy foot from the bangle*, and much 'seraglio music'; what the production lacked was sensitive staging and adequate ritual dancing, so that a very promising concept may have been spoiled.

Arthur Sullivan is 'never dull' and has exceptional gift for ballads which touch on the dramatic. Such a talent, one infers from Shaw, would not be helpful to the composition of symphonies or grand opera, and Sullivan's success stands, even against his wishes, only on his contribution to comic opera. By implication, Shaw disposes with Sullivan's grand opera, *Ivanhoe*, which had a remarkably short career.

Shaw praised the succession of Gilbert & Sullivan's Savoy operas, and none moreso than *Utopia Limited*, which he considered Sullivan's finest music, a most enjoyable late collaboration with Gilbert, and more lavishly produced than any other. Two songs are credited with accompaniments worthy of Mozart in his great operas. The plot makes great play with Gilbert's view that limited companies are fundamentally dishonest; that made total sense to the socialist Shaw.

Gilbert's extraordinary satire, and the condemnation of government through political parties, certainly impressed and may have influenced Shaw years later when he wrote *The Applecart* which he called a political extravaganza. But was *Utopia* too subtle for its audiences? Its lack of popularity is attributed to Philistines and 'the mob' whom Shaw subjects to an elitist battering. He had no difficulty, unlike most present-day socialists, in reconciling elitism with socialism.

Perhaps Shaw was unjust to three opera composers whom his near contemporary, opera specialist Edward Dent, considered in the 20th Century to deserve reappraisal. The prolific Charles Stanford and Goring Thomas who died perhaps before fulfilling his promise: Hamish MacCunn was a Wagnerian who evoked the music of Scotland, as we still hear in his tuneful overture *Land of the mountain and the flood*. Shaw surely had the opportunity around 1894 to comment on probably his finest opera, *Jeanie Deans*, a Walter Scott adaptation.

The one unprecedented development given most sympathetic treatment was Rutland Boughton's annual musical festival at Glastonbury, his Bayreuth. That man had a vision for British music but unlike Wagner, he had no King to finance him. He

> began in village halls in Somerset, with a piano for orchestra and his wife as scene painter and costumier . . . the singing and acting was done by anyone who would come; and a surprising number of distinguished talents did come.

Boughton staggered from one financial crisis to another, but the enterprise continued into the earlier decades of our century and became respected as a unique form of English music-making. Shaw does not of course mention that he helped to finance it.

Amateurism? In the best sense, yes, but Shaw had witnessed some inspiring examples, and also known erratic or inferior performances from professional orchestras:

> From voluntary enterprises, I can often recapture something of that magic which music and drama had for me in childhood . . . commerce in art seldom achieves the things that do matter.

In the professional field, grand opera no longer had any monopoly on the finest singers, who might appear in the theatres for lighter works and the increasing number of 'musicals'. Of these, Shaw distinguishes in the early 1890s two categories: one created by a team of talents dedicated to one aim, such as at the Savoy Theatre, and not dependent on the whims and ruinous salaries of famous artistes: the other the consequence of a 'speculator' finding a libretto and an empty theatre, then fishing around for diverse personalies to expedite and popular artists to sell a product of uncertain quality. In any case, London had an excess of talent which might guarantee success for any entrepreneur that could wisely select and manage talent; so he had no sympathy for those that fail. He was of course writing at the peak of the London theatres' popularity which would begin to decline between 1900 and 1914.

In 1894, he pays tribute to a fine Parisienne artiste, Mlle Yvette Guilbert, notably for her *Chansons* (1) *ironiques* and (2) *legères*. In *La pierreuse*, he is exceptionally moved by her dramatic presentation of the guillotining of a man. Yet her delicacy,

wit and gaiety would be an object lesson to the best artists of
the English music hall.

These also have their strengths, which are mainly their
excellent intonation and sense of rhythm, certainly in the case
of Marie Lloyd, and not the vulgarity of their songs. Shaw
regrets that no-one wrote witty lyrics worthy of Miss Lloyd's
capacity for humour.

I can imagine Shaw in knickerbockers performing a knees-
up to the riotous *Ta-ra-ra-boom-de-ay*, with, as he says, *three low
kicks . . . and high kick on boom*. In May 1892, he ventured to
observe Miss Lottie Collins' rendering, and was delighted with
her self-possession, restrained tempo and planned artistic
achievement. To me, the tune sounds like a debased, accelerat-
ing version of *La donna è mobile*, but Shaw calls it a *figuration of
the common major chord* such as to be found in themes from the
opening movements of Mendelssohn's Violin Concerto and
Beethoven's Septet.

He often called at music halls, especially in the comfort of
the great Alhambra Theatre at Leicester Square. It was here
he ventured to comment none too favourably on current ballet
practices, and he must have upset most of the purists by
elaborating on the artificialities:

> The monotony and limitation of the dancer's art vanishes
> when it becomes dramatic. The detestable bravura solos . . .
> belong to the same obsolete phase of art as the 18th century
> florid arias written for the singing virtuosi . . . would soon
> fall into ridicule.

We are inclined in England to assume that one is not a
fanatic for both opera and ballet; some might have concluded
that Mr Shaw was not a balletomane. Perhaps, like me, he
generally prefers ballet to be seen in opera, with courtiers,
soldiers, devils and seductresses briskly adding to the drama.
It would be consistent that he argues for ballet to be dramatically relevant; and he was writing nearly 20 years before the
phenomenon of Diaghilev and the *Ballets Russes* occurred.

When war broke out in 1914, Shaw was one of the first to
condemn it as a form of madness. He remained concerned
with peaceful activities, such as arguing for municipal orchestras in seaside resorts – like the one playing at Torquay – to
attract the sophisticated holiday-makers who could no longer

travel to the Continent. Encouraging the enterprise of the Torquay Council was intended ironically; he would have sued them for overcharging him to hear a Beethoven symphony with a band of merely 20, if the musicians' efforts under such strain had not been so commendable. Why not employ German prisoners-of-war to make good the number?

He wanted every child to have access to good music without charge, which I assume would require symphony orchestras and substantial music theatres in every county. He suggested a state-supported theatre for at least 1,500 capable of performing Wagner and Shakespeare, and proposed for the purpose, a site on Richmond Hill overlooking, or at Hampton Court alongside a beautiful stretch of the River Thames.

He lived to see established a new theatre for opera in English (Sadlers Wells, 1931) and a full-time company at Covent Garden (1946); but not London's ultra-modern concert Festival Hall (1951), now an architectural classic, or the National Theatre (at the Old Vic, 1964, and in a purpose-built complex, since 1976).

After 1914, Shaw's musical writings were only spasmodic. He enjoyed an occasional protest, supporting a long-term musical cause, wrote the previously-mentioned tributes to Beethoven, whilst in 1922, he wished to place Elgar's *Apostles* in the rank of Bach's *St Matthew Passion* and Beethoven's *Missa Solemnis*.

He did not trouble himself to comment on later developments in popular music; no doubt the microphone would have signified the end of singing. Yet he did make a comment which dealt effectively with what would have been a topical misapprehension in 1927:

> Greenhorns write of syncopation as if it were a new way of giving the utmost impetus to a musical measure; but the rowdiest jazz sounds like the *Maiden's Prayer* after Beethoven's third *Leonora* overture; and certainly no negro corobbery that I ever heard could inspire the blackest dancer with such *diable au corps* as the last movement of the Seventh Symphony.

In 1938, he attempted to interpret the views of younger music-lovers who tended to regard Mendelssohn and Schumann as *drawing-room composers*, whilst Bruckner and Mahler were *expensively second class*. He reinforced the current vogue of Sibelius, *the inventor of a new art form and a new harmony technique*, having escaped from the past more easily than Brahms and Strauss had escaped respectively from Beethoven and Wagner.

His unfulfilled ambition was to become a youthful centenarian, but physical frailty defeated him. Playing music at home remained a valued pastime, even when his old voice could only suggest the melody. At the age of 94, he was still susceptible to female charm; the talented Irish-born film actress, Greer Garçon, called and persuaded him to accompany her in music hall ditties on the piano. It was his last known performance.

# 4   A Dissenting Critic

I n 1846, an emerging 22 year old Austrian music critic, Eduard Hanslick, wrote an article in praise of Wagner's recent opera, *Tannhäuser*, which he had just seen in Dresden. He declared it to be *epoque-making*, just as *Don Giovanni* had been in 1787, *Freischütz* in 1821 and Meyerbeer's *Huguenots*, 1834. He acknowledged the exceptional scope of the work, the great dramatic power, its originality in orchestration, enthusiastically expressed:

> The magical trembling and fluttering of the music, the diabolically alluring upward and downward rhythmic curves, the fairy-tale weaving and dancing and singing . . . pictorial fantasy, sentiment, medieval atmosphere, German character and customs.

Diabolical? The knight Tannhäuser would be a hero more attuned to the 1990s than the 1840s as he emerges from the lustful arms of Venus to disrupt a national song contest with verses which would have shocked medieval society. His earthly lover, Elizabeth, eventually dies, seemingly of distress, and the story would be reprehensible if Tannhäuser were not also to arrive in Rome as a sincere penitent seeking the Pope's forgiveness.

For anyone wanting evidence of Wagner as a 'very tuneful' composer, the work has splendid examples: Elizabeth's festive greeting, the well-known march, the pilgrims' theme, the love song to Venus: whilst the overture fits comfortably into programs of 'popular classics' which still fill London concert halls. The work is not overplayed, mainly because it is so demanding of resources, from its scenes of pageantry to the elaborate portrayal with large corps de ballet of sensual love at the Venusberg.

Wagner's forthright melodies and intrusive orchestration implied a decisive move away from the decorativeness of traditional opera, and from *bel canto*. Yet he had once written a coloratura aria in respectful imitation of Bellini, and Hanslick wrote affectionately of such works as Bellini's *Norma*:

> Who has since written a melody with the long, sweet breath of *Casta diva*, or a song more expressive in its ultimate simplicity than that of the final duet, *Qual cor tradisti*? . . . Sensuous beauty and vocal charm dominated opera in those days, just as the specifically dramatic dominates now.
>
> (Written 1885 concerning the soprano Lilli Lehmann)

The 1840s were an interim period in Italian and German opera; Verdi was maturing and Wagner was about to change direction. *Tannhäuser* and *Lohengrin* (1848) might be thought of as close siblings, operatic giants, but for Hanslick, they were not:

> Who is Lohengrin? What is the Holy Grail? . . . Our first requirement of a drama is that it presents us with real characters, persons of flesh and blood whose fate is determined by their own passions and decisions . . . How meagre are the individual characters in *Lohengrin* compared with the life of the masses within it – a collection of stereotypes without development and without climax . . . What lifeless stage props are Telramund and Ortrud compared to similar characters in Weber and Spontini.

Criticisms of aspects of the music are equally devastating:

> That Wagner understands declamation is one of his most decisive attributes. That he presumes to replace melody with rising and falling recitation is at once the root and flower of his error. I know of nothing so fatiguing as these half-recited songs in *Lohengrin* which never stay more than four bars in one key but with infinite evasiveness, continue from one deceptive cadence to the next until the ear, exhausted and resigned to its fate, lets them go where they will. In this cold plunge of harmonic surprises, the listener soon reaches the point where he is incapable of further astonishment . . . Wagner's music affects the soul less than the nerves; it is not moving so much as externally exciting, painfully concentrated, sensually and poetically exquisite.
>
> I find in *Tannhäuser* incomparably more freshness and vitality. In *Lohengrin*, Wagner is more single-minded and

consistent, but he has become a fanatic in his tunelessness. What counterbalance has he . . . ?

It is to be found in his treatment of the orchestra, his instrumentation with clever use of tone colours and its elastic application to the text . . . makes the music seem dazzlingly new, exotic and fabulous and completely acceptable as a substitute for real music.

Written in 1858, such statements were early references to Wagner's move from 'opera' towards composing 'music drama'. From that time, Hanslick would at best refer to moments in Wagner which pleased him or damn whole works with faint praise; for Wagner, the composer of the ultimate in 'the comprehensive work of art', such criticism was intolerable. Wagner was a vindictive man, and Hanslick whose words in 1846 had earned his gratitude became seen as the bitterest of enemies.

In the comic opera, *Die Meistersinger von Nürnberg*, Wagner decided to pillory an appalling musician and critic in the character of Veit Hanslich, a name later changed to Beckmesser. That provided a good deal of knockabout humour, though as satire, it is crude and 'over the top'; even so, the word 'Beckmesser' still carries its symbolic meaning in music literature. In 1874, Hanslick wrote about this opera, of course ignoring Beckmesser's implied association with himself, but concluding that musical humour was not Wagner's strength. Yet here:

Wagner has given us lively pictures of the German people of the Middle Ages. These artisans of Nuremburg with their simple, Philistine adventures and plain doggerel verse are preferable to the ecstacies and bombastic, stuttering alliteration of *Tristan & Isolde* or *Das Rheingold*.

Hanslick much prefers the third act to the other two, and can hardly fail to praise the great vocal quintet or the exemplary songs given to the drama's 'Romantic hero', Walther von Stolzing, yet in general he considers that *Meistersinger* has the faults of the later music dramas, such as excessive length, too much importance given to the text, the dominance of the orchestra over the voice, and the *continual use of dissonant chords when the ear expects a concluding triad*.

To us a century later, these last phrases indicate that the argument goes beyond Wagner, so that Hanslick stands as an early protagonist in the debate over melody and 'modernism' which has continued even to our own times. He takes a critical look at Wagner's associates, in particular Liszt whom he does not appear to regard as a significant innovator, except of the symphonic poem:

*The main prerequisite is that music be based on its own laws and remain specifically musical, thus making even without program a clear, independent impression.*[1] *The main objection to be raised against Liszt is that he imposes a much bigger – and abusive – mission: either to fill the gap left by the absence of musical content or to justify the atrociousness of such content as there is.*

Of Liszt's 12 symphonic poems, Hanslick by 1857 had heard or sight-read nine, finding *Les Préludes* the best of an unimpressive group. This is today the only one ranking as a popular classic, with its two striking main themes, I would say even memorable, but thought by some to have no more than a 'vulgar' appeal. Hanslick admitted the work could have a very 'stimulating' effect, but found traces of banality, the themes being neither original or profound. In fact, Liszt had transferred the melodies from other works, so Hanslick was right to suggest they had been *added to a finished work by mere cerebration.*

Hanslick lived until the turn of the century, long enough to pour cold water on the early, world-shaking symphonic poems of Richard Strauss, whom he likens to a chemist that prepares heady concoctions which he would rather avoid. Another *substitute for real music*?

So Hanslick is remembered as an opponent of 'program music', his criticisms going back from Strauss, Wagner, Liszt as far as Berlioz. Against it, he posed the concept of pure, 'absolute', music of whom Brahms by the 1870s was to be the master, such as in his four great symphonies. Wagner and his disciples had (allegedly) denied the possibility of writing symphonies after Beethoven, or the need for purely instrumental music. The symphony was to be superfluous once he had transplanted into his music dramas. Hanslick asserts that this 'nonsensical theory' is contradicted in Brahms' long succession of instrumental works.

Nor was Hanslick to be isolated, as the dispute, and other differences over Wagnerism, spread into western Europe's music circles. For decades, there were distinguished names 'for' and 'against'.

In 1886, Hanslick visited London and in the limited time available, looked for signs of promise among England's composers. His written conclusions were hardly encouraging, and he noted that opera generally was not flourishing in London. These remarks could not have offended Shaw; even so, he wrote nothing about this visit, which is not surprising.

# 5 *Brahms' Piano Quartets*

**B**rahms is one of the few composers whose greatness cannot be disputed, like J.S. Bach whom he so much admired. It is difficult to imagine him being neglected at any time; nor is there much argument about his inferior works, because he destroyed or recycled nearly all of them. Yet some of the admirably crafted works of his maturity may lack the inspiration of his greatest.

I was still at school when I felt the impact of those major compositions which he addressed to the world at large, their spiritual quality, the uplifting sound, massive architecture, control of rhythmic patterns such as I had never conceived. He soon posed just one problem for me because he had not composed any symphonic works to be played in the concert hall beyond the eleven for orchestra which were well known: a *German Requiem*, two serenades and a few shorter choral works, and those *Hungarian Dances*.

That forced me to look further, for the first time into the realm of chamber music, songs and the piano. Only a relatively few works had been recorded, and one did yet not conceive a time when all of one composer's works could be heard and analysed in the leisure of one's home. I recall that still into the 1950s, individuals were advertising in the magazine 'Gramophone' to buy second-hand copies of Brahms' Piano Quintet, marginally the most played of his great chamber repertoire.

No-one's compositions for the piano are more substantial than Brahms', starting with those three youthful sonatas whose exceptional size alone must have daunted some new listeners. That quintet is well complemented by three quartets in which he combined piano, violin, viola and 'cello with great assurance, opus 25, 26 and 60. Conveniently, I recently found them issued as a set recorded by the Borodin players, and set off after so many years for a new experience, at least in the opus 60.

Brahms' private life would not have made many headlines, as we think of headlines today. His first attempts to complete a piano quartet are therefore of unusual biographical interest, the years of emotional stress and indecision of his mid-20s, the death of his friend Robert Schumann in 1856, and his ambivalent feelings for Schumann's wife, Clara. She in turn appeared to suffer confusions, such as possible jealousy that Brahms might be eyeing her daughter, Julie. She may also have influenced his decision not to marry the daughter of a Göttingen University professor, Agathe von Siebold. That abortive love-affair was sublimated in several of his works, and a late novel by Agathe.

Brahms is generally remembered, from the late photographs, as a tubby, bearded old gentleman, but when in 1853 Clara's daughter first saw him aged 20, she described him as handsome, with a mane of fine blond hair. Very sensitive and retiring, he suffered his emotional torments without revealing much to others, and, not without some regrets, gradually assumed the characteristics of the inevitable bachelor.

All that certainly remains of that early quartet reflects the deep conflict which he felt concerning Clara. Its first movement has a similar starkly dramatic quality to the start of the First Piano Concerto which dates from that period and is also related to the Schumanns. It opens with a terse, atmospheric passage such as one might expect in a late Beethoven quartet, but which surprisingly serves only as introduction to the fiercely driving first subject, building up to a movement of exceptional power. It is possible to hear a disparing call of 'Clara' in a descending violin phrase, as suggested by some biographers. The serene second subject is Schubertian.

That quartet movement existed for nearly twenty years before it appeared as the first movement of the Third Piano Quartet, opus 60, with only small modification. Brahms even gave a literary reference, to Werther's suicidal passion for a married woman in Goethe's novel. That melodramatic work, named after its self-destructive hero, had astounded an earlier generation of literate Germans and acting like a drug, had itself brought disaster to some impressionable young minds.

The *scherzo* which follows is probably a cut-down version of the finale from the early quartet, and has some affinity with what has gone before. Though the troubled feeling is not dispersed, it is vigorous even by the standards of the youthful Brahms, though once again there is a brief interlude nearer the style of Schubert. The remainder of the work dates from about 1875; the gently flowing slow movement has the deep beauty one finds in middle-period Brahms, and there is a characteristic cross-rhythm passage which brings soothing release. The finale though sombre seems to inhabit a different world. It uses frequently the disturbing rhythm of Beethoven's 'fate' motif, though the piano gives a pleasing diversion by slightly mocking the chorale-like second subject before the work abruptly ends.

Before meeting the Schumanns first, in late 1853, Brahms had worked from Hamburg as a piano accompanist to a violinist, Edouard Remenyi, who was a Hungarian refugee and had brought much of his native folk music. That had increased Brahms' enthusiasm, which explains why concert-goers today are likely to be familiar with purple patches of Hungarian ('Magyar') or gipsy inspiration in two finales: the magnificent rhetoric of the Second Piano Concerto and the gipsy fiddling of the Violin Concerto. Brahms also exploited the excitement and rubato in his *21 Hungarian Dances*.

Yet the Hungarian influence was first most clearly apparent and even dominant in his second youthful undertaking of a piano quartet; this was completed in 1861 as opus 25, and therefore numbered one. Though it is a masterwork, it is unconventional, such as in its wanderings from chamber music into what sounds like symphonic territory.

Has the work a larger number of cohesive melodies than any other in the repertoire of chamber music? It is possible to identify by ear at least six in the first few minutes of the opening, more than most composers could satisfactorily deploy in fewer than 15 minutes. They have so much fire and colour that Brahms was able to dispense with a *scherzo*, and used instead for an *intermezzo* the most gentle tempo in the whole work. Then what starts as a slow movement with a very noble melody turns into a triumphant march which suggests blazing trumpets.

The finale begins and ends with a wild *csardas* which has a scampering little running-mate. The second subject is treated like a parody of Hungarian dance gestures, the swaggering male and overtly seductive female. This is exuberantly 'light' music of a very high order.

Arnold Schoenberg often performed in the work and decided to give it the orchestration which it merited, even needed. The outcome later produced some joking comments about 'Brahms' Fifth Symphony'. Though Schoenberg is widely regarded as a symbol of musical austerity, he cut loose here to give the work the most colourful treatment it could stand, and one which Brahms would never have contemplated, even apart from the astonishing use of the percussion instruments. It has the qualities at any time to become a very popular concert show-piece.

The originality of the youthful Brahms' structures appears to have confused at least one of his early admirers, Eduard Hanslick. In 1862, his conservatism led him to regret the lack in Brahms of a 'continuous stream of development' whilst a century or so later we would see this favourably as an expression of turbulent Romanticism. He considered that Brahms used themes less for their inner content than for their contrapuntal potential, which was only sometimes the case. Most surprisingly for me, Hanslick described the opus 26 melodies as 'insignificant'.

This Second Piano Quartet followed almost immediately and is seen as a close sibling. It still finds Brahms willing to let his hair down and looking beyond Germany's frontiers for inspiration. It is slightly less flamboyant but equal in quality of inspiration.

It starts with an incisive rhythm on a commanding theme which the piano possesses, later in delicious contrast to some lush string playing with a suggestion of a slower, sinuous gipsy style. As with the First Quartet, there is a wealth of melodic variety, and this confident movement runs luxuriantly to nearly 20 minutes. It is followed by a magnificent singing *adagio* whose dreamy lyricism is briefly interrupted by a passionate melody, under-used considering that it is so fine. Though Brahms calls the third movement a *scherzo*, it is unusual because it is developed in sonata form and the more relaxed tempo which he employs might call for some very graceful 18th century dancing, so belying the title. The finale's main theme is memorable for its special energy, and the contrasting one is near to the German folk idiom. Brahms gives this movement plenty of space before bringing a genial and unusually long work to a satisfying conclusion.

These three compositions, then, with nine or ten movements virtually completed before Brahms was thirty years of age, show the confidence and vigour of his earlier years. The first two quartets have those jubilant finales which would have been inappropriate in the third, where Brahms could not find a fully convincing conclusion to such an emotional work.

These compositions say more about his relation to the music of Schubert than about the often-repeated saying that he was the heir of Beethoven, and Hanslick saw the influence of Schumann's later style. As for beauty, if I were permitted to take one hour of Brahms' chamber works to my desert island, these three slow movements, and that to the First String Sextet, would probably be my choice.

# 6  *Proms & Monsters*

L ondon's promenade concerts have now achieved one
hundred consecutive seasons and been broadcast to 45
countries. The program format has generally followed
a similar aim, which has been to present mainly large-scale
works by the great composers.

The initial concert of the 1895 summer season, though not
intended to provide a pattern, cautiously paid tribute to the
relatively low-brow tradition of promenade concerts which
had occurred spasmodically during the previous half-century
in London and some other cities. What the new organisation
had in common with the earlier conception was a policy of low-
prices but good quality of musicianship, and a one shilling
entrance charge, enabling far more people to attend than at an
all-seater event.

That first program of 1895 played works by 21 composers of
whom over half are still very well known and admired, whilst
eight are forgotten: ten songs, several instrumental solos, a
grand march, the highlights being the overture to *Rienzi* and
selections from *Carmen*.

The pre-1895 promenade concerts in London are less well
documented. They took place in theatres with the seats
removed from the stalls, and offered the same kind of entertainment as many all-seater 'instrumental concerts'. An adver-
tisement for two such events on Friday 20 February 1846 is
specially eye-catching. These were to take place in Cheltenham, and without promenade facilities, the cheapest entry was
two shillings.

The organiser was Monsieur Louis Jullien, famed for his
activities in London and beyond throughout the 1840s and
1850s. He and some of his companions had travelled by the
new railway system, of which a main-line extension to Cheltenham had recently been completed, so that its good citizens
were specially privileged by comparison with most other
provincial centres where such visits were not yet feasible.

M. Jullien conducted, and of his seventeen credited assistants, nine had foreign names, a modest proportion even though most of them were almost certainly English. Signor Sivori was in the afternoon to follow Paganini's example by playing a fragment from Rossini's *Moses in Egypt* on one string, but without the help of the Devil who was said to have presided whenever the old maestro performed that prodigious act.

Herr Koenig was perhaps the most valued member of the entourage, frequently enthralling everyone with a cornet-a-piston and playing his own composition, the *Post Horn Galop*, which is still a curiosity that everyone has heard but which has not earned him a place in Grove's *Dictionary of Musicians*.

The overture would be a lively alternative, from Auber's opera *La Barcarolle* or Flotow's *Stradella*. Beethoven would be represented by his triumphal march and a movement from either the 5th or 8th Symphony, sufficient for Cheltenham though London might hear a complete work occasionally with one or more military bands. Nor were the infernal elements to be excluded: the afternoon interval would be followed by four arias from *Robert the Devil*, an opera so notorious as to be correctly written-up as *Robert le Diable*. Its creator had his name mis-spelt as Meybeer, a strange error concerning a man thought by many in the fashion of the time to be the greatest living composer.

For the evening, the diabolical Robert was to be replaced by excerpts from Donizetti's *Lucia* and Bellini's *Puritani*, but with clarinet solos instead of being sung.

Apart from cornet pieces by 'Roch Albert', M Jullien had composed the remainder of the program. His skill in special orchestral arrangements would be shown in his set of quadrilles from Verdi's popular *Ernani*, and his polkas would take us in our imaginations as far as Hungary, Bohemia and Douro. His *Cricket Polka* was not related to the hard-ball game but to Charles Dickens' *Cricket on the Hearth*.

He assures the readers that his new *Redowa Valse* will be as great a favourite in the 'Salons of the Nobility' as his polonaises and mazurkas. Well, a decade previously, the waltz had not been quite respectable because it enabled a man to get at least one hand onto a sensitive part of a woman's body, and even France's poet of the future, Victor Hugo, had condemned it as having a *lascivious, circular flight*.

M. Jullien had immersed himself into popular British culture, resulting in a composition which had to be performed both afternoon and evening: the *British Navy Quadrille*. The fleet takes to sea, the men dance a hornpipe, the Bay of Biscay and the origin of gunpowder are celebrated in song, there is heroic declamation and *Vulcan's Forge* is not forgotten.

Seats for the afternoon show were sixpence more expensive than the evening one. Since it began at 1.30 pm, why was it called a morning concert? This suggests linguistic association with the term matinee, but perhaps also that the idle Rich did not take breakfast until mid-day.

The great impressario-composer-conductor had numerous tricks available, including someone to play that mighty serpentine bugle, the ophicleide. His showmanship was nowhere better displayed than in his 'Concerts Monstres' which he had initiated one year previously in the comparative remoteness of the Royal Surrey Zoological Gardens before 12,000 spectators. For the 1849 show at the same venue, advertised in English, excerpts from Meyerbeer's latest operas had to take top billing: his relatively unknown Prussian work, *The Camp in Silesia*, and almost straight from the printing press, his Parisian sensation, *The Prophet*. Alongside them, a composition which was much famed in its time but is now regarded at best as an interesting museum piece, Felicien David's symphonic ode. *The Desert*.

24 'Roman' trumpets, led by the formidable Herr Koenig and double orchestra, were to play Bender's *Triumphal March of Julius Caesar*. Each bar of *God Save the Queen* would be accompanied by an 18-pounder canon, and there would be an enactment of the storming of Badajoz, presumably without the rape and pillage. The whole performance, including fireworks, would be over in five hours.

Though we laugh at some reports, Jullien was no vulgar commercialiser, but a daring entrepreneur with musical flair and vision, in addition to white conducting gloves and a jewelled baton. He could be very adventurous by introducing relatively unknown works, such as Beethoven's and even attempted to popularise opera in the English language. The reward for that and bringing Hector Berlioz to conduct a London season in 1847 had been bankruptcy: but that had been a common experience in those days of bold private enterprise. He recovered in time to become very prominent in London's International Exhibition of 1851, where he exerted himself to achieve even wider fame. Even so, he was a fine example for other undischarged bankrupts not to follow.

Yet the final words on the 1847 failure can perhaps be left to Berlioz' distinguished *Mémoires*, if we remember that his writings had an imaginative force second only to that which he lavished on music. Jullien's invitation that Berlioz conduct an opera season, in English no less, at Drury Lane seemed to offer hope of relief from accumulated problems in Paris. Jullien had engaged an impressive ensemble, but allegedly had given little time to the choice of works. The venture depended upon a new opera, *The Maid of Honour*, from Richard Balfe but it would fail to produce enough revenue. A safety net was to be Donizetti's *Lucia*, which could not take the estimated £400 nightly needed to cover initial costs. Jullien's final emergency plan was that Berlioz should prepare in six days from scratch the monumental *Robert the Devil*, including non-existing translation and stage effects.

Berlioz wrote that Jullien had an equally ineffective selection committee which included Sir Henry (*Home, sweet home*) Bishop, famous for his efforts to popularise operas through altering even the finest foreign ones before the British could hear them, and therefore a man who must have been anathema to Berlioz.

Berlioz wrote that he received no payment for London commitments, having written the sum off against Jullien's presumed 'madness'. Years later, he waived his claims when the debtor appeared in a Parisian bankruptcy court. Jullien's gratitude took the form of an improbable commitment; having recently heard *the music of the spheres* and received from God (*seen in a blue cloud*) an exhortation to make Berlioz' fortune, the wretched man then offered to 'purchase' his latest masterpiece, *The Trojans*, for 35,000 francs. Jullien (1812–60) was by then on his way to a debtor's prison and death in an asylum.

# 7  *1866 And All That*

Paris is the foreign city which most inspires the fantasies of the English. It is the image of the 1890s and also that of the Second Empire (1852–70) which are most likely to provoke a wish to recreate the past. If I could obtain a time-machine for 24 hours, it is to one of these periods, on which so many words have been written, that I would choose to return.

Republican France at the turn of the Century is quite familiar to us through photographs, and we can still envisage central Paris as the Impressionist painters revealed it. Not that it has changed much superficially, the boulevards and fashionable high buildings retaining their places whilst many other European cities have altered almost beyond recognition, and not in all ways to the good. I often try to imagine the old Boulevarde de Clichy at night, and on a recent visit looked from outside at the Moulin Rouge, which is now no more than an expensive tourist theatre, far removed in spirit from the popular dance-hall where Toulouse-Lautrec painted and fraternised or more with the artistes.

By contrast, Paris of the Second Empire is far more difficult to visualise; because so few painters and cameras had reproduced it, we are left with the lifeless impressions of the lithograph. At the start of the period, 1852, much of the ancient city was intact but in two decades, many of the slums were torn down to make way for the great thoroughfares we still recognise. Those fundamental changes were followed by the destruction of historic buildings in the cataclysm of the 1871 civil war.

The spirit of the times is best felt in its literature and music, the materialism, the extravagant living of the privileged and the grinding poverty of the majority. With the sudden collapse of the Empire, Emil Zola was collecting data and descriptions of those years, including the low life. He sought the guidance of a distinguished man of the theatre, Ludovic Halévy, before writing his classic novel about the demi-monde, *Nana*. This opens with a description of a banal play, decorated with inferior popular music, about the Greek gods.

The anti-heroine, Nana, like many of her modern counterparts, has a weak voice, cannot act but, as the 'Blond Venus', wins the enthusiasm of her male audience by displaying her tall body almost nude. She is destined to seduce, humiliate, reduce to poverty and eventually destroy rich men, but she is also a metaphor for the Second Empire. They both reached the height of their success in the 1860s and expired in 1870; as she lies on her death-bed, the mob outside, seized with war fever, shout repeatedly 'To Berlin!'

*Nana* shocked many by its alleged realism, or more especially, by its concentration upon human weaknesses; but it is, in my view, a moral tale narrated with some sophistication. Nana despises both her banker and her aristocrat patron and is drawn to the violence of the criminal class; retribution comes to her in the form most certain to destroy her youthful beauty, small-pox.

Nana was in part a characterisation of Parisian celebrities, such as singers Blanche d'Antigny and Hortense Schneider. Yet Schneider had a good voice, and a striking stage presence, which, to judge from photographs, was more likely to attract men than any exceptional beauty. She performed in the finest musical plays of her time, and, though she may have had even more lovers than Nana, she ended her days as a pious old lady in a convent.

It is to a day in the June of 1867 that I would most like to direct my borrowed time-machine. The International Exhibition which had opened in Paris during the Spring was the most important display for world technology up to that time, and rivalled in scope Britain's 1851 exhibition. Foreign visitors included most of Europe's leading statesmen and the world's monarchs, who would therefore have their evenings free to meet more informally, and enjoy entertainments probably more numerous and varied than in their own countries.

It was an opportunity for the Emperor Louis Napoleon III to impress with the more prestigious aspects of his regime; it was also his second and last Exhibition and in retrospect a most ominous feature of the show was the appearance of the latest in long-range artillery, manufactured by Herr Krupp in the Ruhr, a western territory of Prussia.

The arts were well represented, reflecting also the increasing interest in distant civilisations, with the exceptional musical culture of Brazil making its mark even among the broader populace.[1] France could boast of progress in the development of wood-wind instruments, the modern clarinet and its new offspring, the saxophone.

It would have been a rare chance to attend a promenade concert to hear Johann Strauss play with his own orchestra. He had been glad of the invitation to the Exhibition specially as he was under a cloud at Vienna. A recent composition had been a flop, mainly because its words had given political offence, but it was worth trying again in a foreign place. It had enormous success there under the title of the *Blue Danube*.

The Parisian theatre was, creatively and socially, the most influential in Europe. In particular, it set the criteria for grand opera, which in length was to last a whole evening in its vast 5-act format; with elaborate ballet sequences late in the performances, permitting the more privileged among the male audience to eye the female performers perhaps in hopes of making closer contact. Such theatres attracted cross-sections of society, from the aristocracy, politicians, foreign dignitaries and the intelligentsia to the courtesans, young fortune-seeking men and *la vie bohème*.

French opera had achieved over decades a dominating international prestige, and as an institution, it was therefore a suitable target for humour and ridicule. One of the first into this field had been a German boy who had settled in Paris at the age of 14, revealed an early talent for musical parody and soon applied it to the stage. With the support of Halévy and other writers, he had extended the scope of such works with topical social and political comment. By 1858, his first large-scale stage work had been converted into a satire of classical Greek legends, grand opera and of the French Imperial court: *Orpheus in the Underworld*. The composer, Jacques Offenbach.

On 14 April 1867, his seventieth stage composition, the *Grand Duchess* had its premiere at the Théâtre des Variétés. It was a glittering occasion famed for a unique non-political revolution planned by a leading Parisian socialite, the Princess Sandor-Metternich, in collusion with several other ladies. To

public astonishment, they appeared without wearing crino-
lines, and at a stroke destroyed a fashion which had lasted for
decades; society women were suddenly liberated from the
tyranny of steel wire. Unencumbered by a crinoline, the
Princess had decorated herself with brilliant red coral on a
much-admired gown of Havana brown. This colour was
henceforth, and for confused reasons, associated that summer
with a most distinguished visitor, the Prussian premier, Count
Otto von Bismarck. He, however, also made the gossip for his
resplendent white cuirassier's uniform.

It was one of many enjoyable and profitable times he had
known in the city. Earlier, as Prussian ambassador, he had
often spoken to the French Emperor. This Louis Napoleon
had taken his famous uncle's name with a view to emulating his
achievements. Bismarck had detected Louis' ambition to
extend France's territories, and had speculated on how to
manipulate this knowledge to Prussia's advantage.

Bismarck came from the Prussian land-owning class and
shared their prejudices. Germany had consisted of about 300
small states until just before his birth, but that absurd feudal
system had been abolished at Napoleon I's intervention. The
new German confederation contained a handful of viable
states, and a further 30 that were still extremely small. Prussia
was by far the largest and most powerful, and the rising
Bismarck schemed to end Germany's ramshackle political
system by asserting Prussian supremacy in some kind of unity.
This would involve ending the privileges of the petty rulers
and their politicians, an aim which would require vision,
determination and presumably other, less admirable political
qualities.

Within four years of becoming prime minister, he had
advanced these aims by defeating in turn Denmark and Austria on the battlefield. The political settlement of 1866 placed
Prussia, through its voting power and its army, effectively at
the head of a new North German Confederation.

That settlement was a blow to the tradition of Particularism,
which legitimated the rights of small German states, but the
south German leaders were the more suspicious of Bismarck's
aims, especially as some of them had in 1866 sided with
Austria in war. She was now excluded for the first time as a

major political influence in the German situation, but conditions were not yet ripe for total unification of north and south Germany.

The arguments for such a move were economically very strong, and popular sentiment among south Germans was not as opposed to the idea as their governments, so Bismarck required some external factor such as a foreign enemy which would help to solidify German opinion. Might France be manoeuvred into such a role?

Louis Napoleon had often expressed his belief in the principle of national unity, so should not have opposed it in Germany's case. Yet he was also looking for an impressive international success, such as annexing Belgium or Luxembourg, and Bismarck allegedly hinted that some deal to that effect might be possible. Yet by 1867, Bismarck was pulling-back from any commitment, creating in Louis' mind an impression of bad faith.

At that stage, but with an aura of victory and statesmanship which impressed his hosts, Bismarck arrived in Paris accompanied by Moltke, the distinguished strategist who had planned the Austrian defeat and achieved it in 18 remarkable days.

That June evening, the two men visited the fashionable Théâtre des Variétés and during the interval, they could walk in the adjacent narrow streets without apparent fear of anarchist violence. That was just a few years before the start of a cycle of assassinations against leading European politicians. Moltke was a man of few words but Bismarck is quoted for his approving comments about this musical, including the play which had been written by Ludovic Halévy and Henri Meilhac. It was their fourth to appear as a very successful collaboration with Offenbach in three years, and it presented a comic-strip view of war and diplomacy.

The first of the four had been *La belle Hélène*, the ultimate send-up of Homer and the Trojan war. Their latest collaboration, finally renamed as 'the Grand Duchess of Gerolstein', satirised targets far nearer home. Offenbach's music, and the presence of Hortense Schneider in the roles first of Hélène and then the Duchess, ensured full houses. When the Tsar of Russia wired from Germany for a box, some other party had to be dispossessed.

The *Grand Duchess* created more problems for the censor than either *Orpheus* or *Hélène*. The Emperor did not object to the ridicule of high society because Offenbach had the privileges of a court jester, but the latest sensation might give offence to many of that summer's distinguished visitors. It also seemed to point at the sinister sexual life-style of Catherine II of Russia, grand-mother of the existing Tsar.

The stage Duchess is less interested in affairs of state than those of the heart. She is likely to punish a discarded lover or promote to general any man to whom she takes a fancy. The problem was resolved almost at the last moment; Offenbach agreed to invent a ludicrously small German state, Gerolstein, of which she would be head. The joke had suddenly been turned away from the Russian court towards those tin-pot German rulers.

The play's second most prominent character is an army commander, General Boum, who lights his cigars with gunpowder, but has little idea about its more important uses. That is clear from the rumbustious song for bass. *Piff Paff Puff.* Comic though it sounds in the 1990s, it had an extra bite which is no longer generally felt. In Meyerbeer's opera of religious war, the *Huguenots*, a fanatical Protestant soldier had a song of the same title, but with murderous intent towards Catholics; the audience would have applauded the parody wildly.

Some weeks before Bismarck attended, the Austrian Emperor was in Paris, but did not see the *Grand Duchess*. He would not have enjoyed references to incompetent generals who can lose a war in a few weeks.

The stage-play also featured unscrupulous politicians who plan battles as a diversion from domestic problems; and the censor was concerned that the play even made reference to the Duchess' favourite, Fritz, winning an 18-days war. Did the clownish Fritz equal General Moltke? Reference to 18 days was removed; but what would Bismarck think of all this?

He found the humour relevant, commenting:

That's just it . . . We are getting rid of the Gerolsteins.

He was also pleased that the French were so inclined to laugh at militarism: did this mean that they had no spirit for war?

Distinguished visitors were often introduced to Schneider whose private life was becoming a legend in Paris; but off-stage, the two Prussians were not specially impressed with her. She was said to have a special weakness for royalty and had earned the nick-name, *passage des princes*. Edward Prince of Wales made his presence felt with her that summer and at other times, and she went to St Petersburg at the invitation of the Tsar. As a box-office draw, she could name her own terms, but not so easily to Offenbach because she could not separate herself from his music; yet many and theatrical were their quarrels. She also liked driving round Paris being 'mistaken' for the Grand Duchess of Gerolstein, and she appreciated the extent to which her image was accordingly enhanced.

The theme-song is a fiery invocation of the Duchess' father's sabre whilst the ambiguous *Ah, que j'aime les militaires* permits a depth of passionate commitment which might not be fitting in a duke.[2] This was Offenbach's most rampant score, with galops, marches and a new can-can in headlong rush, and might have provoked one critic to speak of its creator express-ing the sexual instinct in music. Yet there are arias with operatic tenderness such as *Dites-lui* (Tell him I love him), a classic expression of a proud woman reduced to humility by love. In a soothing nocturne, the participants seem to want to sing *Bonne nuit* until they fall asleep.

It is now thought that the *Grand Duchess* lacked the consist-ency of *Hélène*, mainly because of the plot-laden second act, but its 'military' panache made it at that time the greatest of all operetta sensations in Europe and the USA, appearing within months at Vienna and Covent Garden, then in Berlin and Budapest. Even the formidable critic, Hanslick, had attended its premiere and was later to infuriate Wagner by references to Offenbach's genius.

If my time machine had conveyed me to the theatre on the evening of Bismarck's attendance, he would no doubt be most curious to meet a *bona fide* time-traveller. He would be appalled to learn of the carnage of the two 20th Century world wars because sometimes he felt remorse for the 80,000 men killed in battles with which he had been associated. For him, war was diplomacy by other means, but to be discharged very rapidly, a *Blitzkrieg*, to be settled round the conference table.

Offenbach would be too busy to entertain someone from outer space. In any case, he had enough creatures of fantasy in his stage works. He was a master of improvisation. After every premiere he might work day and night revising, partly in response to audience reaction, to find the perfect version. He took control of production, then would delegate as he moved-off to another venue. That summer, he took his season at Bad Ems, entertaining in the presence of Bismarck's monarch, King William, and the Prussian court. This should not have been too demanding an activity, though Offenbach's late-night activities, in the absence of his wife, were likely to offset any benefits the water might have had for his rheumatism. Even so, this politically harmless annual activity would later be held against him in certain small-minded French circles.

Exactly three years later, King William and Offenbach were again at Bad Ems. Bismarck was far away in the east on his estate at Varzin, but in no mood for relaxing. A possible diplomatic crisis was at hand. The King was having talks with the French ambassador about proposals for the succession to the Spanish crown, and Bismarck fretted at not being present.

The Spanish royal line had come to an end and the prospect of a foreign successor would not be advisable if the French saw such a development as contrary to their interests and security. One remembered that in 1700, a major war had started over a disputed Spanish succession. Now a prince was being pro-posed from the Prussian royal family, the Hohenzollerns. Whatever suspicions this may have aroused, it is not certain that Bismarck was involved in the plan.[3] The Prussian King was anxious to avoid offending the French and when they objected, the prince withdrew his candidature.

Louis' health was bad at that time, which may help to explain his lack of judgment; and his advisers did not advise caution. They sensed that there was an opportunity to win a diplomatic victory by demanding that the Prussian claim would in no circumstances be invoked in the future.

Bismarck was being kept informed by telegram and imagined the King being bullied. He deliberately altered and publicised the wording of a telegram he received in order to create the impression that the King had snubbed the French ambassador at Ems. The effect was to inflame national senti-ment both in France and Germany. Within a week, France had declared war, and the south German states were drawn into supporting Prussia.

The French could not mobilise sufficiently fast and were outmanoeuvred; seven weeks later, they were defeated at Sedan and the Emperor was taken prisoner. He was forced to leave the country, humiliated after his warlike postures which no longer concealed the suspicion that he had fallen into a trap. Classic hubris; during his final exile in England, he might often reflect that the 1867 exhibition had represented, to all appearances, the last of his international successes.

Bismarck came once more to France, this time to impose a peace treaty. Whilst there, he was able to negotiate with the other German rulers his country's unification as the Reich. He became the Imperial Chancellor, and the Prussian King was crowned German Emperor.

The French catastrophe was not over; under the Paris Commune, citizens rebelled against the central government. The city suffered total disruption, mass slaughter and reprisals, leaving much bitterness after the re-establishment of public order under the new provisional Republic.

National humiliation led to a search for culprits and scapegoats, with some chauvinists imagining that public morale had been systematically undermined. Had not Offenbach helped to corrupt society with his 'decadent' creations? Was he not a Prussian who regularly hob-nobbed with the King at Bad Ems? And a favourite of the now-disgraced Louis-Napoleon?

Implying he was a Prussian is like calling a Londoner a Scotsman, but he had been born in the Rhineland and still spoke with a strong German accent. In a letter to the 'Figaro', he had stated that he felt French to the core, and later, he referred publicly to the 'savage' behaviour of the Prussian army, wishing full retribution on Bismarck and arms manufacturer, Krupp. Certain German newspapers called him a traitor; Offenbach was caught between two choruses of unreason, and was very hurt, concerned especially for his relatives in the Rhineland.

Parisian theatres had been closed during the war emergencies and only recovered slowly. A theatre composer. Lecocq, said that Prussian shells had brought about the end of operetta, meaning that in 1871, it would be expedient to keep off politics and satire. Popular taste wanted to forget the past and new forms of escapism would be welcome, so he intended to benefit. His own talent lay in more sentimental comic operas in which he enjoyed outstanding success for the rest of his life.

Offenbach bounced back with *King Carrot*, a complex satire on kings and republican politicians at a time when France hovered on the brink of royalist counter-revolution. Significantly, it was produced at a theatre in a working-class district of Paris. It was his most ambitious work to date, on a vast scale including a ballet illustrating the earthquake at Pompeii. If the new fashion was spectaculars, he was ready for it. Instead of intimate works in his playhouse, he would offer 4-act productions in large theatres. Cast and musicians might together number 300. The venues would be hired or bought. Fortunately, for him money was no object and he proved it several times by insolvency.

Offenbach had no direct successor or equal in France, but by the time he died in 1880, he had created an original, lasting form of musical theatre. Curious that though German-born, he now seems to embody the lighter Parisian spirit in the years of the Second Empire.

1871 marked the high point of Bismarck's career. It seemed as if he had planned the major developments over the recent years of German history, but one cannot reckon the significance of chance and human error in the outcome. Certainly, he had furthered, for whatever motives, a cause which history approved.

He presided over state affairs for two more decades during which he needed peace and stability to consolidate the new Empire. His image was accordingly modified as time passed and he presented himself to Europe's statesmen as a peacemaker, the 'honest broker'. Nevertheless, the political intrigues of that period make unpleasant reading.

He recognised some of the essential paths of modernisation, such as a state-owned railway which was promptly established, and he had a part in the origins of a German welfare state, what we would term elementary social security. That was motivated not so much by sentiment but because he saw it as a necessary step to prevent the rising socialists increasing their popular vote.

In those years, Germany took the decisive steps towards being a great industrial state, tribute to the efforts and abilities of the nation. Bismarck was a very intelligent man but it is debatable whether he was guided more by vision or by political expedients.

Statesmen tend to receive overall more praise and criticism than is justified whereas in the long run composers generally get their deserts.

# 8  *The Appeal of Viennese Operetta*

The Vienna of Beethoven, Schubert, the Strauss family and beyond into the last years of that quaint pre-1918 Habsburg ('Austro-Hungarian') Empire has passed into musical nostalgia. The City retains something of its old shape, and three traditional music theatres remain active, but many of the little streets, or *Gassen*, have disappeared.

One hundred years ago, the Theater an der Wien and the Volksoper along with perhaps half a dozen other large theatres, were dramatising sparkling music in classical operetta. Many dance favourites were heard in these theatres, alongside the attraction of more varied and exotic rhythms. Operetta was a variety of opera, just as demanding artistically, and with special features, such as the dependence on clearly enunciated speech and the combination of song with movement in set pieces which at the high moments bring audiences to a state of excitement relieved by synchronised clapping.

It allowed persistent rhythms and more melodic repetition than opera so was quickly popularised. It drew a proliferation of beautiful tunes from Johann Strauss, Franz von Suppé and many others during the late 19th century, and acquired also snob appeal as it was frequented by royalty and high society. The chance of social and financial success led to imitation, with hundreds of composers producing operettas of lesser quality. Meanwhile, Englishmen were composing religious and choral music in large quantities.

Vienna's many-sided musical culture, throughout the 19th century and beyond, had interesting racial implications beyond the other important social ones. Some of those in the chaotic 1990s looking appalled at conditions in central Europe might even wonder how far the Habsburg Empire offered for a long time an unusual kind of multi-racial stability. It stimulated an incomparable variety of musical achievements. Talented young people from Hungary, Poland, Bohemia, Croatia and beyond embraced the German language and the cosmopolitan culture centred on Vienna, adding to its achievement.

A thousand operettas came to fill growing demand and varying styles developed from Budapest to Berlin, from Moscow to Madrid, where insistent Spanish rhythms had helped to create the staged musical, the *zarzuela*. Today most once-popular operettas are forgotten but at least one hundred are of exceptional quality and can still be heard in concert extracts. Such performances are still very widespread, partly because they are much easier and cheaper to organise than full-scale productions, though they lack the extra dramatic significance and fun of being seen in the authentic context. The greatest operettas remain part of the operatic repertoire and are correspondingly lavish and expensive. This is of course a major obstacle, along with the cost of media publicity, to their being part of the commercial theatre even though music of comparable quality is in decreasing supply there.

Classical or 'golden Viennese' operetta offered rich material for coloratura sopranos, flighty soubrettes, soulful contraltos, dashing tenors, comic basses and ardent mezzos, often as 'principal boys'. New dance fashions might be introduced, and waltzes moved from dance-halls to the lyric theatre, sensuous or tender.

There was no place for the tragic operatic plots; men praised the beauty of women and the anticipation of sex, sopranos sang of romance and fulfilment. Hatred and other negative emotions were placed out of sight. Jealousy appeared, but only as the object of laughter. Villains plotted and threatened, but must never succeed. Fools were over-confident or misinformed. Heroes and heroines suffered confusion and anxiety, but emerged better for their experiences.

Did this lead to some kind of dull formula in plots? Not necessarily; some very talented men of the theatre were at hand, and even where a story was fanciful, it was expected to follow its own logic, to make a well-constructed play. One mechanism which offered rich possibilities was the arrival of a stranger in the second or third act, to throw everyone into a state of visible excitement or confusion.

Most dance composers could not compete in this new genre, but Johann Strauss the younger matched the drama and characterisation superbly to his music. One only needs to hear *Fledermaus*, in an excellent English translation, to appreciate that. Yet it was well-known that his genius did not extend to selecting the finest stage plays. There are anecdotes about his being shoved-off with second-rate ones which would easily sell on his music, so that lesser composers could have the best ones. That is how he ended-up with *A Night in Venice*, a tiresome story with fine music including the dreamy gondola serenade.

*Fledermaus* and *Gipsy Baron* are more performed than his 14 other stage works, because of their consistent melodic inspiration and more interesting plots. They also had sharp edges which did not please everyone who first saw them; *Fledermaus* flamboyantly ridiculed the idle rich; the *Gipsy Baron* was based on a book which had promoted the rights of dispossessed Hungarian peasants. The plot was modified to become a symbol of Austro-Hungarian solidarity, with one sentimental song calling those peasants 'poor but loyal'. No pressure group has ever been so well represented musically, but the plot had retained its charm whilst losing much of its bite by the time it was translated into English; a slow betrothal waltz later became a Hollywood 'hit' with the title *One day when we were young*.

*Fledermaus* is not just a random collection of beautiful songs; its opening phrase from the overture influences melodically much of what follows. The work stands as a perfect model of the genre, with the teasing *My dear Marquis*, champagne and laughing songs, the liberated *Chacun à son goût* and the flowing chorus of international bonhomie, *Brother Mine and Sister Mine*.

That might well have won the special admiration of his great German contemporary, Brahms, who commented:

That man oozes music, unlike most of us.

After Strauss' death, some of his less successful operettas were chopped-up for commercial purposes, such as the very popular waltz medley, *Roses from the South*, taken from the *Queen's Lace Cloth*. Some material was re-presented as pastiche. *Casanova* is remembered for the *Nuns' Chorus*, but the most successful, *Vienna Blood*, is still widely performed in Austria and Germany.

The best of classical operetta was sophisticated, spectacular and avoided cheap sentimentality. Dialogue was witty and speech in emotional scenes could be greatly enhanced by background music, which fulfilled the original conception of melodrama. There was always an organised 'opinion poll', the theatre claque, hopefully to applaud virtuosity or whistle at inferior products.

In the more subtle works, the action could be enjoyed on two or three levels because burlesque of grand opera as well as social and political satire were optional attractions, though the Viennese did not generally concern themselves so much with this as Hervé and Offenbach in Paris, or as much with the lyrics as Gilbert and Sullivan.

Franz von Suppé had entered the operetta field earlier than Strauss, graduating from theatre duties in which he composed set-piece material for traditional Romantic comedy (*Singspiel*) and farce (*Posse*) which, Suppé felt, needed replacing with a genre which matched words to music, both spiced with wit. His *Tannenhäuser* was a Wagner send-up which followed a vogue of composing farcical 'alternatives'.

He then created a succession of excellently-crafted one-acters. The *Girl's Finishing School* had a sextet very close melodically to the famous one in *Lucia di Lammermoor*. There was a multi-national parade of music styles in *Ten Girls and no Man* (punned in English as *Ten Belles without a Ring* in a 1981 version). A father mounts a stage show to impress suitors with his ten daughters' musical skills; as a travelling actor, he had mated with sopranos in whichever country he visited. The strong burlesque element is bringing this work renewed popularity in the 1990s, such as a reduced one-hour version, *Six Girls*, which is being performed in German opera foyers.

In Suppé's *Beautiful Galatea*, Pygmalion creates a physically mature, flirtatious woman, but the humour lies in her not understanding the implications of sex. It has one of several overtures still very popular in concert halls and including the most dashing of all, for *Light Cavalry*, a 'military' operetta written only for male voices.

Suppé retired for some years, then returned with his two large-scale masterpieces. The first, *Fatinitza*, had a march which became a European and American 'hit' of the late 1870s. *Boccaccio* (1879) had the dimensions of Italian opera, with large choruses, and showed the strong influence of Suppé's uncle, Donizetti. It even enabled Suppé to race ahead of the faltering Strauss in popularity.

It presents Boccaccio as the resourceful hero, serenading in Italian his *bella Fiorentina*, a hectic Italian counting chorus, *Undici*, and there are songs and a march of a decidedly Germanic flavour. Boccaccio's classic story of adultery is flavoured with the bawdy *Fassbinder* (Cooper's) song which is astonishing even for Suppé's taste in unsophisticated rhythms.

In comedy style, one unexpected incident can set-off a chain of piquant situations, as in Karl Millöcker's *Beggar Student* (1882). Colonel Ollendorf, commander of a Saxon garrison in Poland, kisses, uninvited, a local girl on the shoulder, then to be struck by her fan. So a conflict of sex, snobbery and national pride follows. The colonel is aware that the girl's mother is an impoverished snob, and plots to exploit her weakness by palming-off a young 'beggar' as a bogus Polish aristocrat anxious to become her son-in-law; of course, the plan is thwarted by youthful love.

Ollendorf's role has become one of the finest of swaggering buffo parts, and he reminisces as if to gain kudos from his momentous rebuff with the show-stopping waltz melody which changes directions as if to suggest the ambivalence of his gesture. There are delicious 'character' trios for the Polish women and soaring love duets which spell further humiliation for the commander. The music has remained very popular, with Germans and Austrians continuing to laugh at the Saxon accents.

His *Gasparone* (1884) also still competes in popularity with Strauss' lesser-known works, with its opera-type recitative and short, catchy musical phrases, such as that in *Close is the Night*. This duet anticipated the appealing tango rhythm which was to fascinate Europe a generation later.

*Countess Dubarry* (1879) featured a love triangle concerning a poverty-stricken girl rising through court intrigue and an arranged marriage to become the mistress of France's King Louis XV.[1] This anecdotal work was only moderately successful until it was revamped as *The Dubarry* by Theo Mackeben for a Berlin production in 1931, to succeed in several cities including London and New York. Its title song switches from sprightly polka to leisurely coloratura singing, but the dreamy waltz, originally called *Charmant*, was given fresh lyrics. As *I give my heart*, it became Millöcker's best-known melody in Britain and the U.S.A.[2]

Carl Zeller's *Bird-seller* (1891) had a more unsophisticated appeal, local dialect, Austrian folk rhythms rather than Viennese ball-room. It is hardly performed outside German-speaking lands, so is best remembered for the duet *Roses from Tyrol* and the sentimental waltz which the fine 1930s soprano Elizabeth Schumann recorded for posterity, its curiosity being that she whistled most affectively the 'nightingale' flute solo.

Richard Heuberger's great success was the *Opera Ball* (1898), and the flavour of the plot may be guessed from the aria which became famous enough eventually as almost to have a separate existence. It is called *Chambre séparée*, an expression which we have never translated, probably because the activities implied, even though involving only one man and one woman, would have been illegal under English but not Austrian laws.

By 1895, Suppé was dead, in 1898, Zeller, and a year later, both Strauss and Millöcker. It seemed that the 'golden' period of classical operetta could not survive the turn of the century, just decline in the hands of lesser men.

Heuberger's muse was apparently also in decline because he failed to provide music for a new commission. So the play we would now consider a permanent landmark in escapist entertainment, the *Merry Widow*, was in the emergency offered (1905) to a young Hungarian bandmaster, Franz Lehar. He provided a heady mixture of dances: mazurka, polonaise, can-can and wild rhythms from south-east Europe, with an exquisite interlude in the *Vilja* idyll for soprano. The plot moves from a Balkan embassy to down-town Paris of the dance hostesses: the gallantries of self-important men, the deceptions, the jealousies and increasingly near the surface, passions . . . the ultimate Romantic musical. It remains unsurpassed in its youthful vigour, from the witty, tongue-in-cheek *Cavalier* song, to the high-kicking dances and goings-on in the Maxim's night-club scene.

*The Count of Luxemburg* followed quickly with also equal success. Its story moved across Paris to the Bohemian left-bank, and Europe sang its rapturous waltz, *Can it be love?* Every evening, these works were seen in hundreds of theatres; several other very talented young composers were also coming forward to present the early 20th century's style of musical.

Vienna was entering a new phase, the so-called 'silver age' of operetta, more sentimental than the earlier style.

Lehar was not interested in satire or ridicule, but intended to move on from idealised stories; he would find more thoughtful, realistic dramas. *Tsarevitch* concerned a prince that was obliged for reasons of state to reject the girl he loved; such heart-felt melodies as the nostalgic *Volga-Song* were inspired by the music of Russia but it contained episodes that had a Puccini-like intensity.

*Friederike* was a sad love affair in the life of the young Goethe, relating to his famous poem, *Heidenröslein*, which symbolises a girl losing her virginity. Lehar's version of this song makes a worthy option to the great one by Schubert. Even so, he had taken a big risk portraying the life of the German Shakespeare. In the event, he avoided any criticism of bad taste by composing a score worthy of tragic opera. In this vein, there is a song of reproachful tenderness by Frederike:

> Why did you kiss my heart awake before I knew what love could mean?

*Gipsy Love* and *The Land of Smiles* reveal fascinations for exotic cultures which lead to emotional entanglement and ultimate disillusion. Some arias in *The Land of Smiles* suggest Chinese serenity, but this is a work of some emotional depth after its light, extrovert first act. One song, *You are my heart's delight*, was destined for excessive popularity among tens of millions who never heard it in a theatre.

*Paganini* was a passing romantic episode involving Napoleon's sister who had held court at Lucca in Italy before 1815; and was a fine opportunity to compose for the virtuoso violin. Lehar in his last work, *Giuditta* (1934), believed he had attained his masterpiece, and Vienna rewarded it with the status of grand opera. The story concerns a vivacious Italian adventuress and reminds us in plot, intensity and Mediterranean colour of Bizet's *Carmen*, except that Giuditta does not die.

Imre Kalman brought the Hungarian idiom to Viennese comedy and did much to popularise it further abroad, notably with the *Csardas* (or *Gipsy*) *Princess*, the nick-name of its stagy heroine, and *Countess Maritza* (1924), with the slow waltz, *Sister Mine*, and its serenade which with Hungarian gallantry celebrates the charm and ladies of Vienna.

Known everywhere and also out of context is *Countess Maritza's* violin melody that still welcomes visitors to Budapest restaurants:

Love once came and laid me low . . .
Play, Gipsy, play, till my aching heart is healed
Play till the stubborn senses reeled
Play me a haunting refrain,
Play till my heart forgets its pain.

The *Csardas Princess* given its heroine an impassioned introductory *scena* in Hungarian style but is a lighter composition overall, with a least three waltz duets which swept across central Europe in 1916. An almost equal success ten years later was the *Circus Princess*, with exceptionally fine tenor arias including that most persuasive of serenades, *Two wondrous eyes*.

All three works give prominence to the Hungarian *csardas*, which generally starts in melancholy mood before switching to a faster but deliberate tempo to such words as in the song, *When Maritza's heart is set on fire*. Kalman's composing has a clear fraternal relation to that of Lehar, but where Lehar often tended to stress the symphonic feel of his scores, Kalman continued to give his lead singers the opportunity to show their energetic dancing skills. Audiences have always responded, and nowadays with more astonishment, to such novelties as the *shimmy* in the more cosmopolitan *Bajadère*, a show still often performed in eastern Europe.

For the *Violet of Montmartre*, Kalman tried to break away from his 'Austro-Hungarian' idiom for something nearer the spirit of Paris' famous cafes-concerts, adding some 'Parisian' music by Florimond Hervé for local flavour. There are several tender songs, but best known in the West is the tango, *Tonight I dream of you*.

For this he accepted an unusual libretto, entirely fictitious, which brought the heroine of the title into Bohemian contact with three distinguished personalities during their supposedly impoverished youth: Hervé, painter Eugene Delacroix, and Henri Murger who wrote the book later used by Puccini for *La Bohème*.

With the passing of time, the *Csardas Princess* and *Countess Maritza* are judged to be crammed with successful numbers, whilst the others seem to be remembered by individual 'hits'.

The two were exceptionally well received in classic New Sadlers Wells Opera productions of the 1980s. That says much for the music's attraction because the lively plots suffer from quaint pre-1914 social values which cannot easily be hidden.

Even music-makers in the USSR took a similarly indulgent view of such 'bourgeois' confections, and operetta has remained very popular ever since. In the 1992 season, Kalman still stood exceptionally high amongst Russians, with more compositions being performed in Moscow and Kiev music theatres than anyone else's.

Oscar Straus, an Austrian, eventually one more of the 'silver Viennese' composers, had started as a satirist, having been much impressed as a youth by an 1886 performance of the *Mikado* which had been a sensation in Vienna. His early parodies included one of Wagner which later incurred the wrath of the Nazis. He was best known in Britain for the song, *My Hero*, from the operetta *The Chocolate Soldier*. This was based on G.B. Shaw's *Arms and the Man* and was therefore favoured with an unusual amount of dialogue. Only Shaw was not pleased with the outcome, and refused to let his plot be used in the later M.G.M. film of the musical.

*A Waltz Dream* was his other outstanding operetta with a romantic title song which has the unusual appeal of two fine melodies played simultaneously. Straus acquired late popularity with the 'hit' which sustained a highly exportable French film of the 1950s, *La Ronde*.

Leo Fall's style has an Austrian charm and humour rather than the passion of Kalman and Lehar. Slower waltzes such as those from the *Dollar Princess* and the *Rose of Stamboul* are widely remembered by the title of the works they appear in. The *Dollar Princess* (1907) exploited the new fascination with things American, has a startling type-writer song, and in *Olga from the Volga*, a lively parody of a Russian song.

Fall sought more topical themes, such as a court-room divorce scene, and succeeded with his distinctive interplay of dialogue and music. In *Madame de Pompadour* (1922), the King's mistress mockingly tempts a 'shy' courtier, Joseph, as she lies in a bubble-bath; her part in the duet is spiced with the five-note motif which accompanied Don José's murder of Carmen, and suggestions of Dalilah's seduction theme from

Saint-Saens' opera. Joseph's dithering response comes across
well in at least one colloquial English version:

> Won't you let me treat you as a brother?
> Do regard me as a second mother.
> Won't you call me Auntie? That is all I want chez-vous . . .
> What will happen, goodness knows, if I become a second
>     Joseph?
> Once before a king went raving at his spouse's misbehaving.
> If today he finds I've got yer, Potiphah will go much pottier.

Fall's prolific successes came to an untimely end with his
death in 1925, and though a few good stage works were
completed after that, the great operetta vogue was moving
into decline. Robert Stolz was composing from the 1910s to the
1970s, and reflected the changes in style. His early *Two hearts in
3-4 time*, with its fast, Straussian title song, is still often performed and he composed the attractively cheerful march,
*Adieu*, which found its way into that very well-known musical
of many composers, *White Horse Inn*. Away from the stage, he
wrote much film music and an insinuating little romance for
female and male singers known alternatively as *Romeo* or
*Salome*.

Stolz had conducted the first Viennese performance of the
*Merry Widow*, and took conspicuous part in the film-making of
the 1930s. Many operetta classics appeared in German, and
Hollywood was not slow to exploit the genre. Unfortunately,
that led to much debasement of the style, so that though the
films were generally popular on release, in the long run they
are best forgotten because they present operetta in a very
false, sugary manner, with banal dialogue replacing much of
the original music.

London theatres did have frequent revivals of first and
second-class operettas until the war, with highly respected
performers such as Evelyn Laye. The Viennese singer,
Richard Tauber, settled in England and began to devote his
energies in this direction, even composing the music for *Old
Chelsea* which achieved some popularity. He is particularly
remembered here for songs which Lehar composed for his
stage appearances, such as *Girls are made to love and kiss* from
*Paganini*[3] and *Maiden, my maiden* from *Friederike*.

The later, 20th century operetta has had many varieties in Europe's capitals. The Hungarians had enjoyed a specially close cultural link with Vienna, but their works for the Budapest theatres in their own language, inclined towards humorous stories of conflicts over social status, the peasants singing in the folk idiom whilst the aristocrats had the more sophisticated Viennese style[4].

In England, top-class professional operetta can easily fill concert halls for popular excerpts, Vienna sharing the stage with the English and French variants, which in practice means Sullivan and Offenbach. Yet the high costs of full productions has not prevented London from seeing in recent years upwards of 50 operettas, a range far greater than that in any other city west of Berlin. The New Sadlers Wells Opera was attracting a new, younger audience in the 1980s, and the growing number of subsidised opera touring companies are adding such works to their repertoire.

Suppé, Millöcker and Lehar have been well represented in productions by the London music colleges and societies, including *Boccaccio, Fatinitza, Ten Belles*, the *Beggar Student*, the *Count of Luxemburg* and the *Land of Smiles*. Such works are appreciated in training institutions because they often give scope for more naturalistic acting, movement, and projection of personality than the strict regime of opera. The updating of scripts, and other improvisations, are welcome challenges in bringing youthful talent to this genre, and leading London music colleges are giving increased prominence to such courses as well as productions for public showing.

Marilyn Hill Smith who first established her name in opera as a coloratura soprano and sang those Kalman leads at London's Sadlers Wells Theatre explained to Richard Baker on BBC radio why she was equally happy extending her big reputation into operetta. She enjoys the team-work, the high notes, the high spirits and another special quality. As she greatly admires German soprano Ingeborg Hallstein, she played her recording of the scene in which Fanny Elssler, in Johann Strauss' operetta of that name, sings exquisitely of receiving a letter from Napoleon's son. That quality is intimacy.

# 9  A Man of Many Parts

**D**uring the 1880s, a variety of extraordinary reports emerged concerning the goings-on at the Empire Theatre, Leicester Square, one of which was of considerable social concern[1], others relating to pure frivolity.

In April 1884, the magazine 'Era' described the stage performance of the Brothers Tacchi. Whilst the one sang with guitar, the other appeared to have swallowed a bassoon which continued to play internally. An hilarious novelty, but was it not incongruous in a quasi-operatic presentation of courtly events in pre-medieval France, with an enchanted forest, Gothic camp and 'electric ballet' of 50 Amazons? This 'integrated' stage work was a parody of grand opera, *King Chilperic*, of which the musical highlight had been the *Butterfly song* dedicated to the King's promiscuity. Though the work's first London appearance had been in 1870, as a spectacle, according to the 'Era', 14 years later it was still of its kind unprecedented *on the modern stage*. So it had been the clear choice for the opening of the vast 3,500-seater Empire.

In December 1887, the 'Era' reported an evening of ballet, including sprightly young odalisques, boating dances and *female representatives of the M.C.C. and Australian Eleven*. Its music had been composed for London by one who lived under the stage name of Florimond Hervé and who had also entirely conceived King Chilperic. He was known as the 'crackpot composer' because of his remarkable therapeutic experiments as a young man putting-on shows in which hospital inmates, many disabled mentally, had been encouraged to act.

Monsieur Hervé must have been a genius because he spread his talents more widely than one would imagine possible without serious dissipation. That was not the case. In 1886, the Empire Theatre appointed as music director this man, who had been seen performing in his own send-up of Gounod's *Faust* as far afield from Paris as Holborn. At a time of fierce competition between theatres, he could be relied on for the unexpected.

If the Brothers Tacchi were not his creation, they were in the distinctive tradition of his insane buffoonery. Starting as a church organist at the age of 14, he had graduated to stage enterprises by the 1840s, and the severe regulations covering performances at that time in Paris, had, fortunately of necessity, extended his activities to the widest inventiveness.

Minor theatres in Paris were permitted only two or three 'performers', so would it be within the law to have additional actors playing-out dumb-shows on-stage[2]? Walking corpses, singers who don't sing or a headless man who does? The audiences found such experiments grotesquely funny, so they were continued into new works long after the staging restrictions had been eliminated by the end of the 1850s. Charismatic, a handsome ladies' man, Hervé would perhaps sing several parts himself in one show. In his own theatre, the Folies Nouvelles, he gave the slightly older Offenbach an early chance of success with a one-acter, the *Queen of the Isles* (1855), in which Hervé played a cannibal queen whose appetite for a musician can only be assuaged by endless melodies played on a double-bass.

In a period when an exposed female ankle could excite male passion, his chorus girls scandalously revealed their calves. His experiments with revolving props, trapdoor techniques, real and pantomime animals and cardboard armies caused him to be known as a master of stage illusion. In London, a Mr H.B. Farney had to clean-up the dialogue in translating his works.

With his farce, *Don Quixote* (1848), Hervé could be regarded as the inventor of classical operetta, and his own theatre became a centre for musical burlesque, his and that of other young composers whom he encouraged. Opera, ancient civilisations and war were specially suitable targets for ridicule, and if he had considered a story about a theatre manager taking his troupe on a wild camel chase into the Sahara desert in search of his patron, he could have drawn on his own experience.

One evening in Paris, when Wagner was addressing a distinguished audience on his musical theories, explaining why he preferred to compose to his own lyrics, a stranger asserted that he did likewise. It was M. Hervé who proceeded to play his compositions on the piano. According to a witness, the astonished Wagner observed him as a lion would a monkey leaping between trees, before relaxing to laugh at the musical improvisations late into the night. Whereas Gounod and Berlioz in their *Faust* operas each wrote a poignant song about the King of Thule, in Hervé's verses, the King was given a pair of elastic braces which on a state occasion were to snap, exposing government secrets to public viewing.

In this manner, he was prepared to offer 'spicy' versions of *Faust* and other current operatic successes, including transparent musical parodies. His anarchic stage plays even ventured into British 'history', notably with *Robin Hood* and *The Throne of Scotland*, whilst his *Aladdin II* written for London may have influenced Gilbert to write the *Mikado*.

Such works bear a similar relation to his late *Mlle Nitouche* (1883), as does *Monty Python* to a West End bedroom farce. Yet it is the relatively sane *Nitouche* which is most performed today in parts of Europe, and was partly written by the renowned Henri Meilhac, so that Hervé was able to concentrate on composing a superior score. Its plot was a case of art imitating life, concerning a young teacher-organist who secretly composes operettas under a pseudonym.

So he confides to the audience that he is Celestin-Floridor and we learn that his evenings are spent at a 'disreputable' theatre as well as having a non-musical relationship with its lead singer, Corinne. Since he has to creep back to his seminary late at night, he risks the wrath of the strict matron and her brother, a major who is innocently courting Corinne.

Denise, a seminary pupil who behaves *comme it faut* when being observed, has learnt to become a shining example of youthful hypocrisy, and when she uncovers Celestin's deplorable hobby, she also creeps out regularly to the theatre. She learns the operetta by heart and even inserts some of its ditties into the school's religious music, to her young teacher's embarrassment. By the time that the actress quarrels with Celestin and runs-off with the major, Denise passes herself off as Mlle Nitouche and is ready to sing Corinne's part, which she does in Act II. The delinquents return to the seminary disguised as soldiers, but whereas Hervé married his pupil, Celestin does not.

Celestin's role attracted comedians from Hervé to Raimu, then more recently Fernandel, who became well known outside France through the post-war cinema[3]. He can still be heard reciting his role in three of the 15 excerpts, one of

numerous classic recordings of French operetta. He introduces himself in low, confiding tones, then acts as a kind of
straight man to the frolicsome young singers. Act I has some
appealing music for female voices: the childlike ballad of the
lead soldier as a relentless galop refreshed by interruptions, a
schoolgirl's *Alleluia* in which devotion is subverted by impish
feelings. The girl offers a brief review of her English and
German lessons, with Lord Byron, Shakespeare, Hegel and
Schlegel, among others, subjected to charming French
mispronunciation.

Denise eventually is impelled to offer a prayer to the mythical St Nitouche, then in soldier's disguise, sings naughtily
about what her uniform conceals. Some of the music, including a *Rue de Rivoli* march, might still be familiar on French
parade grounds, but one thumping fanfare was 'borrowed'
from Berlioz who had used it prominently in his version of
*Faust*. Berlioz would not have been amused.

The gentle waltz which is the theme-song of Celestin's
composition was also among the highlights sung by some
leading entertainers of the closing century, adding to the
street-song popularity of the whole work. The music sounds
remarkably unsophisticated, giving much prominence to the
words, often a French kind of music-hall ditty, and easily
remembered tunes.

*Nitouche* is an intimate, small-scale work such as was becoming popular in France during the 1880s, and in contrast with
the huge extravaganzas which had made Hervé's reputation in
the earlier years, with their mock-heroism, imposing choruses
and grand operatic finales.

Hervé's output of musicals well passed the hundred mark,
though the quality of much of them suffered in the interests of
composing rapidly to a schedule. At best, his music could pass
superficially for Jacques Offenbach's. The two men had parallel careers, were friendly rivals as theatre entrepreneurs and
must have influenced, even inspired one another greatly.
Emmerich Kalman's *Violet of Montmartre* is the best-known
work to draw subsequently on Hervé's music, parts of *Nitouche*
being played in Act III as an ingenious part of the plot.

# 10  *A Parisian Comedy*

Augustus II, Elector of Saxony and King of Poland, was famed for his physical strength and appetites. The most favoured of his estimated 300 illegitimate offspring was Maurice of Saxony, born in 1696 to the Countess of Königsmarck. With a physique like his father's, he was always enthusiastic for military service, serving in Marlborough's army at the age of 14. He rose quickly to great distinction as a military commander in the service of France though, partly for that reason, he receives only passing mention in British history.

In the European war starting in 1740, he captured Prague but his most celebrated campaigns were in the Spanish Netherlands, where he defeated the British and their allies at Fontenoy, Raucoux and Laufeld. He received the highest honours from the French King Louis XV, who naturalised him in the title of Marshall Saxe.

Armies largely composed at that time of mercenaries, enforced men and serfs should, he argued, in the interests of efficiency and morale, be replaced by a citizen's army. His forward-looking views were highly individual and, more important for our story, he also believed in raising morale by giving his troops theatrical entertainment even at the height of campaigns.

His amorous career might have rivalled that of his father if his energies had not also been absorbed by military campaigns; he enjoyed boisterous living and romantic intrigues, where successes were easily at hand for a conspicuously successful soldier of striking appearance and personal charm. Emotionally immature, he required a string of mistresses including a future Russian empress, Anna, and a very famous actress, Adrienne Lecouvreur. She was thought to be the only woman he ever loved and was to become eventually the heroine of a tragedy with a fictitious ending in which she is poisoned by a female rival. Saxe was presented favourably in that play as her lover[1].

Saxe's enthusiasm for the stage followed predictable patterns. In 1745, he became obsessed with a very promising 18-year old Parisian actress, Anne-Justine Chantilly. In a time when there was a virtual cult of artificiality on the stage, her freshness, spontaneity and rapport with audiences marked her out from the start. Her spirited personality had entranced theatre manager, Charles Favart, and he recognised that his feelings were much more than passing. He asked her to marry him and she accepted him; their wedding was a distinguished occasion.

The corrupt theatre establishment, envious at her success, were able to exclude her from leading roles on the fashionable stage for some time. She was relegated to performing at the fringe in pantomimes, where her exceptional talent and versatility earned great popularity. Some thought her achievement in comedy comparable with Lecouvreur's in tragedy. Yet Favart was in financial difficulties, and an invitation from the national hero and Fontenoy victor, Saxe, seemed most kindly and opportune. He was to take a troupe to Flanders, entertaining the army just before they went into battle at Raucoux. Justine was to be given the honour of announcing to the cheering troops that battle would be joined the following day. Favart did not sense any sinister motive behind Saxe's apparent goodwill, but Justine felt in some way compromised and fled to Brussels.

One of the symbols of injustice in France's pre-1789 regime was the *lettre de cachet* by which an aristocrat could imprison indefinitely, by royal command, a less favoured citizen. It did not require more than a pretext for the King to issue such a decree to the advantage of Saxe. This procedure was duly invoked against Favart, but once warned, he fled to Strasbourg where he was reduced to living by painting fans.

In employing a drawn-out campaign of blackmail against the Favarts, Saxe was able to hide behind agents. Justine was imprisoned within a convent, then moved on to similar localities to ensure secrecy. He was able to send her importunate letters, and she knew she could gain freedom by surrendering herself to him.

This intrigue was later raised to a theatrical legend, with a virtuous woman resisting in circumstances where such an influential man might achieve a form of legitimised rape. Over an expended period, Saxe also used more subtle methods, such as bribing her father to oppose her husband, withholding payments to the Favart troupe. At fifty, he was certainly not the god-like figure of Lecouvreur's imagination.

There are other interpretations, Saxe's biographer, Edmund d'Auvergne, bluntly asserting that Justine had earlier been seduced by Saxe, who had settled an annuity on a child born to her; and that Favart always needed her love, but not necessarily her fidelity.

Was she at first flattered by Saxe's attentions or did she give way just to protect her husband? Was there an arrangement in the traditional French manner? There were no snooping photographers to serve the cause of history, so the complexities will always be in dispute. The Favarts returned to work in Paris when the pressure on them had been reduced or removed and in November 1750, Saxe was killed; whether it was through falling from a horse or from a duel involving the honour of another woman, is not certain. The cultured Madame de Pompadour offered an unflattering epitaph which was thought to relate to Justine, but could have also implied a duel. This was to the effect that he had brought about the downfall of so many girls, it was fitting that one had finished him off.

In the 15 or so remaining years of her life, Justine was able to collaborate with her husband on several of his 60 musical comedies, which were plays with song and dance additions. Then years after Saxe's death, Favart was able to take a more detached view of his rival, writing a play, *The Three Sultans*, about a *menage à trois*.

As a precursor of the modern Parisian comedy, Charles Favart's reputation remains high. The Opéra Comique where he achieved his fame still carries his name, as do the adjacent street and an elegant hotel opposite.

It was over a century after Justine's death that Paris saw her honoured in a 3-act comic opera. Offenbach had perfected the art of musical satire, but fashions were changing, and he was looking for ways to gratify them. The Favarts were a most suitable subject and were favoured with a joyous libretto which would avoid any cynical interpretation of the sinister events. It was written by probably the two best collaborators of Offenbach's later years, Chivot and Duru.

Only a slight alteration of history was required to produce an ingenious plot, full of intrigues, false identities, twists of fortune, and a celebratory finale. At the height of his creative ability, Offenbach interrupted work on his opera *The Tales of Hofmann* because he could not resist the opportunity which this 18th century pastiche would give.

Yet he succeeded even beyond that, creating in his Madame Favart a musically commanding role. The stage persona is a mature woman, far more self-possessed than the real girl could have been in a harrowing situation. Undaunted and resourceful, she is always one step ahead of the enemy. By contrast, the character of Charles Favart displays whatever anxieties that this light-hearted reworking of reality contains. An engaging sub-plot concerning two young lovers conniving to gain parental consent for marriage keeps the drama moving and gives scope for excellent ensemble writing for the two couples. An affectionate backward glance towards *Figaro* and Mozart?

In 1879, the London premiere quickly followed Paris' and operetta queen Florence St John had a big success in the title role. In those days, a run of 500 successive performances for foreign musicals was unheard-of, but at the Royal Strand Theatre, it passed that figure, playing non-stop for two years before moving on. Among the satisfied audience was young Bernard Shaw who wrote that the work had *grace, gaiety and intelligence . . . the restless movement, the witty abandonment, the swift, light, wicked touch, the inimitable élan.*

Unlike the play *Adrienne Lecouvreur, Madame Favart* had no role for Saxe, wisely because such a man would not easily fit into the role of a buffoon. The librettists' master-stroke was to invent his stooge, an undignified marquis who lacks the wit to employ his authority to effect.

Justine joins her husband hiding in an Arras hostelry where a young girl, Suzanne, is in rebellion over her father's plan to marry her off to a suitor she does not want. Only if her beloved, Gaston (Hector in the original French version), is preferred for promotion to police lieutenant will the father relent and accept him as son-in-law. The complication is that the governor who will make the appointment only selects men with 'suitable' wives: for Gaston, Catch 22.

Fortunately, he recognises Justine, having seen her once in a theatre performance, and shows sympathy when she explains her plight. He could whisk the Favarts away to Douai in his carriage as servants.

Justine decides to return the favour by presenting herself as his fiancée to the governor who is also in Arras. In her interview off-stage, the governor is duly convinced she will be pliable but makes no move for instant gratification; she returns with a letter confirming Gaston's appointment.

The father relents and the first act in galloping pace ends with the departure for Douai of the two couples. At Gaston's spacious home, the wedding celebrations are underway when the governor gate-crashes; perhaps he likes a formal introduction by husbands in order to spice his pound of flesh. General confusion. Justine will have to impersonate Suzanne for the duration of the emergency and Suzanne reappears dressed as a chamber-maid.

The governor is the Marquis de Pont-Sablé. His dress and manners are slightly *de trop*, and after ungraciously permitting the assembled company to 'pay homage', he contrives to be alone with the Lieutenant's 'wife', but, a small man in a vast room, has to contend with numerous contrived interruptions, nervously stumbling over a divan and losing his wig. Yet he mistakes Justine's neatly-turned irony for a series of compliments and as the proceedings become overheated, she escapes on a pretext, returning in the guise of Gaston's old aunt to tell the Marquis that the Favarts have fled.

Frustrated at every turn in his clownish advances, he leaves, only to reappear within minutes, triumphant because an informant has revealed a 'plot' with the Favarts still in the building. For the only moment in the drama, he has almost encountered the truth; to save both girls, Favart gives himself up. There ensues a piquant mock-denouement, which satirises the clichés of dramatic confrontation, a lively joke at the expense of Verdi or Meyerbeer-style grand opera very familiar in the 1870s to Parisian audiences[2]. Absurdity rules as the Marquis accuses his Lieutenant of running a mistress, none other than the supposed Madame Favart dressed as a chamber maid. He points to Suzanne, who 'confesses' to being Justine and is promptly arrested, the perfect moment for the curtain to fall.

The finale proceeds at a pace. The King orders Justine Favart to be brought to the military camp to appear on stage. The Marquis is still floundering in the morass of subterfuges and fear of once more being made a fool causes him to reject Suzanne's latest confession, brought on by the fear of facing the King, that she is not the actress. His only moment of self-criticism occurs when he imagines he has disgraced the name of Pont-Sablé by falling for someone described as a 'kitchen fairy'; that his inamorata was in fact Madame Favart only strikes him just before his ultimate humiliation.

The two conspirators not arrested by the Marquis, Justine and Gaston, arrive at the camp as an itinerant Swiss couple singing to entertain the soldiers, who look ridiculous when they attempt alpine dancing. When the King calls for a stage performance, the actress is able to switch roles with Suzanne. The Marquis finally addresses the right woman, congratulates her on her skills but still anticipates arresting her. Yet the forces of evil are to be grounded:

> Justine: *There's nothing to fear, Monsieur de Pont-Sablé. Do you know what this letter says? The King accepts your resignation.*
> Marquis: *Accepts? But I've not given it.*
> Justine: *His Majesty thinks you need a rest. Frankly, I think he's right.*

The Marquis collapses into a drum, but remains bewitched by the 'heavenly' lady. King Louis XV is so delighted with her acting that he has signed a decree reinstating the Favarts at Paris' Opéra Comique.

■ ■ ■

In autumn 1990, East Berlin's Metropol Theatre introduced its second production of Madame Favart with precise period costume and 18th century rococo decor. The staging includes an inn, a large mansion concourse, a military camp and a stage within a stage, with choruses of party guests, lackeys and soldiers.

The first act is in the style of an 18th century domestic comedy, with lively musical interchanges between the two couples. On my first visit to this production, during the interval, I was drinking with a friend when an Englishwoman, hearing us, joined in conversation. She had been surprised by the homely, sentimental nature of the piece whereas liking Offenbach, had been hoping for something with more bite.

She only had a few minutes to wait. The opening of the next act offered a *coup de théâtre*. The wedding celebrations are suddenly disturbed by an astonishing vision of human eccentricity, the first sortie of the Marquis de Pont-Sablé. Expecting to be met only by subordinates and menials, his bullying conceals neither his social inadequacy nor weird inclinations. East Berlin's baritone-comedian, Wolfgang Ostberg, gives a sharp, idiosyncratic interpretation of the Marquis, both knave and fool, an effete specimen of in-breeding. He is almost decrepit, obtuse, snobbish, and with sexual urges which, to the immediate amusement of the audience, seem to emanate from his knees.

Except when speaking, he is in a permanent state of unease, derived partly from a paranoid awareness of intrigue. He tries to impress everyone as to his person and mission. Spitting-out a jerky tune, he shatters the nerves of the lackeys by crashing his stick on each table in turn. When they respond in apparent servility, he peers round, surveying them as if to discover a dissonant note, a subversive comment, innuendo or dumb insolence. The effect is a concertante for cane, military bark and hesitant chorus. He employs his lorgnettes in the hopes of impressing and perhaps entering the soul of whichever person is under examination. He will probably fall on both counts.

The Marquis' love technique is a combination of the grope and the grovel, with an occasional leap. Herr Ostberg's body language ensures that his facial expressions can be 'seen' at the back of the theatre. He gives the Marquis a fetish for touching women's knees without lifting the skirts; this reduces him to an undignified crawl. I speculated that the Marquis de Pont-Sablé's frenzied gestures would vary in inverse proportion to his ability to satisfy a woman. On one occasion, observed in disgraceful conduct, he hides, naughty boy, in the corner, Chaplinesque.

■   ■   ■

Justine's 'sing-along' aria is the 'Rondo among the vines', telling how her mother threw her in at the deep end of life, and that she always comes cheerfully to the surface. It reappears briefly at the end, a rare reprise in a score full of ditties.

The ensembles are very distinctive, pushing the action along, with abrupt changes of pace. When Favart joining in a quartet expresses fear of prison, there is a suggestion of Handelian recitative from his confederates. 18th century pastiche and snatches of later operatic styles brighten the score.

Justine introduces herself to the assemblage to a 'hurdy-gurdy' background, and signs off with a laughter song narrating her stage success with the King. In between, she has two more reflective arias relating to youth and maturity; she sings of convent life with suggestions of schoolgirls' hymns, then whilst impersonating Gaston's aunt she poignantly describes in the tempo of a minuet the four stages of woman's life:

A quarante ans, c'est automne . . .
C'est alors que l'arbre donne ses fruits les plus savoureux
. . .
Le plaisir devient science . . .
Je sus plaire le mieux.
(Autumn arrives at forty, when the tree gives its richest fruit, and pleasure becomes a science. It was then I knew best how to please.)

Two of Charles Favart's three solo arias are interesting beyond their musical content. In his kitchen disguise, he sings of his cream puffs, insubstantial and filled with hot air like too many people in French society; the real Favart was the son of a pastry-cook. His Romance is a rare occasion for Offenbach to throw-off his comic mask and match the poetic phrases:

Le regard si doux d'une femme lorsque sur nous il
    resplendit,
C'est la lumière, c'est la flamme,
Mais son absence, c'est la nuit.
(A woman's tender glance can be the flame, the splendour. Without it, only the night.)

Why is this work not better known? It does not require the spectacular treatment of the best-known Offenbach comic operas, but works well as a unity rather than depending on its highlights. It reflected Offenbach's move in his later years towards more intimate Romantic comedy, and is one of his most interesting works on the path to the operatic *Tales of Hoffman*.

The libretto has a credible plot, with scope for characterisation and sharp dialogue. Fleshed-out, it could stand without the music as a very humorous play, for example, if the reported first interview between governor and actress were enacted. We learn later how Suzanne's father had been waiting impatiently outside, hoping to present the case for the alternative suitor whilst an unknown female was 'entertaining' the Marquis in his office.

As comedies go, it makes big demands on the casting and acting; Madame Favart is rarely off-stage except when making eight costume changes, perhaps a record number for opera. The versatility of her role is always a challenge, and the broad demands of the production should make it specially attractive to modern, highly trained ensembles. There are indications that this composition has a good future in Germany, just as at its inception it was more successful in England than in France.

A newspaper critic who had come far enjoyed one performance but regretted that the light-hearted treatment of typical corruption under the pre-1789 regime was eventually obscured in a happy ending. He had overlooked the requirements of comedy which in this case was assisted by a fictitious act of restitution from Louis XV.

Chivot and Duru would have remembered that, in a more serious context, Moliere had introduced a *deus ex machina* in the form of King Louis XIV to rectify the appalling injustice perpetrated in the play *Tartuffe* against a family. In the case of the Favarts, the King's supposed intervention might well have hung on Justine's stage performance.

The success of the Metropol production became known in West Germany, and an invitation was accepted to perform at Bad Ems in 1992. That made a historical link with Offenbach's summer seasons there throughout the 1860s. The theatre is adjacent to the beautifully-preserved Marble Room where his productions had entertained the Prussian royal court.

# 11   *Burlesque in English*

What is Burlesque? The subtle ridiculing on-stage of ideas and institutions which are fashionable, or accepted over a long period either from conviction, convention or necessity; the more significant the objects, generally the more enduring the satire.

Burlesque can be verbal, visual or musical, and preferably a combination of all three. In our own times it does not flourish on the musical stage, partly because there is a shortage of worthwhile targets, and of new music which is amusing or witty enough for the purpose. Two specially inventive scripts were devised to satirise the clash between the government and the Greater London Council in the early 1980s. These were admirably staged, but the selected music was one hundred years old, the orchestral scores of Sullivan's *Mikado* and *Iolanthe* being important factors in the overall success.

Suitable themes had been common enough in the past: political dictatorships, a dominant state religion, widely accepted values, lasting or false, respected institutions or strictly observed art forms. The last of these has at times offered the greatest opportunity for inventive treatment.

The *Beggar's Opera* (1727) was an important landmark in the development of ballad opera, and is still often performed, such as in Benjamin Britten's exuberant version. It was written by John Gay, satirising the grandiose style of G.F. Handel's Italian operas, among others, and employing many popular tunes. Handel was so impressed by the *Beggar's Opera* that he began to reform his own style, and composed a number of comic operas in English which were exceptionally successful.

Exactly two centuries later, Bertolt Brecht made use of Gay's model for his momentous project, the *Three-penny Opera*. This pilloried in a most entertaining way capitalism and the corruption of its privileged classes; within a few years it had been banned by the Nazis. Today, of its kind, it is the show most certain to fill a London theatre for weeks on end.

With or without the politics, new works in this tradition may make a welcome appearance. Period songs accompanied a version of *Moll Flanders* which reached London in 1993, a moving story of a woman born to poverty and crime, by the 17th century author of *Robinson Crusoe*, Daniel Defoe. Significantly, its promoters preferred to describe it, not as a 'ballad opera,' but by the safer term, 'musical'.

Over centuries, there had been popular forms of political lampooning but no sophisticated tradition of burlesque. A fine comedy writer, Richard Sheridan, had satirised the appalling artistic standards into which the London theatre had sunk by 1775 in his play, *The Critic*. This included an elaborately staged demonstration of how not to produce spectacle and grand tragedy, but it was not given a significant musical score until one century later by Charles Stanford.

By the mid-19th century, writer J.R. Planché and others had established a fashion in small-scale musical farces, too superficial for political or social satire. The extravaganza placed legendary or pantomime themes such as *Puss in Boots* or *Beauty and the Beast*, in fanciful plots and tableaux. The humour turned on the incongruous use of words, gestures and declamation, with relentless application of puns, and rhyming couplets for anti-climax:

His majesty and the Vizir
Have very important biz 'ere.

Most interesting for modern audiences is the hi-jacking of well-known operatic and other pieces, relocated with comic dialogue. Increasingly, Shakespeare and other familiar literary models were used along with slices of popular operas by Rossini, Verdi and others. Misapplying Weber's music, such as building his *Invitation to the Waltz* into an elaborate operatic *scena* with fairies, was a lively joke because Planché had been Weber's librettist for his Covent Garden opera, *Oberon*. In England, the idea of composing music specially for parody and satire had not quite arrived, though it was developing in the Paris of the 1850s.

William S. Gilbert (1836-1911) was a versatile dramatist but also a master of comic verse who staged his own works, insisting on the highest standards in all aspects of production. Authenticity was so important that a princess's gown 200 years old was brought from Japan for his *Mikado*. One aim was to attract respectable society back to the theatres which they had understandably long since deserted. A trained solicitor, he wrote a one-act satire on the legal procedures, *Trial by Jury* (1866), with young Arthur Sullivan (1842-1900) composing the music. It was intended to fill-in a small part of an evening program, but was surprisingly well received, especially for farcical court room scenes and a clever imitation of a Bellini coloratura aria. If that pointed to a strong melodic gift, Sullivan proved it, unusually for a 'classical' composer, with a remarkable sequence of songs which would become popularly known. The two men eventually entered one of the finest collaborations of its kind: 'G & S'. Their output was to include what were to become 'hits' loved by tens of millions who never even saw their productions, the so-called 'comic' or 'Savoy operas.'

*HMS Pinafore* was a farce about absurd characters in naval uniforms and *Pirates of Penzance* a burlesque on the notion of duty, satirising many aspects of Romantic opera, such as the confusions of identity, and the wilder, *Trovatore* like plots. *HMS Pinafore* became a barrel-organ mania in the USA where at least 50 companies soon performed it as far as the extreme south and west, in inferior, pirated versions.

G & S heroes often weep over uncertainties concerning their own births – the much-abused foundling device of jaded Romantic drama, and immortalised in the joke about the baby found in a handbag (from Oscar Wilde's comedy, *The Importance of being Earnest.*)

The *Pirates of Penzance* has English youths being apprenticed to pirates until their 21st birthdays. A confusion of the words 'pilot' and 'pirate' had been written into a contract which was the start to the misfortunes of our young hero, Frederick. That was compounded by the fact that he had been born on 29 February, and was therefore condemned to be a pirate until he would be over 80. This is the kind of absurd logic exploited in the famed Gilbertian world.

*Iolanthe* is an extended joke on the British political system, with a climax in which the son of a lord and the queen of the fairies becomes a reforming member of the House of Lords. It gave the traditional extravaganza a much more sophisticated meaning and shape, superior verse, only occasionally repeating the comic forced rhymes and irregular meter of Planché's day:

> That every boy and every gal that's born into the world
> al-IVE
> Is either a little Liberal or else a little Conservat-IVE.

Its fairy music was Mendelssohnian and, more surprisingly, there were echoes of Wagner's Rhine Maidens and Brunnhilde, his nordic heroine.

*Princess Ida* (1884) laughs at forms of feminism which seek to exclude the companionship of the male sex who, to give balance, are presented unfavourably, and includes a parody on Handelian recitative among other ingenious musical allusions. The satire, however, was considered too sharp for the piece to gain the popularity of its three predecessors.

The *Gondoliers* is a mock-Venetian farce which has reminders of *Carmen*, Rossini and Johann Strauss. The *Mikado*, despite Japanese names and costumes, has characters as English and respectable as Bond Street, if thoroughly eccentric in their thought processes. *Ruddigore* is a satire on the popular horror stories, haunted castles and the 'Gothic' novel which Jane Austen had ridiculed in an earlier period; the villains become virtuous and the good people are compromised. Even the original term 'ruddy' had to be replaced because it suggested a swear-word, a simple example of the kind of problem Gilbert's advanced thinking was facing. The work was rich in good music, but needing operatic treatment, so is staged now less frequently than the most popular of all the collaborations.

Sullivan's fluent melodic style shows the influence of many of the foremost composers of his childhood, including Mendelssohn, Auber and Donizetti. He responded to Gilbert's lyrics with music which received the highest popular acclaim, though, to his annoyance, critical opinion did not view his more 'serious' compositions so favourably. It was his ambition to concentrate on writing grand operas, oratorios and symphonies which seemed to imply a lesser regard for Gilbert's lighter writings. That led to serious differences. Fortunately, he continued with his facility for parodying the serious styles to which he aspired and which many lesser composers were pursuing without much success.

Whereas Sullivan was deferential and urbane, Gilbert was of military bearing, irascible, and particularly in rehearsals, intimidating. They never had a warm relationship, but Sullivan's musical charm complemented and softened the effect of Gilbert's sharp wit. The final product had to be chaste to the point of (comic) naivety about sexual matters, and the music avoided all the voluptuousness of French operetta, which owed its popularity in London partly to its scandalous reputation. To quote Gilbert's song out of context, he offered a *source of innocent merriment*.

With conflict between the two men increasingly likely, the third member of the partnership played an essential role. Richard Carte organised the financing of a new theatre, the Savoy, to produce their works. He also established a company, the D'Oyly Carte, which for 80 years enforced strict, traditional performances whilst travelling around Britain, the USA, Australia and wherever English was spoken, in a repertoire exclusively of their works.

The *Mikado* has always been marginally the most popular of their collaborations, particularly for its melodies, and the Act one finale is an hilarious operatic parody to rival the best of Offenbach's. No wonder the work successfully invaded the Continent, and Kaiser Wilhelm II greeted Sullivan by singing one verse when they met at Kiel.

Gilbert's art employs to unique effect multiple rhymes, alliteration, startling combinations of words and ideas. The abundance of classical or topical references – the latter may be updated – presents no great problem, and the speed with which many witticisms follow one another prevents English listeners worrying about what they have failed to understand, or forgotten, such as in the Major General's boasts:

> I understand equations, both the simple and quadratical
> About binomial theorem I'm teeming with a lot o' news,
> With many cheerful facts about the square on the hypotenuse.

Successive G & S operas offered a musical formula that their public came to expect; up-dated madrigals and minstrel-type songs, mock-ceremonial or military music: an English variety of the headlong tongue-twisting aria in buffo style *à la Rossini:* tense, unaccompanied choral interludes: tenors complaining of unfulfilled romance, and their soprano counterparts singing in gentle waltz-time: finales in the style of grand opera.

This formula continued to the last of their finest works. *Utopia Limited.* Its first act opens with romantic dreams expressed by a chorus of girls: a buffo duet in a pronounced skipping tempo: the arrival of a mature, commanding, contralto; a grand *scena*, with patriotic intrusions and a saucy naval ditty from *HMS Pinafore*: a mini-cantata in praise of the English Lady; and an heroic Verdian finale. This is to celebrate the triumph of capitalism in the conversion of the state of Utopia into a limited company – did Gilbert foresee Britain after the Thatcher revolution?

One song gives advice, equally relevant today, on how to make easy money, a process that we now associate with creative accountancy: set-up a limited company, and if it loses, file a petition and start another one, whilst:

'*the liquidators say, never mind, you needn't pay*'

and the King of Utopia declaims:

'*Well, at first sight it strikes us as dishonest, but if it's good enough for virtuous England . . . it's good enough for us.*'

That was an unexpected subject for musical humour, with less obvious popular appeal than, for example in *HMS Pinafore*, the ballad of the admiral that never went to sea, or from the *Mikado*, the cheerful catalogue on ways 'to make the punishment fit the crime.'

Was *Utopia Limited* too subtle for its original audiences? Would it work better with today's cynicism about business practices and the 'market economy'? Yet the institutionalised corruption of the legal profession is always with us:

Whether you are an honest man or whether you are a thief
Depends on whose solicitor has given me my Brief.

Amateur companies have to play safe by performing the 7 or 8 G & S works whose titles are familiar to whole generations. If *Utopia's* best songs are not widely-known, that must have been to the benefit of several later composers of musicals who have searched the score successfully for ideas.

With any of the libretti, the sophistication of Gilbert's satire may take some understanding today. The Parliamentary issue of *marriage to divorced wife's sister* (*Iolanthe*, 1882) means nothing unusual now, but in those times it was regarded as near-incest. On the other hand, the question of women's rights had led to reform legislation enabling married women to retain their own property after 1885, and the struggle for the women's vote intensified up until 1914. *Princess Ida* is now seen to have a fine satirical edge, and should have a good future.

*Patience* (1881), which Gilbert feared would be one of the first of his plays to lose its topicality, can have greater relevance in our days of grossly hyped film and 'pop' stars, and their 'groupies'.

In *Patience* Gilbert had planned to attack the hypocrisies of the clergy, but realised this was too dangerous an area and switched his target to literary pretentiousness. The reaction against industrialisation had produced from about 1850 numerous cults: admiration for medieval times and handicrafts, 'return to nature' movements, a pre-Raphaelite school of painting, 'art for art's sake' – collectively referred to as (Victorian) aestheticism whose eccentricities were brilliantly caricatured in top magazine 'Punch' by novelist George Du Maurier.

The music, with mock-recitative effusions and martial sounds which skip too delightfully to be used on a real parade ground, admirably fits a plot concerning the rivalry of two insincere 'aesthetic' poets and a troop of honest but unenlightened dragoons for the affections of twenty maidens. They, in delicate health and pre-Raphaelite costumes to match, are, in an opening *scena* that resembles the later one in *Utopia*, swooning over an effete, fancifully-dressed poet, Bunthorne, and expressing their 'love-sickness' in tones of genteel longing.

Left alone, Bunthorne confides to the audience in a witty song the absurdities of the fashionable aestheticism:

> If you're anxious for to shine in the high aesthetic line as a man of culture rare
> You must get up all the germs of transcendental terms and plant them everywhere
> You must lie upon the daisies and discourse in novel phrases of your complicated state of mind
> But the meaning doesn't matter if it's only idle chatter of a transcendental kind.

And everyone will say as you walk your mystic way
  'If this young man expresses himself in terms too deep for
me, why, what a very singularly deep young man this deep
young man must be.'
Be eloquent in praise of the very dull old days which have
long since passed away,
And convince 'em if you can that the reign of good Queen
Anne was culture's palmiest day
Of course you will pooh-pooh anything that's fresh or new
and declare it's crude and mean
For art stopped short in the cultivated court of the Empress
Josephine.
  And everyone, etc.
Then a sentimental passion of a vegetable fashion must
excite your languid spleen,
An attachment a la Plato for a bashful young potato or a not
too french french bean
Though the Philistines may jostle you may rank as an
apostle in the high aesthetic band,
If you walk down Piccadilly with a poppy or a lily in your
medieval hand.
  And everyone, etc.

This starts as a medium-paced patter song which slows
down on *and everyone will say* to a confident stroll, with further
changes of tempo to the mock-oratorio of *this deep young man*.
Leading into this song, Bunthorne has confessed his insincer-
ity in ludicrously monotone recitative.

The ideas allude to Plato's philosophical theories, the
fashionable neo-classicism of the Napoleonic period and cults
opposed to 19th century materialism. The poet whose image
fitted a lily worn with ostentatious clothing was Oscar Wilde, who
was complicit to the point of making a lecture tour in the USA as
part of a publicity campaign for *Patience*, organised by Carte.

Gilbert's women have their romantic aspirations or cerebral
passions, with marriage as a necessary social objective. He can
be cruel to the older female characters who suffer the stigma
of having 'missed' marriage. In *Patience*, Lady Jane accompanies herself on the cello in a lament to lost youth:

Silvered is the raven hair –
Spreading is the parting straight

Mottled the complexion fair,
Halting is the youthful gait.
Hollow is the laughter free,
Spectacled the limped eye.
Little will be left of me
In the coming by-and-by.

Sullivan gave her a very poignant song but often complained about the harshness of some of Gilbert's verses.

At about the age of seven, my imagination was seized by 20 girls spending their whole lives in a trance, pronouncing the words *Ah, misery*. I could not understand why my favourite aunt wanted to spend her evenings singing such mournful songs in a G & S troupe. It was another twenty years before I could come to terms with such activities. I had to love opera before I knew how to enjoy laughing at its eccentricities.

The Savoy operas exemplify the so-called English sense of humour, laughing at everything except their most ridiculous institutions, though Gilbert of course crossed that line. Their works should be played with utmost seriousness in order to maximise the farce and retain the period charm. Since the copyright ended in 1961, there have been numerous attempts to modernise the treatment and make radical alterations to the text: for example, a New York *Black Mikado* was widely admired and London has seen and heard the *Pirates* with microphones – and with additions from other Savoy operas. Yet Britain's amateur companies remain thoroughly traditional, and new musical arrangements are not popular. Underneath the vivacity and sentiment, Sullivan's style is disciplined and classical.

These works were conceived in contrast to the licentiousness of the Offenbach shows and G & S differ even more from Viennese operetta and lack the sensuality which was an important feature in all Continental models. The difference is quickly noticed in the rhythms, especially waltzes which Sullivan used far more than the Parisians. Humour and mockery are often at hand in the music, such as when the villains are threatening or confused.

Gilbert's wit is centred in the intellect and never raises a cheap laugh: he set out to provide entertainment to which one would not be afraid to take the oldest or most innocent members of the family. Sex does not raise its head above the genteel facade; crime, greed, jealousy, deception, – and neurosis in very fast tempo – are no more than the topics of comic songs.

Himself a singer, Sullivan wrote with consideration for the human voice songs which were admired by Johann Strauss and many others, whilst still remaining very popular with opera societies as well as with audiences. Gilbert also has his place in literature with his extraordinary skill in the use of words and many phrases which have passed into the language.

No English composer has been able to rival Sullivan's special kind of high spirits but the *Yeoman of the Guard* marked a change, with tragi-comic overtones. It has remarkable characterisation of a sad clown, English and inoffensive, in sharp contrast to an Italian clown in the opera, I *Pagliacci:*

Misery me, lackaday dee,
He sipped no sup, he craved no crumb,
As he sighed for the love of a ladye.

Some consider it the G & S masterpiece, with a particularly fine madrigal, *Strange Adventure*. Could there be a worthwhile successor in this direction? Later attempts lived very much in the shadow of these collaborators.

Edward German's *Merrie England* (1902) looked back to an Arcadian society of ballads and leisurely dances. In 1960 it was given a new script and operatic treatment by Sadlers Wells, but to judge from the recording made, I would think it has dated in a way that Sullivan never does.

A number of serious composers attempted operettas into the 1920s, but posterity has not given their works the opportunity to reassert their qualities. Yet at least two others contributed important burlesques, and should find a place in the repertoire.

The title of Holst's *Perfect Fool* is a joke on the heroes of grand opera, such as a Siegfried or a Parsifal, and takes as its targets Wagnerian and Italian Romantic opera. It is an esoteric work which requires an outstanding performance and an audience that appreciate the numerous allusions. Its most interesting features include Wagner and Verdi parodies.

Vaughan Williams might introduce boisterous humour into his most serious works, but *The Poisoned Kiss* was an extravaganza which enabled him more than anywhere else to let his hair down, employing fashionable dance rhythms of the 1920s. Unfortunately, the whimsicality was perhaps overdone by his librettist so that the work does not receive the attention the music deserves. It was a sprightly offering to Cambridge University, and its qualities were revealed in a London University opera performance in 1975, such as a soft-shoe-shuffle, the satirical chorus *Today when all the world behaves* and the final gem, *Love breaks all rules*. Fairly recently, I saw a cut-down version which concentrated more on the scope it offered for extravagant acting, lively body movements and horse-play.

There was a curious reaction in 1961 when a pastiche of 19th century burlesque-operetta appeared in London. In its original version, it included a Grand Inquisitor scene aimed at the U.S.A.'s scourge of MacCarthyism. Leonard Bernstein's *Candide*, based on Voltaire's classic satire, went to the wrong theatre, to the wrong audience, and was taken-off after a remarkably short time.

It returned to a successful run decades later when there was more appreciation about its genre. It is now recognised as most suitable for opera houses, and a late addition to classic burlesque.

Its story of endless travel permits the composer to indulge his liking for exotic rhythms, such as Brazilian, and the lengthy narratives are helped along with 'buffo' arias in 19th century style. Bernstein's respectful imitations go as far as Sullivan, Offenbach and, in *We are women*, the youthful spirit of a Mahler *Wunderhorn* song. His addition to the repertoire of operatic jewel songs, *Glitter and be gay*, is a very incisive coloratura aria, a stage highlight.

# 12  *After 'Carmen': Massenet & Chabrier*

By the 1870s, French opera could look back on its decades of fame but was entering an uncertain phase and was badly in need of imaginative change. The older generation of composers had either recently died or were no longer very active, whilst Charles Gounod was turning more to religious works.

In 1875, Charles Bizet had the inspiration to compose one masterpiece, *Carmen*, at the age of 38, and in some ways made a break with the past. Bizet had succeeded in creating two obsessive characters not only credible but among the most vivid in all opera; and with music of compelling appeal.

Yet within months he had to die and straightaway after Bizet's death, attempts were made to tamper with the structure of the work, to convert it from *opéra comique* to grand opera, with superfluous recitative, mainly as a sop to fashion. In its original version with its naturalistic spoken dialogue, it was made explicit that Carmen's lover Don José had previously killed and it might even be inferred that he was a psychopath.

Bizet, then, had moved towards dramatic realism, a story of unheroic people who had neither privilege nor power. Who would continue to remove the artificialities from French opera and bring music which could express feelings wonderfully into closer relation with action and dialogue? Even a composer of exceptional genius might encounter formidable or over-whelming opposition, such as Berlioz (1803–69) had suffered much earlier in his negative, bitterly so, relation to the Paris opera world.[1] In many ways an exception, he had also been gifted in symphonic composition, an area where 19th century French music had, until then, made no impact abroad. France's younger composers would continue to accept primarily the challenge of the stage.

Of these, Jules Massenet (1842–1912) was in the mainstream, closely associated with the teaching establishments, a disciple of Gounod's lyrical art and able to digest the new musical ideas, giving shape to many of them in his own compositions. Could he believe, aged 33 when he broke down at Bizet's funeral, that he would so quickly become, for the remainder of the century, the leading and most prolific exponent of French lyric opera? He was more likely to take Parisian opera by stealth than by storm; and his first big successes had been in the fashionable, elevating medium of oratorio, where he could apply his musical sensibility to the themes of fallen women, *Marie Magdeleine*, then Man's first temptress, *Eve*. These made big impressions on his young contemporaries, Bizet, and Saint-Saens, whilst Vincent d'Indy made the definitive comment, always quoted, on Massenet's special allure: *Discreet and semi-religious eroticism*.

His *Roi de Lahore* (1878) filled many theatres, a traditional opera, very melodious and with an 'oriental' veneer, not unlike Delibes' *Lakmé* (1883). His individual craftsmanship was realised in his fourth extant work for the stage, *Hérodiade* (1882), which was considered by many to be influenced in conception and dramatic structure by Verdi's *Aida*.[2] *Manon* (1884) is a work of similar repute to *Carmen*, as different as one might imagine, on a classic 18th century novel involving a young couple living on their wits mainly at the expense of privileged society.

In the opening scene of the opera, Massenet introduces the two young protagonists, establishing their immediate mutual attraction, with the Chevalier des Grieux completing a verbal seduction with the soft option that the impressionable Manon should rush-off to Paris with him rather than enter a nunnery. Her surface charm is suggested in the second theme of the prelude, then in a gentle rising phrase with which she introduces herself.

She is experienced enough to reject in spirited manner a roué's crude proposition, and three girls mock the men who are finally shocked to realise that the pretty bird has flown. Her cousin, known by the same family name of Lescaut, has an impetuous 7-note theme, a young man always on the make and scheming to deliver her to influential men of wealth. Des Grieux's first reaction to Manon has the musical sweep of a youth experiencing a new range of emotions, and throughout the opera, as distinct from the novel, he is presented as the defenceless victim of Manon's cupidity.

A character defect is suggested in a motif; Manon disclaims responsibility for being approached by a stranger with a nervous little phrase which she repeats when explaining that she is not 'mauvaise', even if drawn excessively towards pleasure. She uses it again in the second act when her lover expresses anxiety about their future.

The linking of drama and music becomes most effective in Massenet, and like Wagner, he moved away from the artificial break which permitted applause; for the 1880s, his technique was very advanced and subtle; Massenet the academician even uses a fugue for a light-hearted ensemble. The orchestra gives such a close commentary that the singers may concentrate on articulation and gesture, often speaking in monotones until, in emotional moments, they are drawn into the melodic sweep.

His shorter scenes tend to be very tightly constructed, such as the intimate second act when the dubious heroine's motivation is revealed. Sufficient time has by then passed for Manon, living without money in their love nest, to decide on betraying des Grieux because she cannot live in poverty.

The third act offers an elaborate diversion, more in the familiar comic opera style: shopping crowds, street entertainers, a ballet, early 18th century musical pastiche, dialogue without music or with a dance heard in the distance. It rejoins the central drama when Manon is by chance informed that her lover is on the lonely path to religious orders, having concluded that their feelings had been a mad dream. This leads to one of the few seduction scenes in opera successfully carried out by a woman[3], and one of Massenet's most intensely sustained duets. An inspired sequence of melodies occurs in the finale when Manon is dying[4].

Manon's music suggests her need for excitement and her fickleness; she is not an essentially tragic figure, is negative to questions of morality and has no fight when confronted with any difficulty. She is credible, but a girl who will not live long enough to mature. The opera has the feel of a sophisticated comedy in four of the six scenes, all taking place in markedly contrasting localities, so making heavy demands back-stage.

Massenet's success in assimilating diverse styles was attracting some informed criticism: did this courteous man who so much wanted to please his audience lack the conviction of firm artistic principles? Did he too readily follow fashions? Was he guilty of religiosity?

*Le Cid* which followed a year later in 1885 was a venture into grand (pageant) opera with a Spanish flavour, but the unbending heroism of the protagonist restricted the musical characterisation, and the work is now most often represented by its dances in concert or ballet form. *Esclarmonde* (1889) was a Byzantine fantasy of Wagnerian proportions and solemnity. Wagner was at that time making his greatest impact among French composers, and his melodic influence was apparent.

Like St George, Thais was a mythical saint of early Christianity, presumably invented as the subject of a cautionary tale. Anatol France had used the idea for a novel ridiculing mysticism in which a fanatical young anchorite monk, Paphnuce (Athanael in the opera), comes out of the desert ostensibly to convert Alexandria's infamous cortisan, Thais, but sublimating the desire he once felt for her as a boy. The sadistic pleasure he gains from dominating her, and its implications, are absent from the operatic version of *Thais* (1894) which offered Massenet a scenario of exceptional promise and stark contrasts: erotic, religious, pagan, ascetic.

The scene in which Thais, coolly erotic, first appears, preceded by her retinue and admirers giving themselves up to abandoned behaviour, was a topic of much discussion in operatic circles[5] some years after the work's first performance. The music reached levels of sensuality for which one had not been quite prepared in French opera. An enticing phrase heard repeatedly in the orchestra accompanies Thais' first meeting with Athanael, and its appeal was one of the effects which soon reconciled the author to the opera's divergent interpretation and overall lack of irony.

Emerging from a meeting of philosophers, Athanael is introduced by a short 'cello motif', but their confrontation ends when Thais' maids start to remove her clothing and he flees. Their later dialogue in which he moralises with increasing effectiveness about Thais' life leaves her confused, alternating between mocking defiance and dread of eternal damnation. Left alone, in an aria of intense anxiety, *Dis-moi que je suis belle*, Thais consults her mirror, reflecting on her life of emptiness and fears for the passing of beauty.

Her spiritual crisis is symbolised in a symphonic interlude, the *Méditation*, with its calming violin solo. That is one of several integrating motifs, and the great effectiveness of this scene has been obscured outside the theatre by the unending popularity of the melody which has been heard at millions of coffee-tables, often played with excessive sentimentality.

The theme returns, but with heightened dramatic effect late on in the action when merged with the former 'cello motif now transformed to the pitch of Athanael's passion[6], which is expressed in richer orchestral tones against music of sparse texture, sometimes with chromatic melody, portraying Thais' decision to take the path of self-denial to God. Athanael, obsessed then distraught as he witnesses her dying in a state of physical decline but spiritual grace, is portrayed without a note of ridicule, and both characters are presented as worthy subjects of classic tragedy.

In the period following its being written, Goethe's novel *Werther* (1893) had driven many young readers to suicide in imitation of its eponymous hero. Massenet rose to this problematic tale of love obsession which in most hands would have been unpromising operatic material; that it became one of his finest works reflects his empathy with the characters, whilst the critics admired its score and innovation such as the symphonic integration of what had been until then a novelty, the saxophone.

The new realism which was arriving during that decade, led to *La Navarraise* (1894), with its battle scenario, dispensing with ingratiating music, but it was very successful with the public. *Griselidis* (1901) told a gentle love story with a sub-plot concerning the domestic quarrels of the Devil and his wife, which gave Massenet an opportunity to return to the broad comedy of his earliest stage works. An opera for male voices, *Le jongleur de Notre Dame* (1902), presented the age of the troubadours, excluding any love interest, and even women's voices. No Paris theatre rushed to produce a work in which Massenet had jettisoned his two strongest selling-points, but new patronage from the ruler of Monte Carlo led to the first of his several successes at its opera house. His stage versatility was even exceeding expectations and the work which reached Paris two years later has since been performed there more often than three of his 25 operas.

He welcomed classic literary subjects which he interpreted in his subjective manner, but his treatment of *Sapho* (1897) was faithful to Alphonse Daudet's contemporaneous novel. Its title is a name that the heroine Fanny has been given because of her fame as an artist's model, and an object of men's lust, whilst the story resembles that of *La Traviata*, except that her state of health is no problem. Thais' mirror aria, and Manon's soliloquy to her dressing table have a most affective, gentle lyricism in Massenet and *Sapho* plays to this strength, Werther without the histrionics or death.

Massenet's *Don Quichotte* (1910) was not strictly his swan song, and four more operas were to follow rapidly, but we may think of it as such, and certainly as reflecting some of his feelings at the age of 68. The distinguished melodies continue, not rising in youth and passion, but descending in regret, such as in the parting of Quixote and Dulcinea.

Dulcinea has become a reluctant sinner, mature for her twenty years, dreaming of some kind of spiritual love, an escape from her insensitive companions. Quixote can strike a chord within her, a fool perhaps sent by heaven, and she can only disillusion him softly at the climax in the penultimate act when he absurdly proposes marriage. The music is often in calmer reflection of Spanish dance rhythms, but a return to more familiar Massenetic song occurs when Sancho Panza rebukes the mocking crowd, presenting the old knight in idealised terms. This is a masterly characterisation of a man who lives only in his head, a wholly tragic interpretation but worthy of the more humorous Spanish classic.

Though Massenet composed much vigorous dance music and a bravura piano concerto, he remains distinguished most by the intimate moment, brief melodic gesture, the sensibility of his female roles which drew on him the jibe of being the *daughter of Gounod*. Modern attitudes would favour his kind of expressiveness and the rise in popularity of Romantic opera now brings his large output once more into prominence[7].

His melodies influenced the lighter style of French songwriting which was popular abroad in the first half of the 20th century, and his music was often plundered without attribution.

An unusual initiative for the time was to bring many of his most beautiful themes into one large ballet score 'shadowing' a familiar opera. Though not welcomed in all critical quarters. Leighton Lucas, who had once danced in Diaghilev's troupe, completed in 1972 this commission for the Royal Ballet. He arranged individual excerpts from many Massenet works but specifically excluding music from *Manon* and the other best-known operas, for a ballet on the subject of Manon Lescaut.

The opening scene, closely following the story of the opera's first act, has a similar appeal. On a sepia, reddish brown canvas, crowded with a picturesque range of characters, we observe the arrogant dealings of privileged men with girls and menials. Lescaut is an unashamed pimp and the image of a compliant Manon is represented here and elsewhere by the delicate phrasing of perhaps Massenet's finest art song, *Crépuscule* (Twilight).

Des Grieux's courtship takes the form of the expected two ballet sequences, first a seductive solo. Almost inevitably, this is followed by the melody which characterised Massenet as much as any other, the *Elégie*. It never found a home in any of his operas, but perfectly fits as the Act *I pas de deux*. Though it has been overplayed for a century, the *Elégie* stands as one of the most searing melodies in all Romantic music.

He was an enlightened teacher, never pushing his own preferences onto students, among whom Renaldo Hahn carried-forward his skills into light opera, whilst Gustav Charpentier, in his often-performed opera, *Louise*, presented a tragic social drama set against the colourful background of a corrupting Paris. Debussy's *Demoiselle élue* (based on D.G. Rossetti's poem) and some other early compositions showed Massenet's melodic influence.

■ ■ ■

Massenet's near-contemporary, Emmanuel Chabrier (1841–1894), was not academy trained, but an original who was free to follow his inclinations with a disregard for conventional taste. His idiom was at first widely misunderstood, or considered too unsophisticated, but he was in sympathy with the new spirit of the age, and his work opened-up new directions which later composers from Satie to Poulenc would follow and including Debussy and Ravel.

Chabrier was attracted to the music of cafés, dance-halls and bull-fights. It was his practical observations entered into his music notebook during a holiday in Spain which led to the composition for which he is popularly known. He was fascinated by the *flamenco* dancers, the women's smiles, flashing eyes, arms and hands quivering, especially the sensual *Sevilliana* with castanets, most of the body remaining motionless . . . the lead dancer *becomes literally intoxicated with her own body* . . . guitarists *strumming anything in 3-4 time which the Andalusian women accompany, clapping off-beat whilst moving their behinds in unison.* Such a description might offend Flamenco *aficionados* but Chabrier was naturally crude of speech.

He was one of the first foreign composers to employ Spanish rhythms to great effect though the Russian, Glinka, had composed a fine orchestral *Jota Aragonese* as early as 1845 and Bizet's *Carmen* had of course sought the Spanish idiom, though not to the approval of the first Madrid audience.

Chabrier crams numerous melodies into the six minutes it takes to play his rhapsody *España*, but probably only two are authentically Spanish. There are two-feet tapping rhythms alternating, and several melodies or variants enter over the top with larger strides, including a famous, sweeping brass theme, and a huge orchestral climax.

That certainly captured the spirit of the dancing in a way that would appeal immensely to foreigners, rather than to Spaniards. It makes startling use of cross-rhythms, two and three beats to the bar, but apart from its orchestral and contrapuntal brilliance, it sounds less typical of Chabrier than its companion piece, the *Marche joyeuse*. This hurls itself forward in irregular rhythm, suitable perhaps for ballet dancers but not for soldiers.

His *Ode à la musique* is the kind of work many composers like to produce at least once - Sibelius' *Autrefois* and Rachmaninov's *Vocalise* come to mind. Women's voices are bathed in delicious harmonies; the lingering after the beauty of sound has an idyllic quality.

Then there are some very distinctive miniatures for voice and-or piano, admired by connoisseurs, such as the three waltzes for piano which in his ironic fashion are not as 'Romantic' as their title. His *Bourrée fantasque* has an eccentric duality: a music-hall notion of a primitive war-dance alongside a caressing melody for the boudoir. It impressed pianists by exploiting the impressionist resources of the pedal. Austrian Felix Mottl orchestrated it, and became keenly committed to playing Chabrier's larger works in Germany where they were well received during the early 1890s.

Chabrier was enthusiastic about Richard Wagner's music dramas, though as far as he was sometimes influenced, that aspect of his work is not now considered the most interesting. Cosima Wagner's severe comment, that he wrote *café-concert trivialities*, can therefore be seen in humorous light.

Frau Wagner would have been appalled by Chabrier's quadrilles on her husband's themes, entitled *Souvenirs de Munique*, and an 'incongruous' song, *l'Ile heureuse* (the Happy Island), which starts almost like a piano version of *Tristan* in the guise of a sentimental ballad. Another piece from the same cycle has a rhythm which imitates the movement of that most ridiculed of creatures, the turkey, and includes the whimsical playing of Don Giovanni's serenade, a Freudian touch before the term was known.

In their admiration for Chabrier's supposed Gallic wit, critics have long since decided that his one important venture into Wagnerism was an honourable failure because it stretched his talent too far. The opera *Gwendoline* undertakes the themes of love and extreme violence in a story of Viking invasion and Anglo-Saxon revenge. Certainly, it must have needed a conscious effort to put aside his effervescent vocal techniques to concentrate, for example, on the complexities of writing for the large choruses of grand opera. Consequently it is praised more for individual items, and the overture's opening, suggesting nordic barbarism, would not sound out of place in a Sibelian tone poem.

He only completed the first act of another opera before he died, yet after a rare concert performance of *Briséis* (1899), fellow-composer Paul Dukas implied that it would have been a gem, with its:

> tender, voluptuous grace . . . ingenious connections of chords, internal contradictions, unexpected streams of cadences.

What there is of it does impress in the concert hall, illustrating how Chabrier's style was developing in sophistication, and with increasing expression of sexual passion, as had been anticipated in a short cantata for mezzo-chorus and orchestra, *La Sulamite* (1884). Of this, composer Alfred Bruneau had written: *It is a long cry of love, formidable in its last paroxysm.*

Chabrier's range of inventiveness is most apparent in the opera, *Le roi malgré lui* (a reluctant king), completed in 1886. It suffers from a weak plot which can be the only reason it is neglected. The confusing story is coloured with courtiers who play card games, assassination plans, switched identities, a neurotic conspirator who has an unfaithful wife, and a gipsy girl who diverts with relaxing Arabesques and a love interest. Though there are references to an episode in Franco-Polish history, it can be enjoyed as a fiction which gives pretext for the appearance of Polish, Hungarian, Spanish and French styles of music.

In a charming, idiosyncratic work, elaborate crowd scenes are given striking polyphonic resolutions; two of these are so compelling that for concert performance, they have been given virtuoso orchestral versions: the *Fête polonaise* and the *Danse slav*.

Chabrier's flexible rhythms help the clarity of the words and the concise melodic phrasing works well with comic dialogue. As the meaner human emotions do not really surface in *Le roi malgré lui*, no problem of expression arises.

The score insinuates distant times and places. There are archaisms of modal scales and quaint brass flourishes. The startling harmonies of the opera's opening bars and the chords of the ninth[8] used in that prelude have been much discussed for their influence on Debussy and others. They are related to the conspiracy scene in which Chabrier creates an ingenious parody of the fourth act of Meyerbeer's *Huguenots*.

There are lyrical passages for women's voices which float voluptuously in delayed resolution. Starting with a clear reference to the famous Offenbach original, a barcarolle for soprano and tenor drifts off into more anguished harmonies which are uniquely Chabrier. That can be seen as symbolic; if Chabrier as a young man had worked in the Parisian theatre instead of being a civil servant, he could have become a leading figure in French operetta. He had the flair, humour and versatility to follow Offenbach, lacking only the opportunity and perhaps the desire. It was the success of two compositions that persuaded him to become a full-time musician at 38, at which age Rossini had retired from composing operas.

*L'éducation manqueé*, (a defective education), successfully matched musical devices to whimsical subject matter. It starts with a square melody, appropriate for a self-satisfied teacher but who is to be accused of not telling his favourite pupil something about the facts of life. The youth expresses his innocence in the simplest pentatonic language but when he become angry, switches to a much more assertive key. The pair then recite a long catalogue of academic subjects in a curious patter-song.

The teacher has to confess that he is not competent in the requisite discipline. Perhaps like Adam and Eve, the boy, a mezzo-soprano, and his girl-friend are to gain carnal knowledge as a result of clasping one another during a storm. As their naivety falls away, the style of singing seems to move from Gounod and Massenet to authentic Chabrier, a sensuous waltz rising in anticipation.

'*L'Etoile*' (the Star), launched Chabrier's success at the age of 36. In the style of French operetta, it was first performed at Offenbach's theatre, the *Bouffes-Parisiens*, in 1877, so boldly original that it must have astonished even the old master, and not much later, Debussy used to sing the whole of it, accompanying himself on the piano.

The plot makes a valid point without trying to do more than create laughter, and cannot be more absurd than the spectacle of millions of humans regularly consulting their horoscopes. It concerns a mythical despot who in the absence of T.V. and cinema, gratifies the Sado-Masochistic urges of his subjects annually with a public execution including ritual torture. The victim is always someone who falls into the trap of insulting the disguised monarch in a public place: in this case, a spirited young stranger to the city.

There is a neat twist to the story. By chance, the King's astrologer does a reading, with the conclusion that his master will die within 24 hours of the victim. From that point, the King lives in a permanent state of anxiety, and will give anything away, including his favourite princess, to keep the youth alive and contented.

A clear parody is *Chartreuse verte*, which opens in the buffo style of Donizetti, though the humour seems to come mainly from the 'alcoholic' phrasing of the song and the sight of two inebriates dancing a stately gavotte. There are some curious, sprightly songs, two being interrupted in turn by tickling and sneezing, and melodies with broad sweeps for the two lead sopranos whose highlight is the *Romance de l'Etoile*.

Being an amateur musician at the time, Chabrier gave-up a secure career to join Paris' *vie bohème* and the famous artists of the age with whom he had a creative rapport. He became an art connoisseur, and friend of Manet, purchasing his *Bar aux Folies-bergère* and several paintings by Monet and Renoir. His early death held back the wider recognition he deserved before the end of the 19th century.

Chabrier's musical personality is easily recognised by the shape of his melodies and original use of modal and harmonic language. He can blend two disparate, even uninteresting phrases into an exciting unity. He is perhaps less known today in his homeland than in Britain[9] but his influence on several French composers of the generation following his, and Poulenc still later, is often apparent to the ear, and they were generous in their praise; Maurice Ravel selected an airy tune, Siebel's aria, from Gounod's *Faust* and re-wrote it in the style of Chabrier.

# 13  *National Music*

In the 18th century, Europe's privileged classes shared a cosmopolitan music culture that became subject to the prevailing classicism which was then thought to be uniquely self-sufficient. There was no appreciable attention given to the music of the peasants, or to that of non-European societies. Asiatic music could be presented in comic stereotype for special purposes, such as background effect in operas, with the assumption that 'it' – that is, a fascinating variety of musical styles – would be more complex in its melodic shape, sliding along unfamiliar scales generally in a higher pitch than we enjoy, and lacking harmony.

There were isolated attempts to suggest such lands as Turkey. Composed as incidental music for a play about Athens, Beethoven depicted the occupiers with a Turkish march, repetitious, with occasional melodic leaps, in his most jovial style; would it have reminded any Turk of his homeland? The notion that a Turkish band consisted of shrill wind and percussive instruments playing fast, repeated notes guided Mozart and Rossini in their occasional need for 'local' colour.

For his *Singspiel* (light comedy with music), *Abu Hassan*, Weber[1] produced just one appealingly exotic melody racing up and down on the strings, whilst the accompanying opening duet, and the other nine songs, sound nearer to Mozart or Schubert. This hurried string theme reappears for a 'Turkish' finale, suitably preceded by a slow march of triangles.

There was occasional use of the terms 'alla turca' (to be played in the Turkish style) or 'alla zingarese' (in gipsy style) on a music score. The Turks had exercised some cultural influence in territories they occupied, such as Greece, Bulgaria, Albania and Serbia, and traces can now be heard in those countries' folk music.

There was an assumption that the gipsies were the dominant force in the music of Hungary and adjacent lands where they provided the itinerant musicians. In fact, that influence was not so concentrated, reaching the warmer European lands from the Ukraine to Spain, where it is still specially popular as *flamenco*.

Gipsy melodies influenced even Liszt and Brahms when they began to prepare arrangements of what they considered Hungarian folk music. These small-scale compositions had immense melodic and rhythmic appeal, setting a fashion followed by many other composers, and helping in the West to create picturesque images of distant lands long before the age of international travel by any but the rich.

Liszt and Brahms had obtained music data second hand, in some of the more sophisticated parts of the Austro-Hungarian Empire. Wandering players, mostly gipsies, had brought their skills to Budapest and Vienna, and worked their musical charms in restaurants and open spaces to delight customers: folk, and more recent popular tunes were played side by side. Liszt was proud of his Magyar (Hungarian) birth but was really an outsider, speaking German and French; yet he was able to acquire some very inspired melodies for use.

His tribute to his native land included songs and 19 *Hungarian Rhapsodies* displayed in virtuoso piano versions, a slow section followed by a contrasting fast one in the style of the *csardas* with its sad then exhilarating moods. Of the six rhapsodies that are known in renumbered orchestrated versions, the first contains themes which Liszt thought so distinguished that he used them in an extended work for piano and orchestra, the *Hungarian Fantasia*. The Second Rhapsody with its astonishing acceleration is sometimes quoted as evidence of Liszt's tendency towards vulgarity, but is popular with conductors who want to show the fastest speed an orchestra can be expected to attain.[2]

Two decades later, Brahms was completing a set of dances in a two-piano version mainly for young people's entertainment in their own homes. He did not fully anticipate their popularity and only orchestrated three, but others were at hand to do so for the remaining 18 of these *Hungarian Dances*. He set aside his formidable symphonic techniques to present each dance in a simple, direct form, with a middle section contrasting in theme and rhythm. Only in the later ones did he use some of his own melodies which are not easily detected. Most dances were to last less than two or three minutes, though the two more extended ones have been especially popular: the 6th with its unexpected changes of tempo and the 4th which gives a languorous impersonation of 'gipsy romance'. Nor was there anything condescending about Brahms' approach because respect for folk melody generally inspired his composing.

Through the commercial success of those dances in sheet music form, Brahms was able to recommend a younger friend, Anton Dvorak, to his Berlin publisher, Simrock. Dvorak was able to provide equally successful dances and the first of these appeared in 1878. He had already been concerned with projecting the Slavonic folk idioms into academic prominence in his native Bohemia where with a mixed German and Czech population, Austro-German styles of composition had predominated. He brought a fresh Slav melodic flavour to his serious compositions whilst continuing to embrace the great Viennese tradition[3].

Unlike Brahms, he used his own melodies from the start in his two sets of *Slavonic Dances*, completed in 1886. He looked well beyond his native Bohemia, specifying the dance rhythms and the lands where they had originated. He was also more inclined than Brahms to develop each movement and the last one, the 16th, is virtually a symphonic poem. It is, along with number 4, a *sousedska*, a very graceful dance from an earlier century. The Czech *furiant* (nos. 1 and 8), with its cross-rhythms, the *polka* (no 3) and the headlong Serbian *kolo* (no. 15) are very energetic. The Ukrainian *dumka* (nos. 2 and 10) has been of special interest to composers because of its complexities, often with two melodies played simultaneously and subject to rapidly changing moods.

Even a century later, these compositions of Liszt, Brahms and Dvorak can generate a special excitement in the concert halls. Meanwhile, preparing small dance-like compositions under a national title, initially for domestic playing, was to spread to several countries in the 1880s and 1890s. As in Norway, with Grieg and Svendsen prominent, it became a colourful ingredient in concerted efforts by national movements to establish their cultural identity, and was not primarily intended for foreign ears.

The fashion was not without its critics, on grounds of artificiality. It had become associated with the salon and the concert hall, refined and not played on the characteristic folk instruments. Melodies would be transposed often from strange modes into (for us) familiar major and minor keys. In England some protagonists of folk music turned against classical forms of music-making; an extreme position was taken by the influential Cyril Scott who would not tolerate 'tampering' with original folk material.

After 1900, an invaluable development in several countries was a scientifically researched method of collecting traditional songs. Hugo Alfven listened to a recording of the *Devil's Polska* by a local fiddler before orchestrating it as authentically as possible in his *Third Swedish Rhapsody*. *The Lark*, a breath-taking example of musical acceleration played on traditional pipes, became a virtuoso violin passage as the climax of George Enescu's *First Rumanian Rhapsody*.

As a result of musicologists building-up volumes of notated folk melodies, the emphasis turned away from imitation of perceived styles, and two most important trends followed: arrangements of authentic folk music and the study of traditional techniques to enhance composers' own methods. Those that were most committed to finding inspiration from folk music helped to establish nationalist schools of composition. More ambitious larger-scale works began to appear; impressive among these is Zoltan Kodaly's *Psalmus Hungaricus*, whilst his *Spinning Room* is probably the greatest and most inspired of all genuine folk operas.

In the later arrangements of folk music, it became more common to refer to individual songs or districts of origin; to the length of symphonic poems, Kodaly composed the *Dances of Galanta* and *Maroszek*, and Vaughan Williams the *Sussex* and *Norfolk Rhapsodies*.

With certain compositions becoming popular classics, one disadvantage is that many others of similar value will be neglected. Some music is born for permanent stardom; Brahms' *Hungarian Dance* no. 5 has been performed countless million times, not always to perfection, in hotels and restaurants from Helsinki to Valparaiso. Whenever a T.V. document is produced on Rumania, one or other of the exquisite melodies from Enescu's rhapsodies are almost certain to be heard. Radio once put a so-called 'Swedish Rhapsody' into the popularity charts, but it merely consisted of a few minutes plucked from Alfven's generously long *First Swedish Rhapsody*. The superficiality of such contact did not lead to more interest in the other works of that composer.[4]

We come to think of national music idioms as being quite distinct but much research has been carried out into the historic links. The great melodies crossed frontiers, so one should not be surprised if old songs, including many for children, appear in different languages and guises[5]. Stylistic similarities are more likely to appear in the Westernised or sophisticated versions; that same *Swedish Rhapsody* resembles in moments *Hungarian Rhapsody* no. 6, (The *Carnival of Pesth*). With the exception of some extreme areas, such as the southern Balkans with their Turkish influence, we all share a great European musical heritage.

# 14 *Before The American Invasion*

(MUSICAL ENTERTAINMENT IN THE EARLY 20TH CENTURY).

On those old accoustic recordings, every one of those voices is now beyond the grave, sadder to hear with the passing of the years; nor could their performing have been as imperfect and strained as it sounds.

Those records produced mainly between 1900 and 1924 could be expensive, nearly half a working man's weekly wage, and had to be treated with care because they were so fragile, though that did not prevent soldiers taking them to play in the trenches of France. Most homes were proud to possess a few; in that less sophisticated age, even their appearance must have had a magic, an evocative quality.

Nor can we make the final break with accoustic recording, because of Caruso, Emma Calvé in an historic *Carmen* role, Nellie Melba, Chaliapin, Amelita Galli-Curci singing some impossibly high notes, the original Dixieland Band, and the *Laughing Policeman* which sold for over 40 years. From British music hall, there were the archetypal Marie Lloyd whose voice was prematurely silenced in 1922, Harry Lauder, the Scot that *loved a lassie* and kept *right on to the end of the road*, and George Robey's 1916 version of *If you were the only girl in the world*.

The status record was the high-priced, yellow H.M.V. 12-inch label, restricted mainly to the best opera and 'classical' singers. The voices sounded much less distorted than the instruments, and despite the advertising hype about 'life-like' reproduction, orchestras were realistically beyond the scope of accoustic recording which could only cover the middle range of pitches and could hardly differentiate certain instruments.

Unlike later sound developments, early technology, including mechanical pianos, did not adversely affect other forms of entertainment, or the traditional home music-making. It was only from the mid-1920s, with the development of efficient radio broadcasting and electric recording, that the consequences began to amount to a revolution in leisure activities.

The piano's dominance of the drawing-room reached its peak around the turn of the century. The middle-classes continued to enjoy their *soirées musicales*, the daughters showing-off their superior or modest talents, but if ballads of unrequited love, delivered with great show of passion, were no longer so fashionable, there were thrilling songs of mysterious Araby, and heroic deeds of British manhood in India to be relived. The most refined songs on the program would probably be from opera, especially Italian, or a German *Lied*. Singers with piano accompaniment might try to recreate the drama of the great stage, and sometimes succeed with a degree of emotion too strong for the drawing-room.

The daughters as pianists would be keen to make their families proud, whilst many sons might escape these genteel activities, or impress girls by playing the latest novelty, the banjo. Women were less disadvantaged than otherwise in pursuing music, and Clara Butt, a splendidly rich contralto, was also able to give stature to popular music, her rendering of *Abide with me* having retained currency. Liza Lehmann was not the first successful woman composer to use exotic themes, selecting superior lyrics, such as Omar Khayyam for her *Persian Garden* song cycle[1], ideal for a display of discreet emotions.

Such ballads were extremely fashionable for many decades, and were often tastefully illustrated on sheet music which had become big business and partly for this reason, some composers prepared songs for dual purpose: the ballad and opera. That does not say much for their conception of opera as a distinct art form, but home music-making had a great variety of first, second and third class music to choose from.

The early 1900s were favourable for the street musicians but not necessarily for members of the general public who, almost unbelievably, might have found them as intimidating as today's 'ghetto-blasters'. Yet they did serve to popularise the classics, with barrel-organs, concertinas and cornets predominating.

Free or subsidised concerts, especially military bands in the parks, were increasing. Popular until 1914 were the German street bands, but the proud home product was the brass band.

There were over 40,000 of these with amateur status mainly in the north of England, and competitions could attract crowds passing 50,000. That tradition had largely replaced folk music in the industrial regions of England.

The Viennese waltz and the quadrille had dominated Western Europe's ballrooms for the better part of a century. The quadrille, for four couples in square formation, was often graced with arrangements of at least four items from a popular opera and it would still be prominent at Court dances around the year 1910. Ideally, the fast waltz was for the very young and athletic, as it would be today, from the age when mothers and chaperons could only sit and watch admiringly. Polkas and quadrilles had produced some excellent music, might permit a flirtatious glance, but made demands on the breathing and were not conducive to lengthy conversation.

In the years before 1914, young people were looking for change, to a more relaxed style of dancing, and a free-and-easy walking style was developing, though hardly encouraged by the dancing schools. The cool-blooded English played their part in slowing-down the waltz, and the so-called *Boston* had a vogue. The biggest London sensation around 1912 came from Argentine: the tango had a very distinctive rhythm, was artistic and passionate. High society even held tango parties, but it was a very elaborate dance which only the more skilled could master. The need was for less complicated steps in new kinds of rhythm. Successful dances begin as a simple movement and gradually become more elaborate. What is now the smooth and elaborate slow fox-trot was, to judge from cinema clips of the early 1920s, without the 'slow', a jerky shuffle with much elbow movement. That and the genteel English waltz became in sophisticated forms the basis of popular ballroom dancing, and there were *Palais de Danse* established in every large town for the increasing numbers of enthusiasts.

Until radio broadcasting arrived, the main hope for widening interest in 'classical' music depended upon local funding for cheap entrance charges, such as town hall concerts. London's Promenade Concert seasons became an annual occurrence from 1895 under the direction of a find conductor, (later Sir) Henry Wood. Almost immediately, he up-graded them by concentrating on the great composers who were to dominate the programs. He stayed in charge until his death in 1944.

Opera of international class was mainly restricted to short seasons with foreign singers, for the benefit of London's rich. Provincial theatres had occasional visits from a touring company, but most opera was heard on the piano or in orchestral excerpts of the most popular melodies. 'Classical' music was being played constantly, by bands, countless varieties of instruments and most importantly in the theatres and music halls. The distinction between 'serious' and 'popular' music was not drawn strictly in the way it is today.

The institution of the music hall had developed successfully from the 1850s. It had been informal, democratic and the more enjoyable because people were permitted to drink alcohol at the tables. The rapport between stage and audience was also encouraged by the ever-present chairman, or master of ceremonies, who was skilled in reparti and a range of adjectives splendidly articulated.[2]

The system was being transformed long before 1900. Many old or small halls had failed to pass the new legal and safety regulations, and large theatres were taking over. Alcohol began to be discouraged as a more respectable image was being sought and a new name, 'variety', became used.

A remarkable number of singable, catchy songs had been turned-out by composers mostly obliged under the terms of contract to stay in the background. That was done to the advantage of the leading artistes, who might become famous on a handful of well-known songs. On the whole, however, performers had to be talented, charismatic, hard-working and, without microphones, also needing strong voices. Much of the public identified devotedly with them as they told poignant stories of the street and 'cheerful' poverty, of social ambition, of love and disappointment.

The splendid London Coliseum, purpose-built by 1904 with 2,500 seats, in Italian Renaissance style, had the first revolving stage in London, essential for what it intended to offer. There were to be up to 15 variety items, some commonplace and not all musical. This however settled into a twice-daily routine; there would be a major act of some 45 minutes, perhaps a spectacular staging of an historic event, a scene from an opera, even a Diaghilev ballet, Sarah Bernhardt, or Edward Elgar conducting the premiere (1912) of his *Crown of India*. Yet that theatre soon gained a reputation for expensive seats and stereotyped, even dull entertainment, the consequence of excessive commercialisation.[3]

Generally, it was increasingly difficult for young talent to reach the top; they were poorly paid whilst seeking the mystique of rapport with their audiences, and surviving strenuous routines. The main problem was that the most famous, with a standard, familiar routine, could command high salaries and might earn more than their talents deserved. A familiar story. Women could take their places on the stage for the first time without being regarded as 'immoral', though Marie Lloyd, who might have been extremely rich if she had not been so generous, had difficulties over her risqué mock-Parisian style. She had a husky voice, a smile in the eyes, restrained lady-like gestures and natural charm on- and-off-stage. Despite her achievement, she was never invited for the annual Royal Command Performance, and in the USA she was unsuccessfully prosecuted for her 'corrupting' influence.

It became common for the best songs to be passed-on over decades, and Marie took one which became her signature tune: *The boy I love is up in the gallery . . .*

Male impersonators, such as Vesta Tilley, thrived – an application of the historic travesty role – and Florrie Forde, though not quite as charismatic as Lloyd, had probably the most heart-warming songs, such as the teasing *Hold your hand out, naughty boy*, and *Down at the Old Bull and Bush*.[4]

Simple old songs with pleasing rhymes and gentle innuendo could be put across with facial and body gestures which assisted the audience's imaginations, especially in regard to sex. In *He led me up the garden path*, one might have envied the lovers' ardour which appears to have lasted a long time:

> The stars were brightly shining but the moon was on the wane
> Still we lingered like a pair of cooing doves,
> I missed my bit of supper, for we wanted once again
> Just to interchange the story of our loves.

Every town had its variety theatre and some in London's suburbs, such as Hackney, were at the top. The Alhambra theatre, conspicuous at Leicester Square and boasting a fine

permanent orchestra, witnessed the changes in music hall
from 1860, but presented fewer variety shows after 1900 when
it began to give seasons of English ballet dancers. They had
been growing in popularity over many years but when the
Ballets Russes arrived in 1911, all others were eclipsed.

The decline of music hall-variety was to be terminal with the
arrival of broadcasting and the talking cinema. The historic
Alhambra was demolished in 1936 to make way for an Odeon
cinema, and Daly's theatre likewise on year later.

■ ■ ■

Around the turn of the century, British musical comedy
peaked, with its sentimental songs, contemporary dress, celebrities, fashions, spectacle and glamour girls. The titles of such
works were important selling points: poor girls or rich aristocratic ladies from Utah, Lyon, Japan, Danzig, Gothenburg,
Kensington or even the Hook of Holland. There were numerous actor-singer 'stars', and many of the male audience, the
'mashers', came specially to admire one or more of the Gaiety
Girls, the dance troupe from the theatre of that name. Many of
these girls married into the British nobility, which appeared to
be in need of genetic renewal, and they were rumoured to
have the appalling inclination to drink champagne from chorus girls' shoes.

The plots were predictably trivial, the characterisation weak
and the lyrics lacked the vigour and wit of the best music hall
songs. One exception was *Floradora*, which had drawn vitality
from unexpected sources, such as the coloured minstrels, and
strutting rhythms like the syncopated trot, *Floradora* succeeded also when performed in the U.S.A., with music by
Leslie Stuart, who also gave music-hall exceptionally popular,
alliterative songs such as *Little Dolly Day-Dreams* and *Lily of
Laguna*, and the 1900 war's patriotic march, *The Soldiers of the
Queen*. All of these are still very well known.

Paul Rubens, Lionel Monckton, Sidney Jones and Belgian-
born Ivan Caryll were other successful composers, but their
shows would hardly stand revival now. One of the better ones,
Monckton's *Our Miss Gibbs*, (Gaiety Theatre, 1906) had the
heroine singing:

*I'm such a silly when the moon comes out.*

Edward German wrote superior scores, such as one
occasionally performed today by amateur operatic societies,

*Merrie England,* recalling the 16th Century and the imagined loves of Queen Elizabeth I. Its theme and musical treatment reflected the vogue in seeking the folk culture of pre-industrial England.

The war gave a boost to theatrical entertainment partly because soldiers wanted to take their families out before returning to the front. A chinoiserie, *Chu Chin Chow* (1916), broke all records with a run of 2,238 performances at His Majesty's Theatre. This was the first of the new productions which spent far more money on spectacle than on its performers. The guiding hand was that of Australian-born Oscar Asche, a distinguished actor-manager who played the fearsome robber, Abu Hassan, in his own version of a story from *1001 Nights.* Audiences found its escape into a glamourised Orient irresistible[5], and its clear-cut melodies by Frederic Norton were most singable. *Any time's kissing time* has charm, but the robbers' march became so familiar as to attract alternative lyrics considered impolite. One of its best remembered songs has a cobbler regretting a problem of conducting private enterprise honestly:

> The better my work, the less my pay,
> but work can only be done one way.

George Edwardes had died the year before but would have been astonished by this success at a rival theatre. He had made his name from the 1890s as the most successful impresario of musical comedy. Anything but a purist, he never guaranteed a musical its artistic integrity and insisted that contracts permitted alterations and interpellations in any work. Yet he had an eye for commercial success, taking some big risks on the unknown, and a production team that knew *what the public want.* He had also commercialised 'glamour' with his Gaiety Girls who were selected from the hundreds that queued on Mondays for interview, to be judged more by their physical appeal on stage than by their dancing skills. He often switched musicals between his two theatres, the Gaiety and the slightly up-market Daly's, to maximise success.

By 1907, he was aware of the need for change and looked to the Continent, starting with two compositions by a distinguished Parisian opera conductor, André Messager. Of these, from his operetta *Véronique,* two duets are still often performed as party pieces, one which takes place on a garden swing and the other referring to a donkey.

Yet no-one could have anticipated the prodigious social effects of a Viennese product imported as a stop-gap before Leo Fall's *Dollar Princess* was ready for his stage. Edwardes went to Vienna to see *Die Lustige Witwe* (The Merry Widow) before deciding to premiere it at Daly's theatre. Though he had contracted the distinguished Mitzi Gunther for the lead, when Edwardes met her in London, he decided she looked unglamorous, sent her back to Vienna and paid heavy compensation. Leading man, Danilo, was to be played by an American, Joseph Coyne, who was no singer. For this reason, they tried to prevent the composer hearing Coyne at rehearsals, when Lehar was already worried about the small orchestra and a mere 21-year old, Lily Elsie, as the widow. When Edwardes had to explain that Coyne was popular and funny, Franz Lehar exploded:

*But I have not written funny music.*

The public were delighted by the young widow, the novelty of Coyne's almost speaking the climactic love scene, particularly when he shouted that he was going straightaway to visit the ladies of ill-repute at Maxim's night-club. Unusually for pure escapism, it was destined to last, the most performed musical of all time.

The London production certainly suited its English audience. It had a breathtaking sequence of light melodies and a flavour of central European passion, which the much-travelled Hungarian composer, Lehar, could conjure-up. The *Merry Widow* ran for two years at Daly's and the commercialisation was unprecedented. In England and the U.S.A., there were Merry Widow clubs, food, and, less surprisingly, corsets, hats, gowns and gloves. Some of the literary intelligentsia considered the London version deplorably vulgar in its praise of wealth and luxury.

The *Dollar Princess* followed, running for a year, but these were Edwardes' last two successes. Continental operetta had become very fashionable; if the English translations of certain works were often inadequate, one from Jean Gilbert's *Chaste Susanna* (called in London the *Girl in the Taxi*) contained the finest advice a father can give his daughter:

*If you can't be good, be careful*

. . . one of remarkably few quotations to be handed-down from musical comedy through the generations.

Edwardes lost heavily after 1911, partly because he did not realise that English musicals were quickly losing popularity. Apart from the novelty effect of the silent cinema, the new attraction was the theatre revue. That was a development from music hall, with separate acts not tied to a plot, therefore permitting more variety, improvisation and dancing.

Yet the English musical still had something to gain from following the Viennese example. There is a story that a British composer, Harold Fraser-Simpson, was asked why he could not have a comparable success. So he took the first four notes of the best-known *Merry Widow* waltz, doubled each one:

> . . . *whate'er befall I still recall* . . .

and thereby set-up another waltz 'hit', *Love will find a way*. He put this into a musical, *Maid of the Mountains* and his songs were in fact more original than this anecdote implies, good enough for another long-running success. Four of the numbers were composed by Harry Tate, and one nearly stole the show, with its sprightly rhythm and reflective words, though the title, *A Bachelor Gay* would now need changing:

> At seventeen he falls in love quite madly with eyes of a tender blue
> At twenty-four he gets it rather badly with eyes of a different hue
> At thirty five you'll find him flirting sadly with two or three or more,
> When he fancies he is past love, it is then he meets his last love,
> and he loves her as he's never loved before.

Asche and José Collins[6] as the Maid were very important in this success. In the despair of the fourth year of trench warfare in France, there was special appeal in the catchy phrasing of one sentimental song:

> For when you're over there and I'm over here,
> The world will be bare and the prospect drear.

This work and *Chu Chin Chow* were the last two significant English musicals in traditional style before the new dance rhythms began to prevail.

The classic ragtime[7], such as that of the fine composer-pianist, Scott Joplin, had a freshness and irresistible rhythmic appeal, and – though communications were nothing like as immediate as in our times – there was no stopping its spreading from the U.S.A. Its first appearance in Britain, at the London Hippodrome, was by the American Ragtime Octette, in 1912, on the same bill as Leoncavallo conducting his own opera, translated as *The Gipsies*.

With the interruption of the war, there was a delay until a jazz band first played in London (1919), when the influential young Frenchman, Darius Milhaud, attended the Hammersmith Palais de Danse to discover what it held of interest for 'serious' musicians.[8] The progress of jazz was slow but steady until accelerated by broadcasting.

Into the 1920s, the British musical was being eclipsed. One of the last traditional composers was Ivor Novello, who had a big success during the first world war with the song, *Keep the home fires burning*. Later, he displayed much versatility, writing and acting in his own plays. Was he 'inspired', when Karl Millöcker's *Dubarry* appeared in London, by the slow waltz, I *give my heart*? His own compositions give that impression and his 'Ruritanian' musicals such as *Careless Rapture* and *King's Rhapsody* drew large, reliable audiences. He was musically the Andrew Lloyd Webber of the 1930s, with a comparable debt to the past and a narrow emotional range. Yet he was additionally a 'matinee idol', enchanting more than one generation of his mainly middle-class audience. He was acting on the day of his untimely death in 1951.

Lehar, Fall, Kalman and Gilbert were composing new works which passed in the 1920s very successful from Austria and Germany to England, and a New York composer, Jerome Kern, had made his mark in London by adding many songs to existing shows. The Astaire brother-sister dance duo arrived in 1923, and two years later, an American musical made a big break-through. In those times, one good song was insufficient to 'make' a show but for *No, No, Nanette*, Vincent Yeomans composed *Tea for two*, of lasting appeal and rhythmically indestructible, and music for the attractive 'hopping' dance, the Charleston. Sadly, the stage play can scarcely be revived in modern times because its plot was so trendy that, with its inane dialogue, it has dated more than most.

Who are the forgotten men of those decades? For volume of output, the lawyer and Oxford don, Fred Weatherly, was remarkable; he wrote the lyrics of 1,500 songs, understandably not of the highest literary quality, including *The Holy City*, probably the major 'hit' of 1905. Also his was the poignant *Roses of Picardy* which commemorated the 1914–18 dead and was composed by Haydn Wood.

Albert Ketelbey started as a symphonist but had to settle for transient popularity. His *Monastery Garden* is a bizarre piece of *kitsch*, and his *Persian Market* was much played for its mock-oriental sound, as well as having become known as circus-music, more recently being borrowed occasionally for pop-music.

During the Victorian age, there had been a strong tendency to present the mass of the population with uplifting music, in the churches and public places. It had been anything but a complete success, whereas new styles in popular music were developing to make an increasing impact as communications and recording expanded.

By the early 20th century, the U.S.A. was beginning to produce a fine succession of popular Romantic composers, from Joplin to Jerome Kern and George Gershwin, then towards the mid-20th century, Duke Ellington, Richard Rodgers and others. They were offering sophisticated, well-crafted compositions with a distinctive American melodic appeal, for the radio, dance-hall and theatre. Decades after their departure, their finest recordings are now widely respected as classics.

On the back of such talents, but also taking-in the second rate, a whole industry of music marketing emerged associated with the term, Tin Pan Alley, and a steadily widening popular culture began to emerge, no longer a spin-off from middle-class tastes.

# 15   *Love in a Culture Clash*

At the height of international popularity, in 1910 Franz Lehar received from his librettists, Willner and Bodzansky, a tragi-comic text for which he composed a passionate work, more symphonic than earlier ones and set mainly in minor keys. As a young man he had shown a talent for opera, and this new stage work, *Zigeunerliebe* (Gipsy Love), was a move in that direction, to be presented to audiences that had enjoyed the light touch of the *Count of Luxemburg* and the *Merry Widow*. The risk was fully justified.

Located near the Carpathian Alps in a land of myths where Hungarian, Rumanian and other folk cultures meet, it is the story of a Rumanian girl, Zorika Dragotin, anxious about being pushed into an 'approved' betrothal to Jonel Bolescu. Fascinated by a strange culture and its music, she conceives of running away with a gipsy fiddler, then after two years returning home disillusioned to complete the marriage her father had wanted.

The turning-point occurs in Act II when her lover, Joszi, agrees to a Romany wedding but not a legal, Christian one. A vivacious Hungarian land-owner, Ilona, displays the beauty of her native songs and dances whilst pulling him away from his commitment to Zorika. Act III has more the feel of Viennese operetta, as Zorika returns to the affluent surrounds of her home and to Jonel, the man who always wanted her.

Zorika's rebellious feelings may be dramatised either in the form of a real or an imagined elopement. Early scenes portray musically her bewitchment as she approaches the River Czerna whose waters, according to legend, if drunk may give brides a vision of their future. It is this experience ominously elaborated which comprises Act II, so that in the original stage version she awakes as if from an amorous dream. She resolves her confusions by deciding in favour of her betrothed without his being conscious of anything more than a troubled moment of uncertainty.

The prelude's opening motif, a defiant expression of the gipsy's need for freedom, will recur in song, illuminating the central theme of woman's desire for love set against man as the restless hunter:

I feel your wings fluttering; still, before you escape
Give me what I long for, Blubird of Happiness.

In one of Lehar's most inspired instrumental scores, the Hungarian cimbalon is specially evocative. It gives the melting background to Zorika's early rejection of Jolan and leads, set against a violin solo, to the enchanted river scene. It is the instrument which later hurls Ilona into the *csardas*, the song being loosely translated as *Gipsy fiddles playing*. It is now widely known outside its theatre context and often assumed to be a Hungarian folk dance belonging to a long list of the world's most characteristic national melodies. In the original, Ilona introduces it in German, then breaks into Magyar for the wild dance section; first-class productions favoured Hungarian sopranos for the role, the accent once being as familiar to Austrians as Scots to us.

Zorika's two waltz themes, one shared with Jonel, are far from the Viennese model, giving voice to her desires but also her anxieties whilst the duet with Joszi, the *Garden of Love*, expresses a sadness for the passing of life.

The dramatic highlights are surrounded with folk-like dancing and choruses, the lighter songs being mainly related to Dragotin and the sub-plot concerning his niece. These became popular in England with such titles as *Two hearts beating as one*, *He's got something the others haven't got* and *It's love which makes us young*.

George Edwardes was keen to see *Zigeunerliebe* in Paris, thought it a masterpiece and signed it up for his theatre, Daly's, to follow the success of the *Count of Luxemburg*. Even so, he could hardly fail to notice a striking difference in tone; much as he admired its operatic features, he persuaded Lehar to add lighter numbers and to permit the plot in translation to be revised. Some of the symphonic accompaniment and an ominous storm scene near the start of the work were eliminated. The experienced Basil Hood was not quite the dramatist he imagined, though he believed that Lehar preferred his version to the original.

Hood deprived the play of its most imaginative feature because he thought London audiences would feel cheated if Act II were perceived to be no more than Zorika's dream. Instead of a gipsy encampment, it takes place outside a country inn, not a drastic alteration. However, Viennese operetta was not normally subject to interpellations and I'd be surprised if Lehar was delighted with the addition of a cheery song, *Home Again*, by composer Lionel Monkton in which the aristocratic father sings of such trifles as ordering trousers from London for the spring season.

Zorika's name was changed to Ilona, and the Hungarian Ilona was replaced by a Lady Babby, a role invented for the charismatic London actress Gertie Millar who could temper romance with earthy realism. How an English lady had mastered the intricacies of Magyar dancing and came to be reminding a gipsy of his ethnic origins is partially explained in the added lyrics of *Cosmopolitan*.

Edwardes spared nothing in achieving a remarkable success, importing the very young Budapest operetta soprano, Sari Petrasz; the production had an excellent one year's run at Daly's. Yet the Edwardes regime was soon to end; he died soon after the war began, but Lehar and other 'enemy' composers demonstrated their regard for him by having a wreathe smuggled out of Germany in time for his funeral.

In the even more down-market plot used later, such as in amateur-English performances, Carpathia or Transylvania are forgotten, and the drama is concluded in an English ballroom. The father, Dragotin, becomes Sir Peregrine Plomley searching for his missing daughter in a carriage which breaks down near the inn where the gipsy wedding is taking place. In questioning what they have come upon, he uses the vocabulary of a music-hall chairman:

> . . . anything tantamount to a tavern? A mirage? A fallacious phantasmagorial phantom?

but his foreign pronunciation and race attitudes are suspect:

> I am mad to strum on a cym-BAL-um, humming like a gipsy,
> And, by God, can gipsies hum.

The itinerant Lady Babby disappears and the Hungarian temptress does not return but a gipsy girl enters in Act II to take over some of her most exciting music including that famed *csardas*. Given a vivacious personality, this character can give the drama a welcome lift when the audience return from the interval nearly half-way through the action. On the other hand, the passion of the original Austro-German (and no doubt Hungarian) versions can be in danger of replacement by an innocent garden-party atmosphere, especially in cheerful English productions which are more common today. The operatic atmosphere was partly submerged by the addition of puns, limerics and topical references which any producer today would immediately replace.

Such considerations tend to make *Gipsy Love* as performed something of a hybrid. The more versatile amateur companies like it for the rich melodies, and its title is thought to draw even patrons who know nothing of the music but hope for 'something different', exotic. They should not be disappointed and conceivably, the work could reappear soon in a British opera house, having the voluptuous appeal to repeat its original success.

Lehar's verdict was clear; it was his only composition to be reworked as an opera, performed as *Garaboncias* at Budapest in 1943. Though received enthusiastically, whatever significance that version had for the musical world was obscured by the fact that within months, Nazi and Soviet troops were using Budapest as a battlefield. Outside Hungary, *Garaboncias* is at present for the archives.

A modern English language translation of *Gipsy Love*, such as that used for a BBC radio performance, has fortunately reverted to the original conception, with the book and lyrics by Adam Carstairs which could now admirably serve a professionally-staged production:

> When others tell us of their humdrum daily life,
> Crying babies, church on Sundays, quiet, obedient little wife,
> Then the wand'rer's blood within us warns that this is not for me.

# 16  *Elgar, Germany and the 1914-18 War*

The man who brought a new passion into English music might have passed for a country squire or an army officer; Edward Elgar (1857–1934) had a handsome, sensitive face and was of a shy disposition. Companions noted his reluctance to show his feelings and, in preference to music, he might have preferred to discuss the day's horse-racing.

Unpredictability is an artist's prerogative. In 1921, when he was suffering severe alienation from music, on impulse Elgar took music writer Compton Mackenzie to London's Queen's Hall, describing the march to the scaffold from Berlioz's *Symphonie fantastique* as 'tremendous'. During the opening Strauss' *Don Juan*, Mackenzie (in his book *Echoes*, 1957) reported: *to my fancy, the whole of the orchestra and the whole of the audience was being conducted by my companion.*

The effect of Berlioz' march made Elgar like *a man in a strong gale of wind*. When the oboist who was to play the last breath of the man on the scaffold observed Elgar's glance, he showed *horrified surprise*.

As the next item was Rachmaninov's 4th Piano Concerto, Elgar received indignant glances as he walked out before the great virtuoso-composer reached the piano.

Significant clues to Elgar's earthiness were his liking for Sousa marches, his great admiration for the skill of a Suppé overture, and recording his own sensuous piano improvisations on a Rossini theme. That side of his musicality helps to explain why, almost throughout this century, Edward Elgar's music has been thought of as part of the national heritage, whilst he is particularly well-known for his marches and other short works that have become popular classics. During his creative lifetime, however, even stronger claims were made and informed opinion has now swung back to the view that he ranks among the greatest of Europe's composers of the early 20th century.

Though he was one of a family of musicians, he also had scientific interests, and as a young man, it was not certain where his greatest talents lay. A big influence then came from his frequent visits to Germany in the 1890s where he used his meagre income for such activities as joining the Wagnerite pilgrims at Bayreuth. One of his better-known early works was inspired by the Bavarian highlands, with his wife writing the verses imitating the folk idiom.

From that period, he established two friendships which were to influence his progress. The German, Hans Richter, had been an inspirational conductor in Britain over two decades, and he performed the premiere of Elgar's first popular large-scale work, the *Enigma Variations*, also taking some of his works to Germany. The best-known *Enigma* movement, *Nimrod*, is widely regarded as typifying the serene, 'English' side of Elgar's music. Yet it was intended as a portrayal of another German friend, August Jaeger, who had settled into English music publishing and had greater insight into Elgar's music than many other colleagues; Elgar confided specially in him about his creative plans.

Performances of the *Dream of Gerontius* several times in Dusseldorf and other German towns in the Catholic Rhineland were highly praised before this work was heard in London, only a few years after he had been struggling for recognition. English composers over several decades had risked comparison with Germany's but here was one that came off well. He was praised by the statements of the man who at the time, 1903, was considered Germany's most dynamic living composer. Richard Strauss did not encourage imitators, but he was quick to regard Elgar as an equal talent with a similar musical vision.

A mutual admiration developed between these two masters of orchestral colour. Elgar's overture *In the South* is one of his finest compositions and its 20 dramatic minutes provide remarkable material for discussion. One vigorous passage sounds as if it had been written by the other man; there are moments of Straussian swagger, a sinister passage with arresting Wagnerian brass. His later *Falstaff* is worthy to be placed alongside Strauss' finest symphonic poems.

Interesting comparisons can be made between Strauss' *Till Eulenspiegel* (1895) and Elgar's 'cockney' overture, *Cockaigne* (1901). This starts with a perky tune, which seems to represent the bustle of working people and the horses in London's streets, and later comes another melody starting with a similar rising three notes, relaxed, uplifting, suggesting more leisurely parts, the ceremony, and the classic buildings of the capital.

In his enthusiasm, Strauss described them both as musicians of the future. 'Immediate future' would have been more precise, because they had only two decades before they were seen to belong to the respected past. In that time, Strauss was to astound the musical world with his earlier operas and Elgar was to compose several choral and symphonic works of a scope and grandeur unprecedented in British music.

He had been drawn to epic themes from Britain's early history, such as *Caractacus* (1898) and the Irish *Grania and Diarmid* (1901), but his first venture into a profoundly spiritual text was most decisive. Cardinal Newman's poem, *The Dream of Gerontius* had attracted Dvorak, who was deeply religious, but he was deterred on a visit to Britain by friends who said it was too 'Catholic' to be popular with the English.

Though also a Catholic, Elgar's religious beliefs were less firm but he was deeply concerned about the impending death of his mother and found Newman's poem affecting. It is a modern morality play, following a dying man, Gerontius, through to a sight of God and acceptance in the next world. This stark theme is one which no other composer might have dared to set to music, combining solemn oratorio and elements which took Elgar nearest to composing a mature work in operatic style.[1] The outcome would predictably be either a work of genius or appalling anti-climax.

*Gerontius* is of an unprecedented intensity which owes much to the spirituality of Wagner's *Parsifal*. I find this most pronounced in the scene when Parsifal has gained heightened awareness after surviving the temptations of *Klingsor's garden*.

Choral music had been viewed as an ennobling social force, and was one area where Victorian England had made remarkable progress in popular participation. Many composers, talented or otherwise, contributed choral works which eventually had become stereotyped. Following traditional examples, they would contain edifying fugues, heavenly harps and other familiar celestial software. Elgar disdained all this, even refusing to permit his publishers to describe *Gerontius* as a *sacred cantata*. Technically, it would also be too complex to be given a routine church performance alongside other works, still less by amateur societies.

Even the conservative Gounod had, in his Requiem of 1894, the year of his death, produced some disturbing chomatic passages. Yet to some English ears, *Gerontius* was not only ultra-modern but alarmingly emotional, a 'foreign import' in Catholic garments.[2] This challenging work was of exceptional length, calling for chorus of hundreds and an orchestra of Wagnerian size. Its climaxes are among the most powerful in all choral music, and the vocal parts have a sound quite distinct from German models.

Yet Wagner's conception of epic music drama encouraged Elgar to plan a choral trilogy on Biblical themes. Two parts of this, the *Apostles* and the *Kingdom*, were successfully completed before religion ceased to inspire him. They depict episodes in the New Testament and the characterisation indicates a dramatic skill, such as the portrayal of Judas' betrayal in the *Apostles*. Significantly, that work is specially demanding, with its six soloists, and some critics have considered the two works an advance musically on Gerontius. Yet, in contrast with their narrative style, *Gerontius* may be more compelling on other grounds, a personal statement which relates to the whole of humanity.

His two symphonies were the first indisputably great ones to be composed by a Briton, and the first was greeted by Hans Richter as the greatest of all 'modern' ones. Any resemblance in sound to Wagner is more in texture than thematic. Both men used a vast orchestral canvas which meant that sometimes arrangers had to make cuts to suit more limited resources. Vaughan Williams stated that he would rather do that to Wagner because Elgar's orchestration was already a model of economy.

His melodies tend to be more expansive and less flexible than Wagner's later ones, lengthy with exciting upward leaps, such as the opening, major theme of his Second Symphony, with its attractive syncopation. It has similarities in shape and feeling to the leading motive of Strauss' *Heldenleben* – something of the spirit of the age?

Elgar's first or second subjects might consist of three or four themes. There are a specially uplifting motto theme and sections of leisurely opulence disguising a tight symphonic structure in the First Symphony (1909). Jaeger commented on the joyous scope of the *scherzo* of this symphony, the *abysmal depths of tone colour* of its *lento*, and the spirited, optimistic finale. Listeners were enthralled, but the Second Symphony which followed quickly and was of comparable length and splendour, seemed to contain a disconcerting message, even a funereal tone in the beautiful slow movement. With hindsight, it is as if the evident confidence of the creative world in which Elgar had lived was about to be challenged by some external threat.

The Edwardian decade, and the years to 1914, represented for Britain the climax of the age of Imperialism, and a period of exceptional brilliance in literature, of colour and vigour in music, of style in living among the leisured classes. To modern ears, Elgar's symphonies give an added attraction, a sense of nostalgia for the spirit of that period.

Both he and Mahler were making grand symphonic statements at that time but though Mahler was known personally to Strauss and Richter, he was not receiving comparable praise. Yet Elgar reacted with excessive sensitivity to the Second Symphony's early reception, and there was no successor. In these works most characteristic of Elgar's style are the spine-tingling, expansive passages often marked *nobilmente*.

Similar in sound and excellence to the First Symphony's motto theme, but faster and in a cheerful major key, was the melody described by Elgar as *something which comes only once in a lifetime*. It shares with Haydn's great *Emperor* theme and Sibelius *Finlandia* the feeling of a patriotic anthem. Performed as a march, the *trio* within a bustling outer section, it quickly achieved unprecedented popularity.

Elgar had stated that, like troubadours, composers should be proud to inspire armies with a song. At the time, the full horrors of the 1900–1 South African war were withheld from the public. Conflict in distant continents could still be presented in picturesque language:

See that thy navies speed, to the sound of the battle song,
Smite the mountainous wave and scatter the flying foam . . .

but this rhetoric from A.C. Benson's *Coronation Ode* of 1902 is
soon followed by more realistic images:

Under the drifting smoke and the screams of flying shells,
When the hillside hisses with death . . .

Elgar set the whole poem, yet it was the final affirmation which
was to accompany his great march, and henceforth be intimately linked:

*Land of hope and glory, mother of the free . . .*

Elgar's final large-scale work before war threatened was an
optimistic celebration of his vocation, the *Music Makers*. Alongside serene melodies he places the First Symphony's motto
theme, and fragments from the *Enigma, Gerontius* and other
landmarks. Female soloist and chorus luxuriate in this
show-piece.

The fashionable conceptions of war were quickly dispersed
by the appalling experiences from 1914. Many perceived
there was little of hope and glory in the eyes of the thousands
of men returning with injuries after experiencing the unimaginable horrors of trench warfare. For creative minds with
cosmopolitan sympathies, the European war must have
seemed a hideous perversion. Elgar had been distressed by
Jaeger's death five years previously. Retired and living in
Germany, Richter renounced his British honours but not the
friendships.

Elgar volunteered for war duties suitable to a man of nearly
60, but composed no more stirring marches like the five he
had written around 1900. Yet he showed humanitarian sympathies by writing works for charity in aid of two countries
which had unwittingly become battlefields, Poland and Belgium. In the style of the compositions, he offers both nations a
message of hope, and includes Poland's traditional song of
rebellion, the *Dombrowski mazurka*, later to be their national
anthem.

*Land of Hope and Glory* was to become England's unofficial
anthem as it was played constantly to cheer troops off to fight.
Elgar had never approved the words attached to it, considering them too jingoistic, and he eventually turned against his

own song. That feeling added to his general pessimism about the way the world was moving.

He was, however, moved to compose (1915–7) his last great choral work, *The Spirit of England*, rising up against

> The barren creed of blood and iron
> Vampire of Europe's wasted will.

This idea is portrayed in a startling orchestral outburst within a soaring anthem; then a movement recalls the sacrifices of women in wartime. Finally, an elegy *For the Fallen*, dominated by a tragic, falling two-note phrase. The words became familiar from the traditional November 11th ceremonies, including the promise:

> At the going down of the sun and in the morning,
> We shall remember them.

The poem by Lawrence Binyon represents a conventional patriotic view of the war, quite out of tone with the bitterness of the younger poets who experienced trench warfare, and whose work would be set to music by a later generation of composers, such as Benjamin Britten.

Elgar's style and sympathies could respond naturally to Binyon's more idealistic vision. *The Spirit of England* maintains the high level of inspiration but is almost Elgar's last significant address to the nation, and his few remaining compositions would be of a more intimate nature. Three of these, all chamber music, occupied him during the last year of the war when he had moved to the tranquillity of Sussex, though not beyond the sound of guns from the Western front. The first movement of his Piano Quintet bears an interesting similarity to that by Brahms, whose music he specially loved.

In 1905, he had given a lecture to Birmingham University students on the genius of Brahms' Third Symphony and its significance as 'absolute' music[3]. Why had he spoken in this way at a time when he was so engrossed in compositions with a literary association? Part of the answer might be inferred from his symphonies and late chamber works.

In Britain, he is now regarded as one of the greatest late-Romantic symphonists, along with Gustav Mahler whose First Symphony was conceived on an equally large scale before he proceeded to others which were even larger. One does not go far among British music-lovers to find many who hold both composers' music in the greatest affection, without wishing to compare their divergent geniuses.

Elgar's Cello Concerto solved the problem of giving the solo instrument adequate room in which to move by the most skillful use of the orchestra in its highest and lowest levels of pitch. This, his last undisputedly great work, is intensely personal and at first was not widely understood. It is now seen as partly reflecting his feelings just after the war, and with its deep, elegiac beauty, has become in England today one of the most sought-after of all 'classical' recordings.

Though Elgar was always very conscious of his humble social background, he was not in sympathy with the more democratic spirit which inevitably arrived with the mass participation of men and women in the war effort. He was just one among many who vaguely realised that society, and his world, would change decisively as a result of the upheaval. He began to live in the past.

His wife had always been able to give him the needed encouragement, and had contributed a poem for his fine orchestral song cycle, *Sea Pictures*. Her death in 1920 appeared to bring to an end his creative period, compounding whatever effects the war had had upon him. A man prone to nervous depressions, he often wanted to withdraw from public view, though he carried out the duties appropriate to his status. He would avoid repeating himself in composition, but derived much pleasure in recording his own music[4], probably the first man of such distinction to do so systematically.

The music of Debussy and Stravinsky were leading influences in the new age and Elgar felt no affinity. Romanticism by 1914 was being undermined and, as it were, was killed-off by the disillusionment of war. Elgar, a characteristic late-Romantic composer, dying creatively with it. He would inevitably influence some younger composers, and among these, Bliss and Walton, but he had no direct followers.

There was a fashion for more light-hearted compositions with which composers based in Paris were experimenting. For Elgar, it seemed that a more frivolous age was emerging in the arts. By contrast, he had achieved self-fulfilment within familiar spiritual values and using the firm Germanic music structures of the late 19th century. The new generation fixed him in the illustrious past; by the 1930s, he was increasingly remembered by his more traditional and popular works, whilst his challenging large-scale creations were less performed; significant exceptions to this were his two symphonies and the lyrical Violin Concerto, with its three spacious movements.

He did in fact have a late impulse to write one more symphony, apparently on a more modest scale, in response to a commission from the BBC, but in 1934, his preparations were overtaken by death. He had added immensely to the power and expressiveness of English music.

# 17  *The English Music Renaissance*

## MUSIC WITH ORCHESTRA, c. 1900–1950

In his inauguration speech as professor of music at Birmingham University (1905), Edward Elgar was caustic about the tendency of our composers and musical institutions to imitate foreign models:

'25 years ago, some of the rhapsodies of Liszt became popular. I think every Englishman since has called some work a rhapsody. Could anything be more inept? To rhapsodise is one thing Englishmen cannot do'.

The previous year, Charles Stanford had published his piano rhapsodies inspired by the image of Beatrice and the story of Francesca and Paolo in Dante's *Inferno*. Dante was widely known to have been an important literary inspiration for Liszt. The reference was so pointed that the two composers never again spoke to one another.

How did England acquire the reputation abroad of being a musical backwater? It was assumed there had been an almost total lack of great English music composed throughout the 18th and 19th centuries, since Purcell. There was a vague notion that the most inspired music in our islands came from Welsh, Scottish or Irish sources. Such composers as had been in vogue were long forgotten by the middle of the 20th century and there was remarkably little curiosity about this.

English folk culture had been more seriously damaged than that of probably any other country as a result of social disruption from its early industrial revolution. Music had begun to occupy a less important role in people's consciousness, and performers did not generally enjoy a high regard, unless they were distinguished foreigners. A simplified view was that the upper classes regarded music primarily in terms of social status, and the middle classes were too busy making money to want their children to become involved as professional musician. Art music had been mainly financed from private sources, and this attitude persisted though many European cities were taking great pride in their official contribution to the arts.

London's Royal Academy of Music had been established in 1822, but there was not much advance in training facilities until the 1880s when three more London colleges began to take full-time students to a total rising steadily from 4,000, with composition at last being treated as an important subject. If that would help produce later generations of talented composers, from where would the large audiences come?

After 1871, Kensington's Royal Albert Hall occasionally witnessed concerts with choruses of up to one thousand singers, and some eight times that number of listeners, whilst the Crystal Palace continued to house the largest musical gatherings in Britain. Yet there were remarkably few permanent concert halls in England's cities, and generally high entrance charges were a deterrent to many.

England's more popular music-making was basically amateur. Church-based choral music had been England's special strength in the Victorian era, such concerts being considered almost the equivalent of religious services.

In the promotion of great music a few individuals gained the prominence which might otherwise be reserved for towns and institutions. Henry Wood worked very hard from the 1890s to improve British orchestral playing which the German Hans Richter had initiated. Thomas Beecham used the fortune he had inherited from pharmaceutics to try and establish all-the-year-round opera in London; he also founded two symphony orchestras still internationally famous some thirty years after his death.

Until the 1900s, if our serious music was at best an imitation of Continental models, the recent scope for recording forgotten works has tended to underline this. When Elgar burst into fame, Charles Stanford and Hubert Parry were composing in the style of the great German Romantic tradition, so that Parry now sounds like a close disciple of Brahms, and often appealingly so. The British public understandably preferred the German and Viennese models, having done so for a century. Sadly, Parry may be remembered mainly for *Jerusalem*, a noble Christian anthem, and a beautiful concert piece for voices, *Blest Pair of Sirens*. A competent, prolific composer, Stanford is now referred to primarily as a teacher of greater ones at the Royal College of Music.

On the operatic stage, there had been a considerable London flowering in the age of bel canto. The Irish composer and singer, Michael Balfe (1808–70), was sufficiently talented to draw melodic inspiration from the more famous Italian works of the period immediately before Verdi. One century later, Beecham was bravely attempting a revival of his once very popular opera of 1843, *Bohemian Girl*, with its Bellini-esque soprano aria, *I dreamt I dwelt in marble halls*, which remained popular as a single item well into our century.

Balfe's much ridiculed song, *Come into the garden, Maud* is worthy of Tennyson's lyrics, having a curious intensity which suggests at least a slightly down-market version of Beethoven's *Adelaide*. It is known nowadays as an example of the over-seriousness of Victorian song-making. His duet *Excelsior* is a period piece which dramatises religious idealism, a most effective drawing-room ballad and a spiritual equivalent to the charge of the Light Brigade.

Two contemporaries mentioned alongside Michael Balfe are another Irishman, William Wallace, whose tuneful *Maritana* was very well received even in Vienna (1848); and the German-born, Julius Benedict, whose opera *The Lily of Killarney* was based on a tragic Irish legend. Yet composers often wrote 'Italian' or 'French' operas because the English language was not acceptable to fashionable London society; Weber's *Oberon* (1826), to an English libretto, was an historical curiosity.

■   ■   ■

During the middle decades of the 20th century, with opera not yet possessing the broad appeal it has today, there was a steady increase in the popularity of orchestral music. Concert programs of that period generally had a precise pattern: a symphony probably not too long to be proceeded by a concerto, after a 19th century overture. BBC Radio's programmes tended to reinforce the popularity of these categories, a few 18th and 20th century composers sharing the audience with Beethoven and many Romantic composers from north-western and central Europe and Russia; and a surprising number of contemporary British composers.

These had become respected through symphonic works which could compete in excitement with the show-pieces of Tchaikovsky, Rimsky-Korsakov, Berlioz and the like. All had reached maturity before or during the 1930s, using a familiar musical language without being much attracted to the experimental or revolutionary trends which had shocked but gradually gained credibility on the Continent.

Edward Elgar, who had learned music in his Worcestershire family, was not academy trained, but became acquainted with the momentous developments in Europe from the time of his arrival in London shortly before 1890. That was decisive for his late maturing, at around the age of 40. His orchestral music was eventually established in the British concert halls as firmly as Brahms, whilst some of his marches and light music became familiar to half the nation.

The audience in Gloucester Cathedral for the annual three-choirs festival of 1912 awaiting Elgar's *Dream of Gerontius* heard a fairly short new work for double string orchestra. They might have been astonished to find themselves thrown-back four centuries by the magnificent clusters of vast chordal sounds floating off into the sky. It was a Fantasia on a theme by the 16th century composer, Thomas Tallis, seen in its austere beauty; it would eventually be regarded by some commentators as representing the spirit of English Protestantism, in contrast with the Catholicism of Elgar's *Gerontius*.

It was composed by Ralph Vaughan Williams (1872–1958) who after the death of Elgar in 1934 would be recognised as the leading British composer, remarkable for his mastery of symphonic, operatic, choral and instrumental works. Though his musical personality is unmistakable in any context, it often bears a similar relation to the English folk idiom as Falla to the Spanish or Kodaly to the Hungarian.

As a young man, he had not rushed to imitate the fashionable Continental composers whom he admired, but studied pre-classical music, notably J.S. Bach and England's of the 16-17th centuries. His musical personality was to be strongly influenced by the modal scales which he intended to use in the context of contemporary musical forms.

If we take the common tonic solfa notes and invent a melody centred on Re instead of Do, it will suggest the modal, Doric, scale which had been much used in English folk-song. This evolving style must have sounded very bracing in 1908 when used in his incidental music to Aristophanes' comedy, the *Wasps*, a tuneful open-air romp. This was continued in his folkish opera, *Hugh the Drover*, where the hero fights a boxing match and is arrested for a Napoleonic spy. There are lyrical interludes for festivities and simple melody, with the ballad-seller singing, to off-stage confirmation by a girl:

As I was a-walking one morning in spring
To hear the birds whistle and the nightingale sing,
I heard a young damsel so sweetly to sing
O, I'm to be married on a Tuesday morning.

This was presenting the past in fresh, entertaining style, and Vaughan Williams also intended to express great themes relating to mankind's struggles, choosing the rhetorical, nature-loving American poet, Walt Whitman, for some of his early choral work. The vast *Sea Symphony* (completed 1909), was conceived in the adventurous, optimistic spirit of the previous decades. Its wildness is often set loose by the use of jumping 5-note (pentatonic) scales, and Vaughan Williams praised the influence of Elgar, to be found especially in the opening of the finale. It was the nearest the two composers ever came in style.

Vaughan Williams believed that 'impressionist' techniques and acquiring some 'French polish' from studying with Maurice Ravel would be valuable in completing another symphony, the *London*. It was to evoke the city's bustle, street scenes with sounds which recall a moment in Stravinsky's *Petrouchka*, dancing to a barrel organ and a snatch of music-hall song. Also invoked is the River Thames, the tranquillity of a nocturne which is joined and merged with a melody suggested by the repeated call of a flower-seller, the sad note of humanity and the calm of night. It is a London more lively with human effort, celebrated in leaping song fragments, a less sophisticated society than our cosmopolitan, automated age, and so it comes across to us with added nostalgia.

In gentle modal passages, there are also reminders of a more rural age; this becomes explicit in the Third Symphony (1922), the *Pastoral*, which was widely considered to reflect England's gentle, undulating landscapes. It has spawned many imitations, especially for films about the countryside, and its detractors suggested it pictured a cow gazing over a gate; but it has a calming beauty, with its continuous melody and a haunting finale for a solo, wordless soprano. He retained a large orchestra to portray a fertile layer of sound, and related the disarming trumpet sounds to his recollections, as a stretcher-bearer and later artillery officer, of beautiful sunsets in war-torn France where he first began to sketch the work. There is a brief interruption by what sound like country dancers from Oxfordshire or Somerset.

The 4th Symphony (1934) was astonishingly harsh and modern, though it is in its tight structure comparable with Beethoven's 5th, including a dramatic transition from third to fourth movement. The tension is set from the start with the fierce motto F, E, G flat, F, which returns during the dance macabre of a *scherzo*: whilst a march seems to be led by wild people. The violent conclusion has some affinity with *Mars, Bringer of War* composed by his friend, Gustav Holst. Public response to this work was so strong that the composer admitted laconically:

I don't know if I like it, but that is what I meant.

Much of his 5th Symphony (1943) evokes a religious feeling, and was related to music which had occupied him intermittently over decades. Based on John Bunyan's classic *Pilgrim's Progress*, the theme of the proposed opera completed not before 1949 traces man's quest on earth for the path of virtue and Godliness. This symphony is generally seen along with *Job* as his most representative work, and its ennobling *romanza*, the symphonic movement by which he will be firstly remembered. Because of the need felt for spiritual sustenance during the war, it was more widely welcomed than any comparable work by an English composer.

The 6th (completed 1947) was enigmatic. Its opening is as arresting as his fourth's, but there are to be peremptory changes of mood and tempo. The severity of the first movement gives way to some revelling, as if by those enlivened with alcohol, and there is some irreverent treatment of religious strains, finally put to right by a solemn, uplifting hymn. A slow section is dominated by a sinister repeated note, but even that does not prepare us for the shock of the finale which tails-off into quiet despair.

It is difficult not to see some notion of a 'fate' theme in all this. It seems the British were ready for such an emotional shake-up and they experienced 100 public performances within its first two years.

Of his nine, these three middle symphonies are often viewed as a trilogy of statements directed at the world condition. The 4th Symphony might have been interpreted as an outburst of anger at the rise of Fascism in Europe, the 5th as an expression of hope for the post-war world, and the 6th revealing the pessimism of entering the nuclear age. Vaughan Williams always took such explanations in his stride, then said he had had none of these thoughts. That is not to say that a work of genius may not unconsciously reflect the spirit and beliefs of an age.

He was among many agnostics who have been inspired by one of the great works of English literature, the 1611 translation of the Bible. This and his concern for spiritual values explains the large output of seemingly religious music. Yet it was the *Song of Solomon* which inspired a fine concertante work, *Flos Campi*, in which the viola has the leading role to this Biblical text. Womankind's yearnings reflect sensual love expressed in a wordless chorus in strange, voluptuous sounds, a suggestion of the music of antiquity. Writing simultaneously in two keys, polytonality, is extraordinarily effective here and that would typify Vaughan Williams' approach to such 'new' techniques, or rediscoveries, of the 20th century, to be used sparingly in specific contexts, rather than as a common tool of modernism. He might compose effectively for unusual combinations, such as a Romance for Harmonica and a Bass Tuba Concerto, but was impatient with the attention-seeking devices which he thought was innovation for its own sake.

With a curiosity about new developments in the arts, Vaughan Williams contributed incidental music to the cinema, such as a film on the loves of a country girl, and an account of Scott's tragic 1912 Antarctic expedition. This is introduced by an etherial soprano voice over a frozen landscape; the atmospheric music was so appropriate to the heroic story that the composer reworked it for a new symphony, his 7th: the *Sinfonia antartica* (1953). Expanding on the courageous, wearying march which will end in the death of five men, it is dominated by the relentless impact of untamable nature, and at start and finish, are heard the wordless voice and chorus which both attract and terrify, giving-out the final dirge, the siren sound of impersonal forces.

The work which most concentrates Vaughan Williams' many-sided personality into 40 minutes is the ballet *Job*, an orchestral tour de force. It follows Job through the stages of prosperity, fear, the extremes of misery, hope and into the sight of god. Human and supernatural elements are dramatically contrasted: a Satanic dance, a richly-scored saraband, a much-quoted saxophone impersonation of Job's oily, hypocritical comforters. Lucifer attempts to resume his spider dance, but his lurch is cut short by God's cohorts which rejoice in a galliard. Its sweeping melody seems to place Heaven reassuringly near to England.

The amount of fine music devoted to Shakespeare's Falstaff is extraordinary. Apart from the Verdi opera, the Elgar symphonic poem and Nicholai's *Merry Wives of Windsor*, there are, among others, Vaughan Williams' *Sir John in Love* and Gustav Holst's *At the Boar's Head*. These last two operas suggest in this lusty story the atmosphere of Shakespeare's time, but Holst's is much the briefer, concentrating on riotous tavern scenes and dancing. He uses throughout traditional songs, finding the words to match them.

In contrast, Vaughan Williams kept closer to the original text and used his own tunes, but including two traditional songs. These were extracted to form the *Greensleeves* Fantasia for string orchestra, a short work destined to become Vaughan Williams' best-known composition and widely taken to typify the gentler aspect of the English folk idiom.

Producing this opera is a big challenge because it has the scope of a full-scale Shakespeare play, scored for many voices and a large orchestra. The composer had not compromised on his conception even if it was to result in far fewer performances; that is also true of his *Pilgrim's Progress*, with its 41 soloists.

■ ■ ■

Whilst Vaughan Williams devoted so much time to the problems of symphonic development, Gustav Holst escaped from them after his early attachment to the music of Wagner. He made an uncompromising break with recent traditions, taking a lone path into the unexplored so that he had mixed reactions when a major composition not publicly heard until 1920 established itself quickly as a popular favourite.

No-one else need have been surprised about that. *The Planets* is a most unusual work in its conception, relating to the remote and the timeless, but rich also in bounding melodies and displaying a rare orchestral virtuosity. The planets are conceived in their astrological forms, so that for example *Venus*, the planet of Peace, is a serene interlude. The *Mercury* pays tribute to Rimsky-Korsakov and the Russian strain, whilst the greatly admired *Saturn* is nearer to Ravel. *Neptune* recalls Debussy and *Uranus* suggests at times Vaughan Williams as well as the magic and mischief of Dukas' *Sorcerer's Apprentice*. It is the exception, a fortunate one, because Holst was generally disinclined to mirror contemporary styles.

There is a legend that a rehearsal of *Jupiter* once caused some London women cleaners to stop work and dance in the concert hall. With its exuberance toned-down, *Jupiter's* main theme has also become a much-used hymn-tune. The work has made an attractive ballet, and remains one of Britain's most exportable concert pieces. It gives full, uninhibited voice to forces which make their presence felt in two other works: the mock-diabolism in his opera, the *Perfect Fool*, and the suppressed cosmic energy of the *Hymn of Jesus*.

Gustav Holst was drawn to the early monodic style of the Church, and paying homage in his *Hymn of Jesus* (1917), with solo instruments displaying the profound beauty of the medieval plain-song, *pange lingua*, before introducing the male and female choruses separately. Sharp harmonies intrude at dramatic moments and discords for moments of religious intensity. Then fierce dance rhythms are unleashed, hopefully inducing the congregation to put aside prayer-book and join-in. Holst was inspired by this mixture of sacred and profane to his finest choral work, one unimaginable within the English Church tradition.

He researched as far as Hinduism, Japan and Algeria for musical ideas and a sense of ritual, translating a Sanskrit text for his opera *Savitri*. His style could range from the austere or archaic to the extrovert and experimental. Yet there was nothing remote about his social philosophy, and, despite persistently bad health, he remained dedicated to his teaching role especially at London's Morley College with its amateur tradition. Starting in 1908, he pulled it up from the worst to the best that could be achieved in such conditions. He undertook to reconstruct and perform Purcell's *Fairy Queen*, a formidable and most important task for a work which had been mislaid for over 200 years.

In 1918, he spent hours in the air-raid shelters encouraging his students to compose and sing parodies of grand opera. That led him on to a difficult challenge, a broad satire of the most generally admired operatic styles in *The Perfect Fool* (1922) from which the rumbustious ballet music has been extracted for its popular appeal. It also demonstrates Holst's expertise in brass orchestration which owed much to his having been a trombonist.

Particularly in his later period, Holst often used much more sparse harmonic writing, such as in the *scherzo, Hammersmith* (1930), a picture of his familiar London environment, which at first was written for military band, and a symphonic poem that he and critical opinion rated among his greatest works: *Egdon Heath* (1927), to a bleak landscape text by the great 'Wessex' novelist, Thomas Hardy.

■  ■  ■

Frederick Delius (1862–1934) was born in Bradford of German parents, and chose to live mainly in the USA and France. Though cosmopolitan, he was not much influenced by German or other musical traditions which he considered intellectualised in ways which music does not require, nor was he sympathetic to fashionable trends or modernism.

He did however turn to German texts for very important works: Gottfried Keller for the opera *A Village Romeo and Juliet*,[1] Heinrich Simon for his pantheistic Requiem, and Nietzsche for his *Mass of Life* (1905). Delius believed that *Zarathustra* reflected his own philosophy and this assertion of the *life force* inspired him to compose on the largest scale in a mood of exceptional elation. This feeling is enhanced by his original use in parts of a wordless chorus, a device which many others were to follow.

For him, music was emotion and poetry, a song plucked from nature and expanded harmonically. Unique for their creation of mood and atmosphere are many orchestral works of modest length and sensuous beauty: their appeal is often so immediate and emotive that the titles are all we need to know: *Song of the high hills*, *In a summer garden* and *Paris, the song of a great city*. Paris had searing memories for Delius and these are suggested retrospectively in that symphonic poem of his early maturity (1899).

His sensitivity to local atmosphere enabled him to draw valuably on the American folk idiom in the Florida suite, *Appalachia* and the opera *Koanga*; and the English folk song, *Brigg Fair*, inspired his fine set of symphonic variations.

He wanted to set Ibsen to music, but eventually realised that writer's psychological complexities did not suit his musical style. Some compensation stands in two inspired short tone poems: *Eventyr*, an unusually powerful evocation of the legendary Scandinavia and *On hearing the first cuckoo in spring* which was based on a Norwegian folk tune. He had a close friendship with Grieg, but in a late letter, the older man expressed regret about the increasing sensuality of Delius's music. He hoped that Delius would pull back; but there was no possibility of that.

Two of his most admired works completed by 1904 share the rich orchestral style of that precise period, and make an interesting contrast. *Sea Drift* is a simple tale of love and final separation narrated in sad resignation by a baritone against a sea-scape coloured by chorus and orchestra. The same forces are employed in *Appallachia*, variations on a slave song, at times vigorous and optimistic, sounds that could now accompany a superior film about America's southern or mid-western lands.

By then, Delius was becoming greatly admired in Germany, before the 1914 war badly affected musical contacts, but his progress in Britain was slower. His style was unique, and he frankly expressed a preference for his own music over others'. He was not drawn to realism and would not have been concerned at suggestions that he did not have sufficient dramatic sense to write great operas. Each of his six had distinctive aims and personality, from fantasy and poetic tragedy, to a conversational style.

Given an intense poetic drama, he could respond to its emotional extremities with a background score; its combination with James Flecker's *Hassan* in 1923 earned great praise at its London premier. It is regrettable that commercial considerations probably inhibit a revival of this kind of play-with-music and we have to be satisfied with concert excerpts so leisurely moments, such as the *serenade*, are better-known than the anguished sequences. The climax of the melodrama gives the lovers the choice of exile and permanent separation, or one day of ecstacy together followed immediately by the most excruciating death, oriental fashion. They take the second choice.

Delius' vocabulary was late-Romantic supplemented by very large orchestras. Yet he did not develop themes in traditional symphonic ways; he varies the texture, an impression of flowing rather than changing, often creating a dream-like effect. For this reason, he was not much concerned with symphonic structure and his four concertos are nearer to rhapsodies.

Delius' music has found a special niche in Britain and does not need to be justified or compared; it exists for those that luxuriate in the feelings which it generates.

■ ■ ■

The deaths of Elgar, Delius and Holst in 1934 served as a reminder that the decade was breaking radically with the past. This brought in particular to the fore William Walton and Arthur Bliss, who in the 1920s had seemed most likely among the English to respond successfully to modernistic trends emanating mainly from Paris; in fact, they both settled within an easily recognisable tonality.

William Walton (1902–83) had caused a sensation at the age of 20 with an 'entertainment' based on euphonious but non-sensical verses by Edith Sitwell, using a chamber orchestra and a parody of the fashionable Schönberg-type *Sprechgesang* (speech-song). It presented 22 dances in comic guise, including valse, polka, fox-trot, tarantella and a yodelling song. One joke was to dress a banal music-hall tune, *I do like to be beside the sea-side*, in *macho* tango rhythm, then play it alternately with a pasodoble in an undignified hurry. If this chamber work offended purists, it was soon arranged for use as a very colourful ballet, *Façade*, for full orchestra (1922). It has probably earned more royalties for Walton than all his other work, and enabled him to concentrate on more substantial creations, though Stravinsky (on imperfect knowledge) told him he thought it his best.

Arthur Bliss had been influenced by Stravinsky and the 1920s' Parisian composers. He was to make substantial additions to the British ballet repertoire, such as the martial *Checkmate*, before and after settling into a more Romantic style.

Walton took three years to complete the massive, orgasmic finale of a symphony in traditional form, but the other parts had been given a concert performance earlier. The first movement is clearly inspired by Sibelius, with a climax of a convulsive string passage over a brassy ostinato. This was followed by a biting *scherzo* to be performed *con malizia*.

He was quickly recognised as an exciting mainstream composer of orchestral, instrumental and choral works as well as concertos with strong virtuouso appeal and welcomed abroad, especially in the U.S.A., for their undisguised Romanticism. A strong characteristic is the nervous rhythmic energy of Walton's faster movements, such as the racy overtures, *Scapino* and *Portsmouth Point*. In his later years, he felt some affinity with the music of Paul Hindemith and composed a set of symphonic variations on a theme by the other man (1963).

As a native of Yorkshire, he had previously paid homage to the choral and brass-band traditions of that part of England with an exhilarating cantata which exploited to the full in sound volume a declamatory baritone, chorus, orchestra and massed bands, *Belshazzar's Feast*. For a Biblical theme, it was considered by some unsuitable for performance in a church. A fierce, strident paganism predominates, such as in portraying the lust for gold, whilst the sequence relating to the *Writing on the wall* is of exceptional dramatic force.

Bliss (1891-1975) commemorated his experiences as a guards officer, in the war which killed his brother, with his powerful oratorio, *Morning Heroes*, employing a range of classic texts with a speaker. His concert-hall successes included the *Colour Symphony* which has an Elgarian majesty, the crisp *Music for Strings*, a Lisztian Piano Concerto and a more lyrical Violin Concerto. His opera *The Olympians* ventured into a lush Romanticism, for which most British critics were unwilling to excuse him. His skill at writing ceremonial works, marches and fanfares enabled him, in his later career, to perform as Court composer.

Like Prokofief, he was able to give of his best for the cinema, especially for a visually exciting version of H.G. Wells' *Things to come* (1936). The incidental music includes a sinister march, to a war scenario predicted for the year 1940, a scene of human desolation, and an idealistic anthem which looks to a future of science and progress.

Walton achieved similar success with music – showing a skill for Renaissance pastiche – to three outstanding Shakespeare films directed by Lawrence Olivier: *Henry V*, *Hamlet* and *Richard III*. He composed one comic opera on Chekhov's *The Bear*, and a passionate version of Shakespeare's *Troilus and Cressida*.

He expressed little hope for the continuity of the musical tradition he had followed, though regarding himself as 'classical' with a lyrical tendency. He had often listened to atonal music with fascination but not conviction. A late pronouncement from him was that the best hope for the future of music might lay with the liberated non-European countries.

■  ■  ■

Arnold Bax (1883–1953) wrote some excellent miniatures, such as the relaxing *Mediterranean*, but preferred the larger canvas for his impressionistic skills which enabled him to compose several of Britain's finest symphonic poems. There are also seven symphonies, large-scale Romantic works, richly expansive.

Bax was born in South London and was rich enough to have the leisure for writing and extensive travel. Extended visits to Dresden and an amorous adventure further east enabled him to gain enjoyable experience of German and Russian music-making. Essentially a Bohemian, he ridiculed the respectable academic approach of the English establishment of his youth. He was also drawn to the mysticism of the Scots and Irish literary movements, and he found within their countries a major source of inspiration.

The orchestra became his natural medium. His best-known work is *Tintagel* (1919), a description of the sea breaking against the coast of Cornwall, with its memories of King Mark and Tristan. A theme from *Tristan & Isolde* is introduced by a mournful oboe and features in the central section, the rapidly descending melody suggesting Tristan's delirious obsession, and mingling with the surge of the sea. Yet there is no suggestion that this indicates Isolde's approach, or that the work is a commentary on the final scene of the opera.

In a western Irish legend, Fand is a woman who like Circe and the Lorelei lures sailors to destruction on her island. In the *Garden of Fand*, Bax depicts a small boat on the calm Atlantic, Fand's seductive song, the revelling, the destructive storm and the calm when the vision disappears in the twilight. Its long, leisurely central theme, with a sonorous climax in the middle, is characteristic of Bax.

*November Woods* reminds us in part of the orchestral forces unleashed in Sibelius' *Tapiola*, but was written nine years before that work. These three compositions were said to belong to the most inspired time of Bax's life, up to 1920, surrounding his love affair with pianist Harriet Cohen.

Unlike Richard Strauss', these tone poems are not conceived dramatically and Bax seeks the dreams, the fleeting moments, the enchantment of our memories. Bax was clearly influenced by Debussy's orchestral touches, and in *Tintagel*, we are reminded of *La mer*; it is the surge of the Atlantic which dominates the work which had become a concert classic by the time of Bax's death.

E.J. Moeran (1894–1950), born of Anglo-Irish parents, collected Norfolk songs, transmuting them in his own work, and also spent long productive periods in County Kerry, Ireland. His output was sadly restricted by a war wound gained when a young man. The Symphony in G (1943) is even nearer the folk spirit than any of the townsman's, Vaughan Williams. It is a large four-movement work closely integrated, the contrasts being mainly in its pace and intensity. This work, and others in rhapsodic style, justify the description, given to him by the authoritative Bax, as a 'Romantic'. Yet he was also influenced by the trends of the 1920s, syncopation figuring prominently in his neo-classical Sinfonietta (1944) with a first movement which strikingly recalls the Sibelius of the 6th Symphony. According to his biographer, Geoffrey Self (1986), he kept the great works of Dvorak and Elgar in mind when composing his own Cello Concerto. Self refers to an 'Irish tune' in its rondo finale but surely it is a variant of the quasi-folk song, the *Star of the County Down*?

Several fine composers inevitably have become associated with only one major concert work. For example, John Ireland

(1879–1962), who particularly admired Brahms, composed admirable miniatures and songs, and his concerto which is often attractively reminiscent of Ravel had, among English piano concertos, been the most performed. That, and his *London* overture, which has a main theme suggested to him by hearing a bus conductor call out 'Piccadilly', are no longer heard often in concerts, for no other reason than the much increased competition of newer works.

Constant Lambert was very influential in the revival of English ballet, and that, with his untimely death in 1950, restricted his composing. Outstanding in popularity is his *Rio Grande*, a melodious, extrovert work for alto, chorus, piano and orchestra, with syncopated 'New World' rhythms.

Rutland Boughton (1878–1960) was greatly attracted to legends and conceived of music drama as a spiritual experience with massive popular participation in the choruses. He contrasted it with virtuoso opera, and wanted to take it away from the opera houses to the open-air festivals, such as at King Arthur's Glastonbury where a different kind of music is still celebrated. (His ambitious schemes were of necessity subsidised by G.B. Shaw and others). He composed ten music dramas including *The Immortal Hour* (1914), which even had one aria, the *Fairy song*, which became widely known.

Granville Bantock (1868–1946) composed in Romantic vein and up to the 1930s was regarded with similar respect to Elgar, but the immense scale of his major works on classic themes, such as *Omar Khayyam*, has much reduced performances, and he should benefit greatly by the recording boom. His *Pagan Symphony* has several Straussian passages, and as an evocation of ancient Greece, it seems rich with late-19th century sentiment. That is probably an important pointer to how he is seen today.

The folk music movement attracted numerous highly dedicated men. Some, notably Cyril Scott, were purists in their approach to the source material, but the Australian-born Percy Grainger (1882–1961) was prepared to make modifications in his finished products, putting much of his own exuberant personality into them The special attractiveness of his compositions caused them to receive much attention on his centenary.

He visualised a nordic cultural movement – not unlike the Nazis' – including Scandinavia but excluding Germany because it had dominated music for so long. In protest against German and Italian music markings, he resolutely wrote all instructions in English, which can look comical. His *Country Gardens*, *Handel in the Strand* and *Shepherds' Hey* are very familiar, light-hearted miniatures. Teachers used to thump his strident country rhythms out on classroom pianos, and in my earliest childhood memory, followed by a Grieg *Norwegian dance*, without any explanation. We were probably expected to ingest them as an introduction to real music: not a bad notion.

*Mock Morris* is his tribute to England's traditional dance, which most city dwellers find laughable. The *Morris* is danced by men only in loose-fitting white costumes, with hat and bells, and the name is a derivation from *Maurish*, Moroccan.

Strongly influenced by the folk idiom, George Butterworth wrote two beautiful orchestral idylls, *The Shropshire Lad* and *Banks of Green Willow* before dying as a soldier in 1916. He may otherwise have achieved the highest distinctions.

■   ■   ■

These composers were often associated in companionship, but not as one school. Vaughan Williams and Holst are obviously close in many compositional aspects, with their common interest in pre-classical English music, and the help they offered one another. Butterworth was a disciple of the first man.

Of the composers mentioned, only Bax and Bantock studied at the Royal Academy of Music where Wagner's importance was recognised, and perhaps coincidentally, they are nearest in sound to the Continent's late-Romantics.

Collectively they can be seen as a late flowering from the great European mainstream. They shared many important values and a positive philosophy motivated them[2]. If they dealt with death, it was in the context of pure passion or of its inevitability; they were not attracted, like so many foreign contemporaries, to portraying neuroses, or psychopathic killers in a new musical language, which they noted without taking too seriously. They were rather inspired by the glories of English literature, its lyrics, the Bible, folklore, the countryside and the tragic aspects of war.

# 18  *Ralph Vaughan Williams as Writer on Music*

Ralph Vaughan Williams – 'R.V.W.' as he was known – and G.B. Shaw date back some four or five generations, but their musical writings, spanning some 80 years, remain unusually stimulating. Their conflicting opinions on many composers are revealing, and especially over the issue of nationalism in music.

Though a mere 16 years younger, R.V.W.'s published writing dates from his maturity, a time after G.B.S. had completed the bulk of his. G.B.S. the dramatist wrote like a journalist; R.V.W. the composer as a teacher and often like a historian. More than anyone else, he has made me go back, or forward to works which he has presented in an invitingly fresh light.

A grand-nephew of Charles Darwin and related to the Wedgwoods, he received a classical education, and took a history degree at Cambridge. A man of very enlightened social views and a good, relaxing mixer, his broad approach to music is revealed in countless anecdotes, but I particularly like hearing details about the occasion when he gave a street musician a hand in fashionable High Street, Kensington by banging-out tunes on his barrel-organ. The only surprise is that he did not subsequently compose a work for that instrument to which he specially liked to see children dancing. That and the lilt of a chorus joining-in a popular music hall song were among his notions of what composer's 'raw material' should consist.

His teacher, Charles Stanford, whom he also admired as a composer, wanted him to study opera in Italy but in 1896, he made the excellent choice of Berlin for his honeymoon. He then remained there for two terms to study, partly because that was the only city where Wagner was being performed uncut. His reward was to receive more encouragement for his awkward talents from the traditionalist composer Max Bruch than anyone had previously given him. He particularly recalls opera evenings and subsequently wrote more about German composers than any others.

Yet the cult of Wagner at that time was not for long to affect him, whereas J.S. Bach remained for him the greatest of all influences. He dislikes the recurring fashion for playing such music on 'period' (18th century) instruments. Being born in an age when the piano had to serve so many important functions, he sympathises with Bach for having had to tolerate the *nasty jangle* of a harpsichord, which could not even sustain a note, and which in the 20th century is composed for only in special circumstances. Of the traditional 18th century instruments, he thought the baroque organ a 'monstrosity' and oboes 'asthmatic'.

Great composers such as Brahms and Wagner do not just pop out of a hat, they *come at the end of a period and sum it up. Sometimes the potentially right man comes at the wrong time; Purcell was too early for his flower to bloom fully.* Sullivan might have written a *Figaro* but was held-back by mid-Victorian inhibitions.

As an 18-year old music student, R.V.W. had his wish come true when he began to study under Hubert Parry. When writing in his maturity, he still considered Parry's *Blest Pair of Sirens* his favourite piece of English music and was absorbed by his *Job* and *De Profundis*. Yet he had for some time been baffled at Parry's assertion that Gounod's greatly admired *Judex* melody from *Mors et Vita* was 'bad' music, and the theme from the finale of Beethoven's *Eroica Symphony* 'good'.[1]

He had had to learn to appreciate the greatness in Beethoven's early and middle-period works behind the idiom which he did not find sympathetic; sometimes he associated it with fashionable Viennese salons. Yet he admired *Moonlight* and *Kreutzer* sonatas which many of his English contemporaries had been inclined to criticise as 'in bad taste'. He calls the opus 78 Sonata 'a dreary affair', despite Beethoven's known affection for it.[2]

R.V.W. writes at length about Beethoven. It seems to me that he had no difficulty with the late-Beethoven works because they cut through all artifice and prettiness. To critics of the finale of the 9th Symphony (1824) he suggests that 'good taste' is a poor substitute for the dictates of genius. That

movement, in his view, is the noblest conception in a work
which ranks alongside the finest of Bach's. If the finale is
difficult to perform to perfection, that is partly because conductors approach it with too much anxiety and restraint; it is
populist in spirit and if Beethoven had lived a century later, he
would have approved of Salvation Army bands. The technical
problems are formidable; D major suits the instruments in the
melody to Schiller's *Ode to Joy*, but is too high or too low for the
chorus, whilst later, holding a high F for 12 seconds is a trial
for most sopranos.

R.V.W. dislikes the 'tag' on the end of the *Joy* theme, finding
it quite unnecessary. In fact, it does not appear in the early
exposition, though I had always considered it an integral part
of the theme, a cheerful rounding-off. He does however
strongly approve of the 'Turkish patrol' variation played by
the wind band and *probably sung by a drunken soldier*, in a section
referred associated in Schiller's original text with the stars
marching across the heavens. Presumably Beethoven's citizen
army still marches in 1824 even though Napoleon has finally
departed.

One of the symphony's innovations is to introduce a 'vulgar'
new theme in the final two minutes – drums, symbols, trumpets, voices, unrestrained jubilation – and R.V.W. considers
this coda one of the work's finest inspirations.

He sees the *Choral Symphony*, not as the perfection of Beethoven's art, but as a great experiment, an adventure *towards the
unknown region* where *even he could not see clearly . . . seeing as in a
glass darkly what no-one has ever seen before or since*.

As Beethoven approached his life's end, contents became
immensely more important than form. His last period would
greatly influence the following two generations of Romantic
composers, but did some of these go too far by rejecting the
classical rules of symmetrical pattern? R.V.W. also asserts the
permanent relevance of the sonata-movement formula based
on the logic of two sets of contrasting themes and keys.

Liszt in particular is viewed critically for deserting sonata
form in favour of continuous development. In order to tell
stories, he needed the innovation of the symphonic poem, but
it was not a success. Richard Strauss is described as 'Liszt plus
one', not a 'modern', as many had called him around the turn

of the century. but 'overheated' and wallowing in the senti-mentality of the 1850s.

Maurice Ravel said that he did not believe in symphonic development for its own sake, as we might infer also from some of his larger works. That did not worry the 38 year old R.V.W. when he took lessons with the slightly younger com-poser. Their first meeting struck difficulty because he refused to compose *un petit menuet dans le style de Mozart*, not one of his favourite composers. The two men established a good rapport – a curious pairing: the large, likeable English bear who fortunately could communicate in French and the small, remarkably self-contained Frenchman who thought Tchaik-ovsky and Brahms quite 'heavy'. He would have been aware that they were both much more keen on symphonic build-ups than he was.

R.V.W. could learn about form elsewhere, but was specially interested in what is loosely referred to as Ravel's 'impression-ism'; but he only mentions very briefly that Ravel showed him *how to orchestrate in points of colour rather than lines*. His String Quartet written soon afterwards was thought by friends to have been influenced by Debussy whose *Sarabande* he admired as an original example of modal harmony.

He was introduced by Ravel to the colour of Rimsky and Borodin and they had been influenced by Michael Glinka who used 'street-songs' in his operas:

> Fashionable Russians habitually talked French to each other, reserving their native Russian for *droshky* (cab) drivers. They labelled this nationalist style as coachman's music. But the coachman's music has survived, while the sham classical style of Rubinstein has almost disappeared.

Elsewhere, he appreciates the value of Russian nationalists having introduced Western composers to modal harmonies, which they had built-up from bare melodies, since folk songs do not possess harmony. Mussorgsky's *Boris Godunov* carried this technique right through, and we should consider it, not as an archaism but something excitingly new,

Bach used and beautified folk themes. It was his cantata no. 80 which dignified *Ein' Feste Burg* (God is our refuge and our strength), which, in the form Martin Luther had played it on his flute, was 'nothing special'. A Huguenot battle-hymn became the penitential *O Mensch, bewein* and later, an English version of Psalm 113, said to have been John Wesley's favourite tune. It forms the basis of the choral finale of the first part of the *St Matthew Passion*

R.V.W. rejects the notion that in the 16th century there was any clear distinction between sacred and secular music, with examples. Calvin's *Genevan Psalter* (1551) contained many beautiful tunes; it set the 134th Psalm to one of folk origin, very familiar in England and the USA as the 'old 100th'. This theme he gave a triumphant setting to be played at the 1953 Coronation, years after he had used it within his own work, the 100th Psalm, which, unusually, he composed in a style near to Bach's.

He was not a Christian believer, but had a deep literary appreciation of the religious classics, and often in writing uses the imagery of Bunyan's *Pilgrim's Progress*. His sympathetic attitude to Christianity was influenced by his understanding of social history. From the late middle ages until the 18th century, Western Europe's courts had ignored as far as possible the music of the people, but the churches did not necessarily do so. That was despite official policy which was partly designed to prevent the congregation singing 'rude' words to familiar melodies.

His references to the Russian coachman's music had probably stemmed from his study of the way the Norman aristocracy in England had attempted to displace the Anglo-Saxon language by French. They had also imported to England troubadours whose impact was superficial whilst the earthy music of the Anglo-Saxons was far more important. The 13th century song, *Sumer in icumen in*, is a great popular melody, whose genius was *the wonder of despair of historians because it cannot be explained in academic terms*.

Native traditions are to be heeded even though they are not always good, and just as in families, bad habits are to be rectified. Respect for other cultures should be implicit but by keeping close to his heritage, the composer of genius, such as Sibelius, may extend his art in directions undreamed of. Stravinsky had spent too much time shocking the bourgeoisie; his finest works follow Russian traditions, notably the *Symphony of Psalms* and *Les Noces*.

He reveals that Beethoven gave him the idea for at least three themes in his own symphonies, with that for Satan's dance in *Job* taken from the opus 135 Quartet's *scherzo* – though I wonder who would have noticed. To his collaborator, Roy Douglas, he confessed that he was worried the opening of his *Sinfonia antartica* resembled the *Ancient Romans'* theme in Elgar's *In the South* overture[3].

Several examples are given concerning the great composers: Schubert allegedly would have known that the theme from his song *Death and the Maiden* was being cribbed from Beethoven's 7th Symphony. The openings of Brahms' Second Piano Concerto, the horn solo, and the *Inter oves* in Verdi's *Requiem* use identical notes, the same key and vary only on one slight rhythmical change, but sound quite different. He cites Mozart's use in his Quartet (K.465) of a phrase familiar to us at the start of the prelude to *Tristan & Isolde*. The relevant Wagner music is no less than a landmark in European culture, and the comparison cannot make it any less original or significant: there is simply a world of difference in feeling and intention.

It is the context which so often bestows greatness upon a musical idea. Any boy bugler might have invented the *Rheingold* theme in Wagner's *Ring*, but coming where it does, its dramatic effect is overwhelming. The drum passage at the end of the *scherzo* in Beethoven's 5th Symphony is not intrinsically great, but *as a sort of resurrection from the abyss, building up into the glorious outburst of the finale, does it not reveal the master mind at work?*

R.V.W. considers that searching in all worthwhile directions for material is an enlightened approach for composition, and he had a very different perspective in this respect from Shaw. He also resented GBS's hostility to Stanford and Parry, 'pioneers' of the English music revival, and virtually accused him of mischief-making.

Progress comes from cultivation. The world of creativity is like a pyramid; the wider the base, the more chance of ultimate success. We should not rely so much on specialisation; there should be more people playing football and not just watching it: reading music should be as natural as reading books. A profusion of composers will produce a great one; and his lesser works should not be disregarded, leading as they do to his masterpieces.

He was however no advocate of a 'do-it-yourself' craft, that approach to music which has been so fashionable and commercial in more recent years. When he encountered educationalists who simply wanted to give a child a paint-brush and let self-expression take-over, he was suitably impatient.

*Life is very exciting for the young composer nowadays; he is free of all rules* (written about 1924). He may have to rebel against his traditions but should keep a life-line and not be lured to destruction by foreign voices: *the triviality which is so fashionable among the (musical) intelligentsia is the worst of precious affectations.*

The ordinary man can get real vulgarity in his daily life; he wants neither that nor derision nor cleverness from a serious composer. He will not be frightened by a little 'uplift'.

Why should a composer be specially interested in folk music? It draws on intonation and speech rhythms; it reflects communal tastes and feelings, it can be further worked upon; its melodies are free from the restraints of harmony and rhythm. Composers deny their national and local heritage at their peril; Mozart and Schubert were 'national', as were Grieg and Mussorgsky. Haydn's resemblance to Mozart is only superficial, the result of a common musical education, but in his finest works, Haydn the Croat can be heard. Yet what we call the 'classical' idiom is the Teutonic idiom. When Beethoven arranged some Scottish melodies, they lacked authenticity because he had given them a German flavour.

In a similar spirit to Bartok and Kodaly, R.V.W. was collecting folk songs from 1903 and recording local musicians. As music editor of the *English Hymnal*, he then introduced at least 30 folk tunes and set about reharmonising the work for the benefit of millions who had no chance to hear more sophisticated art music. He simply explained that the work was a way of keeping in touch with great melodies of the past, a modest comment considering the importance of the new *Hymnal* (1906) in reviving public affection of folk music, appearing as it did under a disguise.

He noted the value of the initiative under the Emperor Joseph II in the Vienna of the 1780s not only to shake-off the Italian influence over opera but to encourage a genuinely national style. That of course encouraged Mozart to compose his two great German operas, *Die Entführung* and *Die Zauber-flöte* (*Il Seraglio* and the *Magic Flute*, as we say), and though it was only a brief phase, it was part of the chain which led from Hiller, through Marschner and Weber to Wagner.

Young composers should cut their teeth on the familiar, what is near to them, as well as on the compositions of the greatest: no matter if they imitate and make big mistakes in the process. There is a polite rebuke for certain 'modernists' who forget that the human soul is involved in composition; being 'modern' does not mean being trendy but relating one's art to real life. The traditionalist Brahms drew greatly on his love for folk music, whereas Liszt cultivated the reputation as the great innovator. In recent times, does not Brahms appear fresh and exciting whereas Liszt seems dated?[4]

Brahms and Wagner would be *leading nowhere* for young composers just before 1900. R.V.W. and the others had there-fore been like *kittens running after our own tales*. Then one new inspiration arrived in Britain just on time with Sibelius; in *Finlandia*, he hob-nobbed with the man-in-the-street, but had *sublimated human experience into the mysticism on his 4th Symphony*.

Even in the First Symphony, Sibelius merely flirts with symphonic conventions, but his themes give form to a whole movement. He can make a simple C major chord sound completely original, such as in its dominance of the Seventh Symphony. He uses patterns generally on a small scale, with a partiality for the ostinato, a short rhythmic phrase repeated many times against a changing background. Sometimes, the music seems to stand still, but he knows exactly when to break the spell, and let it rush on.

As a composer, R.V.W. saw himself as serving us plain food and hoping it would prove nourishing. He even used to arrange a formal meal-tasting: late in life, a 'committee' including Arthur Bliss and other composers and musicologists used to comment on his latest work served up on the piano.

He had relied greatly on the advice of Holst whose death in 1934 was a deep personal loss. Whilst others spent their holidays in Bayreuth or the Dolomites, Holst was playing in a sea-side dance band and continually benefited from his exper-ience in orchestral pits. Though poor, he risked his teaching post at London's Morley College by losing many rich students for the committed ones who were slow to appear.

Holst had done nothing by halves. In the *Hymn of Jesus* he strains our sense of harmony to breaking point; in the *Planets*, there are disconcerting moments, such as *Neptune* the mystic giving us a glance into the future. The opening of *Venus* is very beautiful, though *Uranus*, despite its remarkable glissando for full organ, is rated lower, just 'good fun'.

Holst was attracted to the Sanskrit classics for their mysticism, not the orientalism. The exception was the orchestral suite, *Beni Mora*, which, if played in Paris might have given him a European reputation, and in Italy might have caused a riot.

The days when English composers were insensitive to the poet's words are past (1937). Ivor Gurney, a 'Georgian', followed in a great song tradition going back far beyond Brahms and Schubert. The occasion for this tribute was Gurney's early death after a period of insanity probably caused by a war injury.

George Butterworth's death in action had also been commemorated in 1916 when R.V.W. recalled how he had not observed the beauty and character of certain folk tunes until he heard Butterworth improvise harmonies for them. This had not been mere cleverness but part of the process of musical evolution.

By 1945, R.V.W. was already a willing recruit to film music. This could be composed with strict regard to action and dialogue, or as a continuous flow; he preferred the latter, but the other method is a good disciplinary exercise for any contemporary composer.

He concluded that the ideal combination of film and music required that one should be completed before the other was started. That was unlikely to happen in the prevailing conditions of haste, though Disney's *Fantasia* had been the exception, since it was easier to plan a cartoon in this way. Problems, from the human factor to synchronisation and sheer expense, have to be overcome before the cinema can achieve the status of a new art form.

He could conduct his own work with distinction, and set forth written precepts; these included a revealing comment, on *tempo rubato*:

Perfect orchestral rubato should be like the playing of a single performer, holding back or pressing on almost imperceptibly as his emotional impulse directs. This cannot be achieved except by a permanent orchestra at one with itself and the conductor, and then only after long and careful rehearsals.

There is comfort for people just starting out on the path of musical discovery. To understand a big symphonic work there is no need to look up text books or read music. One need only develop the qualities of attention, memory and co-ordination to the utmost. The essential is that every passage we listen to *whether it be a folk tune or a symphony must grow, organically, from its roots*.

R.V.W. was guided by a consistent musical philosophy reflected in his compositions during six decades of unprecedented levels of change in musical beliefs and fashions. Despite his faith in the creative spirit, he says remarkably little about the future and is dismissive of Schönberg and the 20th century musical revolutions. I would guess that the only certain development which would please him since his death is the much greater opportunity for musical participation.

He would be totally sceptical of all forms of cosmopolitanism which have dominated musical culture, both elitist and populist, in the decades since his last writings in 1955. Despite his appreciation of Russian nationalism in music, he does not indicate awareness that his views would have been applauded in the USSR. His book on *National Music* has even been translated in the post-Soviet period.

If he could be questioned now, would he agree that we are reaching the end of an exceptionally great period of European culture?

# 19 *Bartok and Transylvania*

Transylvania is a fascinating country of mixed cultures, of history and of legends; in the West, it is considered remote and no more than a subject of weird imaginings. We might be fortunate enough to see an authentic filmed documentary about it, but any other media attention is likely only to appear in times of emergency and should be therefore treated with scepticism.

It is a large province, about the size of Scotland, but generally more mountainous and less accessible. For this reason, it had resisted Turkish invasions over centuries, but had been linked to the Hungarian kingdom until as recently as 1918. It was then annexed by Rumania under the 1919 peace settlements, and has since been the object of friction between the two countries, though that was played-down in the communist period.

Today, Rumanians constitute almost two-thirds of the population, the Hungarians about one third, and there are also German and *Tsigany* (gipsy) minorities. These four racial groups have been able to develop separately and in rural areas with remarkably little intrusion from modern Europe. Even today Transylvania has therefore remained an immense source of historical interest and folk culture.

In 1905, Bela Bartok (1881–1945) set out with simple recording equipment, such as a phonograph, to visit remote parts and obtain authentic folk material from local musicians. It was no easy task, physically or in other ways. Old men whose memories dated back to the 1940s were often reluctant to sing for *strangers from the big city*, Budapest; and when they did, they might break-down with emotion. There are moving accounts of such events and Bartok's reminiscences show strong emotional involvement. His team were also able to use moving cameras for the complex dances which the mainly young performers were proud to be able to display.

The timing of this research was most favourable; recording equipment had only just become available and population movements were much less than later, during and after wars whilst neither branch railways nor the radio had arrived to disturb the culture of Transylvania. The outcome was a priceless written record of living folk music which had been passed down, like folk poetry, through families.

The races live side by side throughout Transylvania, and political division is not practicable. That did not prevent Hitler splitting the province between the two states in his arbitrary fashion in 1941, but the arrangement died with him. The Hungarians had to accept Rumanian control, but have declined in numbers, mainly through emigration and because their birth-rate is relatively low. Second only to their language, they attach great importance to their music as a means of expressing racial identity.

The Rumanians have a comparably rich musical heritage, and the *hora* is the most familiar of their dances abroad, with its strong rhythm. The *briul* is very fast, and the *doina* is accompanied by a melody which seems to hover, suggesting a Turkish influence. The Pan-pipe is one of a sophisticated variety of flute-like instruments, which can provide a range of effects from furious driving rhythms to the atmospheric and the sinister, vigorous rather than sentimental. If their culture is for us a little more accessible than the Hungarian, it is probably because their language has a strong affinity with Italian, being derived directly from Latin. They are proud of having descended from the Romans of the province of Dacia.

Bela Bartok's earliest research in Hungary had started with his friend, Zoltan Kodaly, who however was too occupied to accompany him to Transylvania. Of 7,000 Hungarian folksongs collected by 1920, Bartok's share was one third, but he also showed a similar interest in *Tzigany* (gipsy) material and recorded 3,000 Rumanian folk tunes. He investigated in Turkey for traces of the influence of its music as a result of the Turkish occupation of most of Hungary in the 16th century. He also researched hard in Slovakia and travelled in North Africa and Russia to further this form of enquiry. It was his conviction that cross-fertilisation between cultures was of great value; that put him very much at conflict with the theories of racial purity then growing in influence throughout central Europe.

His folk song arrangements were very few, and a rare example of direct imitation in his composing were his often-performed set of *Rumanian Dances*. His ultimate aim was to understand his musical roots, and use the knowledge gained to help break away from the traditions such as had been taught in music academies for many years. Analysis and synthesis: he would break the folk style down into its rhythmic, harmonic, melodic and tonal elements, then assimilate what would give him most freedom and strength of expression in his own compositions. He experimented to great effect in his string quartets and piano works, making use of chromatically-influenced Hungarian melodies, ancient pentatonic and modal scales, harsh counterpoint, fierce, 'primitive' phrases or complexities such as two dance rhythms alternating at each bar[1]. Within a few years, he was recognised as one of the most uncompromising and important of modern composers.

His researches incidentally cleared-up some old confusions, such as those which had affected Liszt and Brahms when they composed their 'Hungarian'-titled works a generation previously. They had been unaware of any clear distinction from 'gipsy' music which, in its village forms, Bartok was able to identify. The gipsies' own music had been 'tolerated' but as recognised music-makers for centuries, they had also had to play local Hungarian and Rumanian music well enough to avoid a beating, for examples at weddings, and earn payment. There were also later-developing styles, arrangements prepared for the larger towns, performed for audiences in cafes and elsewhere. These may be most pleasing to the ears of us uninitiated Westerners and other tourists, but were of no interest to Bartok who regarded them as synthetic.

Bartok, then, cast-off the influence of Liszt and others on his early work, such as the heroic *Kossuth Symphony*. He had found directions to travel along for the rest of his life; he asserted that *only through the entirely old can the entirely new be born*.

To judge from his ballet, the *Miraculous Mandarin*, he could have composed around the subject of Dracula, even the most violent aspects of Transylvania's most notorious son. The slow movement of the great *Music for Strings, Percussion and Celesta* would make ideal background for a filmed version of a night with Dracula, or for a ballet of insects[2], but it is probably the most accessible large work to give a broad introduction to his folk-influenced composing.

For an opera, he interpreted humanely a fictitious character who is sometimes confused with Dracula. The Bluebeard legend has many versions, the only common factor being of a nobleman who had disposed of several wives. The writer Bela Balasz (born 1884) also intended to evoke the spirit of the Hungarian frontier people, and his psychological drama presented a sympathetic Bluebeard in his lonely environment, anxious that his marriage to the youthful Judith should not be doomed by recollections of his past life. Seven doors in his castle hide symbolically the recesses of his mind, and he implores Judith not to demand the keys. She however, impelled by curiosity and possessiveness, opens each door in succession until the pain and tragedy of what is revealed destroys her hopes.

A two-character drama, it lacks action, but Bartok produces magnificent climaxes for the revelations behind the doors where Bluebeard's realm can be seen and where everything is warped by blood and tears. For the disparate states of mind of the two lovers, Bartok affectively uses remote keys. When the seventh door is opened, three previous wives emerge and Judith can only join them, to become another memory for Bluebeard.

This opera, *Duke Bluebeard's Castle*, which dates from 1911, revealed some folk elements and the Romantic within Bartok, but was therefore a summing-up, not an indication of the way forward. He had three more decades of work from his home in Budapest, where he installed traditional furniture ordered from Transylvania. He and Kodaly survived the political difficulties of those years, and Kodaly stayed on to achieve world fame as the expert on music in schools, latterly under a communist regime which favoured his work. Yet by 1940, Bartok had left Hungary largely because of the political strain and in the U.S.A. and away from his native soil, he was unhappy and never really settled. For a long period, he lost his will to compose, though he recommenced in the few years before his death in 1945. His *Concerto for Orchestra* (1943) is now a concert classic, but in its use of contrasting thematic material, it symbolises in part his joining a more cosmopolitan society[3].

In the late 20th century, societies in most parts of the world are seen to be suffering alienation from their traditional roots. Awareness of this has given impetus in Hungary to a remarkable cult of folk-music, particularly in Budapest. There is much pride in this, such as a keenness to share their heritage with other Europeans, television giving excellent introductions concerning what they call *hard folk*.

The province of Transylvania has a special status within these activities, and this has been sharpened by the fact that it is politically isolated from the Hungarian heartland. Continually, young people have set out to visit and explore its historic appeal, even in times when crossing the frontier was severely restricted. Research teams still report the area's resistance to social change, so that it may even be thought of as a vast ethnological museum. Yet, apart from the wishes of the inhabitants and the effects of stark economic forces, it can only be a short time before Transylvania is also affected by growing tourism and commercialisation.

In Budapest there are clubs where folk music is performed in traditional, contemporary and experimental styles. In one evening, several diverse amateur groups will take turn on the platform and, apart from their pleasure, performances may be assessed by the level of applause which is never less than polite. I attended once in 1992, a large assembly hall reasonably filled with mainly young people, rather like the atmosphere in an English jazz club of the 1950s. The man who served us beer had been playing 'cello in a group a few minutes previously. People were informally dressed but there was no sign of shirts bearing Western-type advertisements.

Young people in the villages may now of course be attracted to popular Western musical influences, but typical of those enthusiasts who intend to keep a great tradition alive and evolving is Marta Sebestyen of Budapest. She spent periods residing with Transylvanian villagers who could pass on to her the secrets of their musical art, and from her explanation, Bartok whom she affectionately calls 'Bela' is often with her. Hungarian television followed her, and has been enterprising in ensuring that the resulting documentary, and others, reach many countries including Britain.

So we may have seen Maria, her young face radiant, as accompanied by three musicians on stringed instruments, she sings so plaintively the *Outlaw's Song*:-

Turn my noble horse towards the sunset
For we are never coming back again.
I'm going into exile, to a faraway land.
Never again will I see my beautiful motherland
Blow away, good wind, the dust on the long road,
Blow away the dust of the long road and the footmarks of my horse.
It was a good horse – God bless the person who trained it.

In a foreign land, foreign people.
I walk the streets, I know no-one.
I would speak to them but they don't understand.

# 20 *Romantic Music in the Works of Ken Russell*

n 1970, a scurrilous if entertaining film about Richard Strauss was shown on BBC television, for the first and only time. There has never been any question of it being repeated, so I have only retained a slight recollection of *The Dance of the Seven Veils: a comic strip in seven episodes on the life of Richard Strauss*. It drew on a book by American George Marek which presented the composer as egocentric and bombastic, to a background of the allegedly declining culture of Germany between the 1890s and the 1940s.

The film was the responsibility of its director, Ken Russell, whose empathy for music, and especially of the late-Romantic period, has been applied widely and very creatively. This has been linked to his talent for selecting diverse elements and episodes of a character's life and juxtaposing then imaginatively, often to remarkable visual effect.

My first encounter, however, with such techniques was unfortunate, in a film that was to prove offensive to many sensibilities and so far *over the top* as to contribute to Russell's long-term notoriety. A *comic strip* of course may be thoroughly irresponsible, and the film pilloried Strauss in unbridled fashion. Far less subtle than irony, there was use of extracts from Strauss's major works: references to his admiration for Nietzsche's superman (*Zarathustra*), the 'hero' and his critics (*Heldenleben*), self-delusion (*Don Quixote*), graphic presentation of his marital sex-life (*Sinfonia domestica*), and a scene of subservience to Hitler, spiced with appropriately comic music from *Le Bourgeois Gentilhomme*.

Though it lay between caricature and fantasy, its most damaging aspect could have been a moral indictment in Strauss's alleged indifference to the sufferings of Nazi victims, on which point Russell held a sincere conviction. Yet where indisputable facts are used, they are hardly illuminating; Strauss may have been materialistic, with a mundane private life and a domineering wife, but that says nothing about his musical genius.

If such a film appeared today, it would probably be unexceptional, for there is a surfeit of media denigration of the famous which has become the easiest path for mediocre talents. Yet Mr Russell is always more likely to lead than to follow fashion; he can suffer creative disasters, but they are unique.

The composer's son had understandably threatened legal proceedings and the BBC made it clear that the film would not be shown again. It was also the last creation of Mr Russell's early association with the BBC, following features of approximately one hour each on Prokofief, Lotte Lenya, Elgar, Bartok, Debussy, Delius, Isadora Duncan and *Douanier* Rousseau, among less famous personalities whose talents he valued. These had been made for BBC's admired cultural programs, *Monitor* and *Omnibus*.

Unfortunately, because in the 1960s I was too busy to watch much T.V., I had missed all these items. Yet I saw *Billion Dollar Brain*, a particularly enjoyable 'cold war' film which had already (1967) shown much evidence of Mr Russell's brilliance as a director, especially considering it was made on relatively small financing. As a result, he was given the chance to make a fine, perhaps classic film, *Women in Love*, on the critically admired novel of D.H. Lawrence.

By the time I had seen two full-length films on musical themes, I thought of him as an original and, despite the Strauss vilification, genial spirit. That was apparent in a parody of the 1930s musical, especially in design and choreography, with affectionate regard for the style of Hollywood's Busby Berkeley. Russell used for the purpose Sandy Wilson's pastiche, *The Boy Friend*, with its story of romance and ambition among the wide-eyed, long-legged chorus girls. An excellent score was arranged and part-composed by Peter Maxwell Davies, from Wilson's original composition, and dream-like, pastel-shaded dance sequences were given the inimitable Russell treatment. Actors and actresses of distinction, or even without experience, fitted well into his scheme, a film which even as a layman I find technically absorbing. Yet many who had admired the original musical were strongly critical of the creative liberties taken by the director.

*The Boy Friend* had received a colourful display of extravagant imagery. Some of the films which followed with light musical associations hardly bear mention; critically, and in box office terms a failure, his bio-pic on Rudolf Valentino did at least have Rudolf Nureyev in the lead, convincingly as a one-time dance-hall gigolo.

As a very young man Russell already had a facility which enabled him to lecture on music during his service in the R.A.F. I have always assumed he makes all important decisions about music because of his unfailing ability to select what is most apt, in addition to his astonishing talent for interpreting it in visual terms.

Whilst this has helped to ensure him a large critical following, the musical element is not important in every film he makes, and as I have not seen all of these, I do not presume to judge his overall achievement. Of what I know, I cannot think of one episode that I would consider corrupting, which is more than could be said of much which appears on film today.

From his statements, it seems he does not take his own work, or that of other film directors, too seriously. Unusually for that industry, there is an absence of hype in his statements; informal, propelled by a youthful sense of experimentation, he is not short of distinguished artistes who are keen to work with him though he has to make do with very restricted budgets. He has also launched some versatile talents.

In his formative years, he developed a strong dislike for the artificiality of British films generally, and a rare work he cites as having influenced him was Fritz Lang's German classic *Metropolis*. His films often contain humorous allusions to pre-war film routines.

The two lengthy films which the music world could not ignore concerned Tchaikovsky and Mahler. Many were shocked by his film *The Music Lovers*; I could live without much of it, but there are characteristically fine moments, a superlative performance from Glenda Jackson in the difficult female lead and gifted use of the close-up. Subsequently, he said he had conceived this film as the relationship of a homosexual, Peter Tchaikovsky, and his nymphomaniac wife, Nina: not the broadest possible view.

Tchaikovsky did put much more of himself than most into his music, which gives particular scope for Russell's merging of reality and fantasy. Idealised love is symbolised in Tchaikovsky's relations with his sister and with Mme von Meck, the patron whom he never met. Physical relations tend towards the distasteful and that between the newly-married couple reaches breaking-point in an hallucinatory scene in a railway carriage to anguished sounds from the *Pathetic Symphony*. Not everyone likes watching such an explicit display of sexual revulsion, and the scene may be more interesting in the long run to cinema technicians than to the general public. How does one get a complete film crew into a space six feet square? Russell has explained how the cameramen were swung, with a lamp, high-up, above a 'compartment' placed on moving motor-tyres, all so precarious that luggage and a technician fell at one stage onto the naked Nina.

There is a fine early sequence which suggests exhilaration after Tchaikovsky and his sister drive by coach to the Moscow Conservatoire, with the intrusion of a yearning phrase from his *Manfred Symphony*. He plays his First Piano Concerto in the presence of his closest companions whose roles are suggested in fantasies of near-balletic movement. The euphoria is finally dispersed by sharp criticisms from his professor, Nicholas Rubinstein, who demonstrates on the piano, to the amusement of the Conservatoire and cinema audiences, the exhibitionist clichés in Tchaikovsky's style.

There were several enjoyable fringe attractions, a firework display, with such impish musical offerings as his *Miniature Overture*: using the story of *Swan Lake* as a symbol of the love entanglement, and the film's oblique tribute to Tchaikovsky's achievement in ballet scores.

In his film about Gustav Mahler, Russell dealt with the composer who is his favourite alongside Elgar, but taking a detached glance at aspects of his life, and Mahler's 'conversion' to Christianity – allegedly to further his ambitions to direct the Vienna opera. This receives treatment as harsh as that given to Strauss. Perhaps because he has to struggle to survive with integrity in a harsh commercial world, Russell takes any opportunity to rebuke great men who prostitute their art.

The most controversial sequence in the film features, as Mahler's judge and torturer, Cosima Wagner, improbably young and sexy, clothed as a jack-booted Nazi. She whips Mahler like a dog through the hoops of Christianity to emerge, knock-kneed but pork-eating, as a reluctant Siegfried who then staggers in a silly walk towards the cave where he slays the dragon. To the *Ride of the Valkyries*, they sing a duet:

You're no longer a Jew-boy, winning Strength through Joy . . .
Dictator of opera, Mahler, Sieg Heil.
You've made me a star.
You'll go very far.
My passport to heaven . . .

There was another idiosyncratic sequence in which I thought humour exceeded bad taste, though many took the opposite view: Alma Mahler dancing at her husband's funeral cortege, an elaborate fantasy on his jealousy and fear of death, to the sinister march from the 5th Symphony.

There are some interesting quotes, real or conjectured:

Stranger: *I hear . . . your Ninth Symphony is about death . . . death the implacable enemy, the joker or even the lover.*
Mahler: *My Ninth Symphony is a farewell to love*
    : *The Kindertotenlieder* (Songs on the Death of Children) *are not about death but the death of innocence.*
    : *I conduct to live; I live to conduct.*

Many of the finest parts of this flawed but often enchanting film relate to childhood, including the boy Gustav's experience of the scenes and sounds which would influence his music – lake and woodland, military bands, folk dancing, his Jewish family life. A baby's rattle sounds in time with the opening of the 4th Symphony, whose description as a child's view of heaven is parallelled by Mahler's infant daughters articulating their ideas of God, angels and death. Did Mahler have a premonition that one of them was soon to die? There are ominous tones from *Songs on the Death of Children* as they in their hurry through a wood during a storm.

The film is set in a train, with a series of flash-backs in the course of a railway journey to Austria, a homecoming to death. The trials of marriage to an egocentric genius are sharply sketched, and Alma's compositions are cruelly mocked by Mahler as amateurish and derivative of her former lover's, Zemlinski. (A pleasingly naïve melody, called *Alma's Lied*, had been provided for the film by another composer.) To the passionate sounds of Wagner's *Tristan*, Alma buries her music scripts in the earth, one of the film's most quietly effective moments.

Russell's liking for in-jokes leads to a short scene on a railway platform when we see a pretty boy in sailor suit, a reference to the central episode in *Death in Venice*, the film sometimes confused with Russell's *Mahler* for no good reason except that it repeatedly plays the lyrical slow movement from the 5th Symphony.

A most effective tongue-in-cheek use of movie cliché occurs in the final sequence. Mahler explains to Alma that his depression in summer 1904 was mainly caused by dwelling on the wasted talent represented by the deaths of his brother Otto and composer Hugo Wolf. That also complicated the preparation of the 6th Symphony but he finds words of tenderness as he tells his wife she is the hope in his life, and that her spirit lies in the most rapturous theme of that symphony.

In Hollywood fashion, Gustav and Alma are reconciled in the train's corridor with a kiss, though a reference to 'eternal love' must be set against Alma's promiscuous life, past and future, with men of exceptional creative talent. The enthralling accompaniment has to be that theme, the second subject of the first movement. It turns into an exultant march, and as the doctor approaches to meet the dying man on the platform, they walk past him into the mist with the words: *You can go home, doctor, we're going to live for ever.*

Well, the symphonies now belong to us, or , as Mahler might have said, of and to the world.


Russell writes that many Anglo-Saxons had, in a derogatory sense, described his style generally as 'operatic'. His musical enthusiasms had been symphonic and he claims not to have liked opera until the Italians gave him the opportunity as a producer, starting with Stravinsky's *Rake's Progress* which he came to admire greatly. He was not prepared to create a conventional *Madama Butterfly*, so by the time he presented Boito's controversial *Mefistofele* at Genoa, armed riot police were standing outside the theatre. He offered Italians the spectacle of Mefisto's rocket ship being powered by nuns thrown into a furnace, the imagery coming close to episodes in his other work. He believes he helped to bring Genoa back onto the operatic map, which must in some sense be true.

He was given a contract for English National Opera in 1992. W.S. Gilbert's *Princess Ida* was an intriguing 19th century essay in comic aspects of women's liberation, and as such a fine opportunity for Russell to demonstrate his satirical inventiveness.

He simply ducked the challenge, stating in a radio interview that he had conceived the work as a Christmas pantomime which he hoped his own children and others' would enjoy. They might well have done so but many adults in the audience did not; what could be a delightfully child-like imagination failed wretchedly. There were of course satirical notions, from the Japanese buying Buckingham Palace to costume designs based upon Prince Charles' large ears, but I was much less entertained than at an amateur performance of *Princess Ida* two years previously. For me, the biggest joke was that Russell's flop had occurred in the house of that trendy Coliseum trio who were soon to relinquish their responsibilities, supremo Peter Jonas (off to Munich), producer David Pountney and music director Mark Elder. It was just one more slice of impertinence to add to several of theirs.

When Russell eventually addressed 12 million TV viewers in a 220-minute serialised film, (1993), I was disappointed that the choice, once again D.H. Lawrence, was *Lady Chatterley's Lover*. This novel had achieved notoriety for its sexual descriptions and the resultant prosecution in 1960 for obscenity. The theme of an aristocratic lady deserting her husband, sexually incapacitated through war injuries, for a vigorously masculine game-keeper, has been used for countless dirty jokes. On a more interesting level, there has always been speculation as to how far Clifford Chatterley reflected Lawrence's fears of sexual inadequacy in relation to his voracious German wife, Freda von Richthofen.

Russell handled the plot with restraint, and despite the condescension of the critics, I thought the interpretation paid adequate respect to the novel, though the sexual incidents were less explicit than in the original. Even the choice of the sensitive Joely Richardson from the distinguished Redgrave family was criticised. She was alleged to be too beautiful or insufficiently buxom for Lawrence's heroine, even though she looked well-endowed when she cavorted, as in the novel, totally nude. The main distinction is that Russell presents her as delightfully naïve about sex, and near-virgin.

Most of my friends had no interest in seeing what they assumed would be a sensationalised version of an over-rated novel, but the first two who did – not unmusical – said that they could not recollect any music.

Russell's extraordinary skill in its subliminal use is typified by the last quarter of an hour of the first part of the televised version. After Connie has watched her father (played by Russell) and her sister dancing at a house-party to the waltz from Offenbach's *Belle Hélène*, left alone, her movements betray her frustrations, accompanied for over three minutes by the tense, elongated chords from Holst's *Saturn*.

Relief comes when the sister slams down the piano lid to have a blazing row with Sir Clifford Chatterley. Then the two girls chat mischievously whilst dancing in liberated style a tango to a jazz trio, with, once more, the *Ride of the Valkyries*, this time as a saxophone solo. As Connie walks into a woodland setting for her last innocent encounter with the gamekeeper, the sense of expectancy is introduced and sustained by the playing of most of Delius' exquisite *On hearing the first cuckoo in spring*. No wonder that Russell is in great demand for directing television advertisements.

For Connie's first fulfilling sexual act, the unpredictable choice was the development section of the first movement of Elgar's Second Symphony. I had never considered this in *Tristanesque* terms, but one part has a distinctive voluptuousness and with a sadness which could be related to some aspect of the sexual experience.

Russell dislikes critics complaining about minor inaccuracies in biographical films; he seeks and works on a poetic truth and the relatively short film has often been his favoured medium. The most recent includes one on an English composer whose music he specially likes, Arnold Bax, placing some emphasis upon that man's inspirational love-affair with the pianist Harriet Cohen, and himself acting Bax. He directed *Salome's Last Dance*, based on Oscar Wilde's play but placed in a brothel. The lascivious words that Salome addresses to John the Baptist are accompanied by that cliché of oriental sensuousness, the slow-movement of Rimsky-Korsakov's *Scheherazade*.

A low-key presentation of episodes in the life of Bohuslav Martinu took Russell into far less familiar territory. The background of Germany's occupation of Czechoslovakia and Martinu's cultural alienation in the USA offers an abundance of images alongside the Freudian treatment of his feelings for a girl student left behind in his homeland, and the effect of that on his marriage. We hear enough to suggest diverging influences on Martinu's style: the folk idiom, especially in ensemble singing, a taut, disciplined neo-classicism such as in his Concerto Grosso, and his individualistic essays in symphonic jazz. There are important references to the symbolism in his work, particularly the *unattainable dream-girl* who inspired his opera, *Juliette*, and the autobiographical aspects in his Fifth Symphony. Yet we had better enjoy the film's surrealist basis because it hardly makes claim as a valuable introduction to Martinu's character or art.

The music-centred film in which Russell went to the extremes of self-indulgence had been *Lisztomania* (1973) which, full of esoteric allusions and cinematic in-jokes, showed no concern whether it might appeal to any particular section of the film-going public. It presented Franz Liszt in a sequence of rock-music cartoons, performing like a Liberace to hysterical fans a piano fantasy on the themes of Wagner's *Rienzi* mixed with the children's piece, *Chop-sticks*, and other absurdities.

Liszt is pilloried for his alleged commercialism, his relations with the two most important women in his life, and the complexities which may have induced him to take religious orders. This unsubtle approach is further vitiated by Russell's obsession with Wagner whose nationalism he always sees, unhistorically, as entirely negative, destructive. With Wagner rejecting democracy and set on creating a Nazi-type Superman, the *Valkyries* and *Siegfried* motives are prominent, until finally an equally strident theme from Liszt's First Piano Concerto resounds in virtuous contrast.

In fact, Liszt did not accept money for public performances from 1847, the year he met the Polish-born Princess Carolyne Wittgenstein. She is presented partly in flattering caricature, at least in visually appealing scenes when she is dressed in the beautiful clothing, and surrounded by the imagery, of traditional Russia. At their first meeting, Russell kindly introduces a fragment of the magnificent coronation music from Mussorgsky's *Boris Godunov*, almost the only time in the whole film when we are allowed to enjoy unadulterated music.

Of a very different order was the appreciation of the compositions of Ralph Vaughan Williams whose widow and former literary collaborator Ursula combined her talents with Ken Russell's in a finely illustrated film. As they both acted in it, she experienced his exhilarating directorship at first hand, with visits to Stonehenge, army manoeuvres and fearfully windswept caves in search of elements which inspired some of the symphonies. They also sped around Parliament Square in an open Rolls-Royce whilst young people in distinctive clothing and heavy boots stomped to the fiercer rhythms of the *London Symphony*.

These and other sequences were, in my view, inspired and there was a very pleasing episode in which Russell discussed the music with his infant daughter. This positive aspect of his work, always at its best when considering great art, brings us to an early film which I have left till the end because it is so widely admired.

The broad view, with which Russell agrees, is that the black-and-white *Song of Summer* (1968) had been his finest film interpretation. It is seen through the eyes of Eric Fenby, a young man who acted as the severely ailing Delius's amanuensis for five years, from 1928 to 1933. We see Delius in his French retreat, appallingly disabled and in frequent pain during the last stages of syphilis, grasping out blindly to whatever he needs, and dictating impatiently by means of exaggerated musical impressions which Fenby successfully transposes into a dreamy orchestral song.

From a prurient neighbour, Fenby learns of the past lives of Delius and his artist wife in which eroticism and orgies were alleged to feature prominently, and of Delius's excursions to Paris which led to his contracting the disease which in those days was specially devastating, such as inflicting blindness.

Despite her impending death, his wife, Jelka, plays a stoic role needed to support his frustrated genius. The contrast between the early and latter years up to Delius' death is poignantly suggested, but there is a triumphant assertion of the power of the creative will. An essential in this was a memorable performance as Delius from actor Max Adrian, who later played Rubinstein, alternately imperious and wheedling, and a hectoring comedy part in *The Boy Friend*.

There are at least three striking episodes which relieve the film's tense atmosphere and, incidentally, in two of these Russell is the music teacher. Firstly, a gramophone playing *Ol' Man River*, with Delius explaining his empathy with the blacks of Florida whose music inspired him to compose. A choral passage from his *Appallachia* then emphasises the link.

Man and wife recall moments in the mountains of Norway when Delius was already crippled but not blind. This is a fine lyrical passage, as he delights in the wind and perhaps his last sight of the sun. With the ecstatic background of his *Song of the High Hills*, we may notice, perhaps clearly for the first time, that work's melodic similarity to the Norwegian idiom and Grieg's style.

Back in France, this is soon followed by a heartening 'scherzo', one of the most joyous memories in all Russell's films. A youthful jester bursts into Delius' courtyard, throws a tennis ball over the roof, then rushes through the house repeatedly to catch it, before taking the old man on an exhilarating ride in his wheelchair. Delius is delighted by this rude interruption and finds enough breath to introduce him laconically to the astonished Fenby:

*This is Percy Grainger. Sometimes he composes.*

# 21　Russian Melody, Romanticism and Soviet Policy (to the 1950s)

*N**arod* (adjective *narodni*) is a term that was most significant and commonly used in the Soviet Union. Meaning
folk, people or nation, (adjective, popular or national),
it was applied widely to terms as disparate as 'people's republic'
and 'popular music'. The *narodniki* were a *back to our roots*
political and social movement of the late 19th century. We
would have loosely called them populists or nationalists, and
they typified one permanent strain in Russian culture.

Another was initiated by Tsar Peter the Great (1694–1725),
the first of Russia's leading Westernisers, who imported ideas,
technology and skilled workers from the advanced countries
of western Europe. These two sometimes conflicting strains
and policies have played major roles in Russia's history, and
eventually in the development of Russian music.

During the last third of the 19th century, Russian musical
culture expanded greatly. Their leading personalities were
influenced in varying degrees by Western musical forms and
the new Romantic elements. Many drew on the rich musical
tradition where, as is often said, one may find Russia's soul.
The vitality and spontaneity of Russian music contrasted with
the more reflective qualities of Western Romanticism.

Some Russians, such as Borodin and Rimsky-Korsakov,
drew on this immediacy, leaned towards picturesque styles
and added touches of the exotic which were coming into vogue
with fresh interest in Russian-occupied Central Asia. Their
compositions in turn made big impressions on younger Western composers, especially in France.

Rimsky-Korsakov adapted a special scale for his more exotic
works and would be widely known by his imposing symphonic
fantasy, *Scheherazade*. Tchaikovsky was quite distinct from his
colleagues, an eclectic who was comfortable in the accepted
forms of Western European music, such as the concerto,
symphony, large ballet suite, and Romantic opera, but with

some influence from Russian folk music. Others sought forms more in the spirit of Russian traditions: short, bright orchestral pieces or dance movements, liturgical works, folk or historical operas. These contrasts of approach, in fact of philosophy, became the subject of increasing polemic.

Mussorgsky broke free from foreign influences, keenly investigating the idiom of traditional folk music and extracting whatever he needed. He aimed for a greater realism, such as in illustrating poems which confronted death, and operas where 'the people', ordinary citizens, played forceful if sometimes destructive roles. For the 1870s, his style was most adventurous and uncompromising, with startling harmonies. Potentially the greatest of his generation, he died early, leaving most work unfinished: friends orchestrated much of it and Rimsky-Korsakov conscientiously removed what he considered many crudities from the scores. Yet Mussorgsky's original conceptions are nowadays restored as far as possible because they are considered of special interest.

The cult of folk music had disturbed the traditions of the conservatoires in many other European countries outside those with a German culture. Yet by 1914, that first great generation of Russian composers had died, and neither late-Romanticism nor nationalism were considered specially newsworthy. Younger composers were appearing to challenge or even reject not only the accepted styles but the very musical language on which they had been built; evolution would be replaced by revolution.

The 'reactionary' protests against modernism were many and famous but the man whose seemingly violent, primitivist *Rite of Spring* caused a riot at its Paris premiere in 1913 can be seen in retrospect to have been very respectful of the music of the past. Igor Stravinsky had a remarkable early success with the ballet *Firebird* which did credit to his teacher, Rimsky-Korsakov, opulent in its orchestration as well as in the decor which it inspired.[1] Its exciting syncopations made new demands on the dancers. This was followed by a work of exceptional originality, with generous use of popular and folk melodies, *Petrouchka* (1911). The *Rite of Spring* set-up unprecedented rhythmic tensions, and showed great virtuosity in the use of orchestra and solo instruments, especially in their percussive functions.

Stravinsky was quickly to move in the direction which marked a sharp reaction against the Romantics; his astringent style became restrained, with more symmetrical melodies and cool harmonies, initiating a cult of neo-classicism. Already established in international repute, Stravinsky was to leave Russia in 1917 and his later drift towards modernism was not approved in the USSR so that he had very limited influence there during the following 40 years.

The years after the Soviet revolution witnessed much artistic freedom and social experimentation in Russia. Yet from the mid-1920s, the new permissiveness in such areas as sex and education were judged to be having undesirable consequences, and in totalitarian fashion, policy was reversed by 1925 immediately from above in the assumed interests of social stability. In education, for example, Soviet policy would henceforth revert to a strict academic approach, with deep regard for the classics. Cultural anarchy, such as we experience at the end of the 20th century, would have been firmly opposed, though they had other terms for it.

This new cultural assertiveness found its way more leisurely into the realm of music. The Soviet authorities were unlikely to be Westernisers, but would they incline towards the internationalist or populist approach? Would they for example regard the academic musical traditions as 'bourgeois', to be by-passed?

Lenin and many others had bourgeois tastes, Lenin specially loved the music of Beethoven and considered the classics should be the basis of Soviet musical education, with a 'levelling-up' in popular taste. His view was rather like the aspirations of enlightened Victorians.

Composers were increasingly encouraged to use their Russian or other national music idioms. An extreme revolutionary view was that classical forms should be discarded, but an all-out cultural revolution was not necessary. The rational compromise was that traditional large-scale forms, the symphony, opera and cantata, would address the mass of the people, portraying the grandeur and idealism of the new communist society. On the other hand, there was a hardening of policy against the new cosmopolitan styles which were making their mark in the West. The majority view, if not explicitly stated, was that musical development had reached its desirable peak with the work of Wagner and the late-Romantics, and that further radical experimentation with melody and harmony was unnecessary.

The ensuing ideological debate becomes most clear to us in the experiences of those composers we know best. When Dmitri Shostakovitch appeared on the scene in 1925, he gave promise of becoming a model of a young revolutionary composer. How did these aspirations work out?

In 1933, Russia's most respected communist writer, Maxim Gorky, pronounced the cult of Socialist Realism; in all the arts, the aim should be to express the spirit of the *narod*, the people. This was a conception which might permit broad interpretation, and it was to become the basis of the Soviet aesthetic.

One interesting side-light of the persistent efforts to exclude undesirable Western influences was the early opposition to jazz, which eventually became 'respectable', as the expression of the American negro. Much later, there was a lasting disapproval of what we call *pop culture*, as distinct from the more general term, *popular culture*. Though it has not always been clearly perceived in the West, the communists saw it as an integral part of commercialism and cultural exploitation. I believe their analysis was correct.

■ ■ ■

Dmitri Shostakovitch (1906-75) had a nervous, diffident personality but the opposite impression comes from the composition with which he first achieved fame, like Mendelssohn, at the age of 19. It was an extraordinary work which, some would say, equalled the best of what followed. His First Symphony (1925) must have astonished as many as it enthralled, starting with an impudent theme[2], and an exciting development section even drags a solemn, halting waltz into the revelry. This continues into the second movement with piano adding percussive effects, and a disarming 'oriental' section, all very confident, as if Shostakovitch were glancing back affectionately at some of the Russian masters, up to Stravinsky. The remainder of the symphony is distinguished by its rich melodic sounds, the unexpected pathos of the slow movement passing dramatically through drum-rolls to a surging military finale.

This is an exuberant, then impassioned arrangement of traditional forces, as if Shostakovitch were shrugging-off the difficulties of composing a major work before proceeding to undiscovered territory. We might be tempted to think it symbolises his youth, then growing up into the tragedy of civil war. He then commemorated the tenth anniversary of the 1917 revolution in a Second Symphony, which, apart from its striking instrumental passages, is very different in conception and feeling. Composed in one movement, order out of chaos, it shows what will become a characteristic use of powerful, steadily climbing themes, and ends in heroic style with fierce choral declamation. To Western ears, it has a Russian flavour but lacks the glowing personality of its predecessor.

Shostakovitch was to prove his command of satire in an opera, *The Nose*, using a modernistic idiom. He was beginning to experiment at the furthest boundaries of his expressive powers in order to establish the most effective creative range. The 4th Symphony is consequently a difficult work, especially for the orchestra. He eventually criticised it as unnecessarily complex, delaying the premiere until 1961. Meanwhile, his highly successful opera, *Lady Macbeth of Mtensk*, was after two years officially condemned in the Communist Party's 'Pravda' (28 January 1936) as *unmusical, neurotic and in very bad taste.*

Those of us who have enjoyed the work in recent years probably find it most acceptable within our explicitly violent culture, but to those more puritanical Soviet authorities, it seemed very corrupting. There is hardly a likable human in the play, and even if the eponymous heroine is a 'victim of society', she remains someone with whom very few rational males would wish to share either a bedroom or a kitchen. Though in *Tristan*, Wagner symbolises the sexual act, *Lady Macbeth* gives a vivid musical portrayal of rape and ejaculation, two gruesome murders and almost incessant expressions of hatred. Artistic 'realism', yes, but not socialism.

Stalin certainly is on record as disapproving of what he saw, and the opera was not performed again until after his death. The composer was so affected by this dispute that he abandoned a plan for a trilogy of works on Soviet womanhood. The 'Pravda' article was issuing a general warning to Soviet composers against modern and cosmopolitan trends. In simple terms, modernism or formalism was defined as paying more

attention to form than emotional content, indulging in disso-
nance for its own sake and failing to compose clearly recognisable or enjoyable melodies.

Shostakovitch appeared to accept such criticism, and he
pointedly turned away from the style and spirit of his 4th
Symphony in the following one. It opens solemnly, in the
questioning manner we might expect from a late Beethoven
quartet. The brooding slow third movement has resemblances
to the expansive style of Mahler but is preceded by a witty
dance movement in triple time which recalls him more directly. The finale starts with an outburst on the brass, a theme
so forceful that it eventually sweeps aside even the magnificent
contrasting second subject.

With its powerful and optimistic conclusion, it was considered a model of a symphonic statement from a Soviet composer. It seems to address the whole human society, in a
predominantly heroic spirit. Many of the subsequent symphonies by other Soviet composers did in fact follow similarly with
strident, confident melodies, but often with an ingredient of
Russian or other folk material.

Shostakovitch was a volunteer fireman in the start of the
hideous siege of Leningrad, and was moved to write an
exceptionally long symphony, the 7th, about that city's suffering. The completed work paid tribute to its people's heroism
and was treated as an important contribution to the war effort,
being played especially in such countries as Britain and the
U.S.A. for its propaganda purposes. It includes an elaborate
section assumed to represent the march of an invading Germany army. Such noisy, repetitive devices are considered by
some to be 'unmusical', and in his Concerto for Orchestra,
Bartok within a short space of time went out of his way to
ridicule this movement.

His other war symphony, the 8th (1943), also exceptionally
long, is more concerned with inner struggles and had to wait a
long time to enjoy equal esteem in the USSR. It has one theme
which recalls Tchaikovsky's *Manfred Symphony*, and these two
works often live in a phantom world, but any similarities may
be coincidental. The 8th has two violent *scherzos* and the
enigmatic finale precludes any sense of optimism.

Some commentators believe in such contexts that the war
gave the composer a pretext for writing tragic music, of which

much really referred to his country's pre-war political and economic strife.

Stalin was less than pleased that Shostakovitch did not produce a large-scale, heroic work to mark the end of the war. Instead, the apparently genial, tuneful 9th Symphony was on a smaller scale than the First Symphony and glanced further backwards towards the classical spirit.

It was as if the composer had lapsed into a boyish refusal to deal in pomp and ceremony. In those years, he was also embarking on many chamber works, where he could experiment with style and technique. In that more private world, it was easier to avoid ideological criticism, whilst completing significant, heart-felt works.

The 10th Symphony fulfilled in style three decades later the hopes lavished on his first one and is among the last of Europe's great Romantic symphonies. With warm, late-19th century harmonies the opening develops leisurely but impassioned, to be followed by a helter-skelter *scherzo*, which has an abrupt, vehement ending; how sinister was it? Simon Volkov in his not too reliable account of conversations with the composer, *Testimony* (1980), may have influenced perceptions by stating that it was intended as a musical portrait, manic and evil, of Stalin who had just died in 1953. The slow movement leads to a sequence of astonishing orchestral convulsions and the finale, with its dominant use of Shostakovitch's signature motif, D, E flat, C, B, was understood to signify his defiance of unspecified adversity. If the work was intended as a celebration of Stalin's death, it was an historically fascinating example of musical irony.

It reinforced the traditional tonal language which the composer was increasingly favouring, and which accorded with official policy. Shostakovitch must have considered he had peaked in his search for fulfilment within the form of the abstract (non-program) symphony, so that he was ready in subsequent works to find fresh directions and forms, especially in the 1960s.

His achievements within his own society impelled him in 1954 to assert that Soviet composers had more freedom than those in the West. This was not forced from him; he had always been aware how commercialism always tends to corrupt artistic purposes in capitalist societies.

Stalin was very conservative in his view of what was musically acceptable, but his representatives did not manage to stifle, if that was their intention. Shostakovitch's creative genius, which had supported the revolution in the programs for his 2nd and 3rd Symphonies. The 11th (1957) dealt with an overtly tragic event, the failure and suffering associated with the attempted 1905 revolution and was exceptional in that it used a large number of borrowed folk melodies. The 12th was a kind of sequel, depicting the Bolshevik revolution of 1917.

Of three large patriotic works for chorus and orchestra, the most distinguished was *Song of the Forests* (1949), with its attractive Russian choral style familiar abroad from the contributions of the travelling Red Army ensembles.

A side of Shostakovitch always important, and given official encouragement for home consumption but now becoming better known abroad, was his large and varied output of light music. He had always had an affection for much 'gipsy' and other popular music. It is arguable that 'vulgar' tunes may sound excellent when played on the right instruments, especially as used by a master of humour. He achieved comically grotesque effects in a sequence of dramatic songs, *Baba the Priest*, and there is an exquisite little song, affectionately Russian, in his *Adventures of Kosinkina*.

For pleasure, he often played even rare pieces of Offenbach, who seems to be present in the love music and the sprightly dances he composed for a film about a young tearaway, *The Gadfly*. If it had been composed much before 1955, its Romance would surely have been added to Sir Thomas Beecham's musical 'lollypops', an exceptionally lush main theme and a haunting middle-section which is consciously northern and Sibelian.

He had a facility for parody, and ingeniously distorted some of Offenbach's glittering melodies so that they represented the tastes of the lecherous and degenerate 'reactionaries' in the civil war of the 1871 Paris Commune. That was part of his incidental music to Eisenstein's silent film, *New Babylon*, in which the heroes were represented by themes somewhere in spirit between the *Marseillaise* and workers' revolutionary songs.

For *Cheryomushki* (The Cherry Tree estate, Moscow), 1958, a fierce satire on Moscow's housing problems, he ventured into musical comedy with its liking for songs in 3-4 time, and he included much strident music as well as parodies of Tchaikovsky and Borodin. Much of his best light music was used in the *Age of Gold*, a most ambitious three-act ballet, with an ideological slant ridiculing Western life styles and sleazy stereotypes within a 1920's night-club. It gives scope for an intriguing range of modern dance rhythms, which the composer clearly enjoyed also for their own sakes.

■  ■  ■

The originality of the style of Sergei Prokofief (1891-1953) is easily recognised and dissected in his piano works, with which he burst into notoriety and lasting fame. Angular themes which last agreeably longer than expected, ironic tunes and 'wrong' notes, clusters of dissonant chords, fierce percussive technique, the briefest pause before a disarming mood change, the piquant effect of one hand playing major, the other minor. One movement might contain Russian folk rhythms, leisurely almost lazy passages, machine-like repetition and soaring lyricism.

If Beethoven's 3rd Piano Concerto was an immensely enjoyable farewell to the classical, Mozartian concerto, Prokofief's 3rd (1921) looks back similarly to Romanticism. This is apparent in the dreamy, lyrical opening theme which awakes to lively transformations, and a final big melody, bathing in a Rachmaninov-like glow. That and the cheeky neo-classical theme of the slow movement, with its impish set of variations, have made the work a concert-hall favourite. It is not far from the spirit of Shostakovitch's First Symphony.

A youthful work which illustrates the extent and variety of Prokofief's expressive powers is the pantomime opera, *The Love of Three Oranges* (1919), based on an 18th century Italian farce. The comic-hero prince suffers a range of moods which extend the conventional operatic aria to extraordinary degrees: excessive melancholia, uncontrolled laughter, fear of cosmic phenomena. It is late in the proceedings before he can declare his love for a princess, who has just been conceived in an orange, in terms which are passionate beyond belief. He rushes around the world on a wind-propelled machine, is almost eaten by a giant with a very low I.Q. and has to contend with an enemy who, taking the shape of a rat, brings chaos to the court. All this leaves so much scope for bizarre orchestration that these highlights are regularly performed in a symphonic suite now as well-known as the opera.

There is a surreal game of fate played with cards between two fantastically-dressed witches conjuring, in shrieking voices, the fiercest infernal forces at their command. The orchestra seems to split in half in splendid confrontation. Yet though the composer may not have wished it, the march was destined to become his hallmark: bold, spiky and manic, it may be suitably presented on stage with soldiers marching backwards at the request of the King of Clubs. No earthly monarch, president or general would dare include it in any ceremony.

All this might suggest suitable attitudes in a composer at the heart of the political revolution. In fact, Prokofief was living among the artistic *avant-garde* and fleshpots of New York and Paris. He enjoyed composing for Diaghilev's Ballets Russes, including the primitivist *Scythian Suite* clearly influenced by Stravinsky's *Rite of Spring*. He put some of his most complex but overwhelming music into an opera, *The Fiery Angel* once more enabling him to enter the supernatural world and grapple with diabolical forces. Its theme mixes religion and sensuality, rising to the most frenzied scenes, and this 'decadent' story never found favour in the USSR so that Prokofief did not see it performed. It was therefore valuable that he used it as material for the 3rd Symphony (1928). That and the 4th, related to music for his ballet, the *Prodigal Son*, are very enjoyable works, but the big advances in symphonic style were to come nearly two decades later.

His sympathy for the revolution extended to naive efforts to write 'industrialisation' music, but that was regarded in Moscow as dillitantism. Yet he grew tired of the West, even though he had unrestricted travel between there and Russia, and returned home in 1936. He was becoming bored with the trendy fashions and attitudes in Paris, needed the musical inspiration of his homeland and hoped the requirement that Soviet composers should select uplifting and relevant themes would help him to achieve his most genuine artistic perspectives.

The earliest works to emerge from his new environment were therefore awaited with special curiosity. At least one

English critic had described that popular 3rd Piano Concerto as *totally devoid of feeling*, presumably thinking of the Parisian fashions of the 1920s. He took back to Russia a new Violin Concerto, the Second, which was admired for its warmth and lyricism, a trend which he would continue.

As complement to that, he always had at hand sprightly melodies with an instant appeal, such as in the music for the satirical film, *Lieutenant Kije* (1933). Specially popular has been his First Symphony, that had been conceived in the style of the 18th century, with a *gavotte*, a Haydnesque finale and symmetrical themes which are given piquant 20th century harmonies.

He threw himself into compositions supporting the Soviet system, of which probably the best was *Zdravitsa* (Greetings), a large scale choral work that also drew on the musical idioms of seven national groups in order to glorify the political union but was criticised in the West as praising Stalin. For the film classic, *Alexander Nevsky*, (1938), he wrote one of the most effective pieces of descriptive music ever heard in the cinema. It portrays a ragged Russian peasant army rushing to fight the historic *Battle on the Ice* in which the pseudo-religious Prussian invaders are defeated and drowned. This cantata also displays a deep feeling for Mother Russia and that won the enthusiastic approval of Stalin; its moving choruses were performed widely by schoolchildren, especially during the war.

In 1948, as spokesman for the Composers' Union, Tikhon Khrennikov, who wrote not inconsiderable symphonies with a political, socialist-realist program, criticised, among others, Prokofief for 'formalism', and having been too much influenced by Stravinsky. Prokofief in reply wrote that to compose a melody instantly understandable, but also original, was most difficult, with the pitfalls of banality, sugariness and unconscious rehashing, whereas complex melodies were easier to find. He was determined to resolve this problem.

He rejected atonalism which had once attracted him. Constructing a musical work with the recognised key system was using a solid foundation, whereas building without tonality was as if on sand.

To explain himself further, he divided operatic accompaniment into that supporting action, recitative, and the song-like, which he called *cantilena* and *arioso*, including the typical 19th century aria. He had been criticised for using recitative too much, or almost entirely in the opera, the *Gambler*. Yet he recalled *painful* experiences of listening to almost one hour of Wagner without anyone on-stage moving. Opera-goers wanted action, which implied the use of recitative, and fear of immobility had reduced his use of *cantilena*. The letter song in Tchaikovsky's *Eugene Onegin* resolved this problem perfectly and he would try to follow its example.

The most official interference Prokofief had to suffer was over his plans for an opera on the sensitive theme of a war hero. Seen as being intensely political, it had to conform to accepted policy, and later critical opinion is that it ended-up as one of his least satisfactory large-scale works.

For his adaptation of Tolstoy's *War & Peace* (1944), he was asked to give more prominence to the war, and less to the love story. His biggest frustration might have been that he saw neither of these works performed as he wished in their completed forms, though we can now see his achievement in *War & Peace*. In the patriotic tones of a pageant opera, it leads on from the style of *Alexander Nevsky*, balanced with a lyricism which suits the love entanglements. There is a moving scene in which Pierre confronts Natasha about her infatuation for a feckless married man. Surely a fulfilment of his wish for the desired operatic style.

Otherwise, there is not much evidence that the difficult political climate affected badly the quality or nature of his output. He could always rely on official approval whenever he composed for children, and that was an undisputed benefit, such as the universally popular *Peter and the Wolf* with its inspired instrumental characterisation of the animals. Nor were all obstacles political. The appearance of his *Romeo and Juliet* in Leningrad was delayed because the Kirov dancers complained it was technically problematic, diverging so much from the traditional ballet scores of Tchaikovsky and others. Yet it is now of course considered a classic, worthily placed alongside *Swan Lake*.

The most important developments of his last years resulted in three fine symphonies. The 5th was lyrical and intense in ways that won approval as an example of what was hoped-for in Soviet music. The official comment which best summarised the Soviet position was clearly stated firstly in connection with *Peter and the Wolf*:

Here we have, in a classically pure and polished form, the melodic and harmonic style of the mature Prokofief . . . the gift for clarity and directness of a new Soviet symphonic style, free from both intellectual self-analysis and a tragic view of reality.

Within these terms was implied a generalised criticism of developments in form and content of the symphony among composers in Western Europe, where allegedly, such works had suffered a serious decline and only 'decadent' specimens were not being promoted.

Prokofief was quoted as relating that symphony to the freedom of the human spirit. That and the 6th were conceived in 1944 when all the leading Soviet composers had been offered a temporary home together away from the war, and were mainly concerned with works which would celebrate the return of peace.

Yet the 6th Symphony (1947) had to be completed slowly after a severe heart attack, which may partly account for its more disturbing passages. In its slow movement, the feeling is such that a melodic reference to a noble theme from Wagner's *Parsifal* blends movingly.

The 7th Symphony (1952) is in total contrast, attractively light-hearted, with percussive sounds such as we enjoy in his ballets. It was at first regarded in the West as not quite worthy of its momentous predecessors. Perhaps some critics did not appreciate the value of writing for young people, which had been the composer's intention. It should settle as a popular concert classic, inimitable Prokofief.

In those years before his death – on the same day as Stalin – Prokofief, born of a privileged family and at one-time considered perhaps wrongly to be enjoying life as a 'playboy' in the West, composed in close consideration of the requirements of the Soviet state. Whereas Shostakovitch, a son of the revolution from a loyal communist family, gradually moved towards a more private and questioning philosophy reflected in his later music.

Much has been written about the problems of both composers within the Soviet system. It may have provided them with, at best, the inspiration and, at worst, the nervous tension which found expression in some of their finest and most loved works.

■ ■ ■

In the West, of the other first generation of Soviet composers, only Aram Khachaturyan (1903–78) is well-known for a handful of works from a large output. He first attracted attention in the West with two concertos, one for violin the other for piano, each with immense vitality, and introducing the sounds of his native Armenia to appreciative 1930s audiences. In movements alternately exciting and languid, he offers us unfamiliar rhythms and melodies sliding gracefully between half-tones (adjacent notes), from a country which lies across an Asian frontier.

Yet in addition to providing for official and state occasions, Khachaturyan was satisfying Soviet demand for lighter music, along with many composers whom we do not know in the West. Several orchestral scores opulently translate his national idiom into a Westernised concert sound. That became specially popular abroad, with his exotically coloured *Gayaneh* ballet of 1942. Its virile sequences make explicit the military origins of Caucasian folk dancing, such as the *Sabre Dance*, in swirling cross-rhythms the *lezkghinka* intrudes, a fiercely exciting dance supported by a strident drum beat which marks it as Armenian or Georgian. The contrasting female response, proud and statuesque, is accompanied by exquisite instrumentation. *Spartacus* (1954) was to make Khachaturyan's name familiar in international ballet circles, and even on television screens. The sinuous music and suppressed passion of its Adagio[3] suggest this method of building-up to triumphant orchestral climaxes, such as in his 3rd Symphony. It concludes in rising suspense around the third note of the scale (the mediant), the cadence being held back to the final chord.

The opening of the First Symphony (1934) is in the style of the lullaby from *Gayaneh*, but the 20-minute movement undergoes sharp rhythmic transformations. The themes are often swaying fragments, recurring but flexible and luxuriantly embellished. All the movements in his three symphonies are lengthy, with dance rhythms integrated instead of being given a separate brief existence, as in traditional symphonic forms. Khachaturian's work in gaining international recognition for his nation's musical idiom was exceptional by any standard.

His achievement was within the Soviet's ideological frame-work, but in the difficult years, he spoke up for a more tolerant policy.

Dmitri Kabalevsky (1904-87) was very prolific, favouring the traditional forms of symphony and concerto, and his work, extrovert and optimistic, has tended to be critically disre-garded in the West. His melodic appeal lies in its wit and frequent Russian folk influence, and in his faster movements could sometimes be mistaken for Prokofief, such as between parts of the 4th Symphony (1954) and Prokofief's 7th Sym-phony. He is best known in Britain for his exuberant overture to the opera, *Colas Breugnon*, and it even reached the last night of London's 1994 Proms. The opera was based on Romand Rolland's novel concerning treachery, plague and the pillag-ing of private armies in the 17th century. To judge from the exceptional quality of the overture, it is regrettable that we have not had the chance to judge the complete work on stage.

Kabalevsky and Khachaturyan represented nationalist idioms in Soviet music-making whereas Shostakovitch inclined towards a cosmopolitan style, especially in his major works. Prokofief clearly had a facility for both approaches.

To justify their exalted positions, composers were encour-aged or expected not only to write for state occasions and other formal gatherings, but also for popular consumption. Works which required large resources to execute were to be capable of attracting and ennobling substantial sections of society.

The belief that the nation's finest composers should pro-duce some compositions with broad popular appeal is not unreasonable, but has never been fully appreciated in the West where very few people with real influence would want to be quoted publicly for stating that popular music in recent decades has mostly been provided by hacks. Conversely, direc-tives to composers would be regarded as interference in their artistic integrity, and much has always been made in the West about ideological influences in Soviet music-making.

The official warning against formalism, directed in 1948 by the Party ideologist and commissar for cultural affairs, Zdha-nov, has acquired historical notoriety. Prokofief's opera *War and Peace* was criticised as being interesting only to an elite group in the USSR. He replied, agreeing with Soviet opposition to modernistic trends, in particular atonalism, which the rulers were determined above all to keep out of the USSR.

He instanced his Fifth Symphony, *Alexander Nevsky* and the *Romeo and Juliet* ballet as examples of his desire to please the widest possible discriminating audience, a reasoned response to musically unenlightened men acting with Stalin's approval.

Not long after that, Kabelevsky, whilst visiting an English university, was presented with an inevitable question: would an atonalist such as Schoenberg be permitted to compose in the USSR? He replied that no such people existed there, not a answer to satisfy a libertarian audience. He might have been on safer ground if he had used the populist argument, that such music was not generally liked and did not merit the spending of public money.

Serious music always had high status in the USSR, public participation was impressive and the output of compositions was correspondingly large, but much banal work may have been accepted for ideological reasons. Yet, whatever we assume about political interference in the USSR, it must be said that all the works most popular with concert-goers in the West – with the exception of *Lady Macbeth* – were officially approved as being worthy of a committed Soviet composer.

# 22  *Finland and Sibelius*

In the mid-1950s, Finland seemed for us English a very remote land, so I was very fortunate to be invited as a guest, rather than go as a tourist. The six-week visit in 1955 leaves me with memories of a country which, I imagined perhaps wrongly, in many ways represented the future, and of an admirable culture closer to nature than our own.

At that time, there was a cult, in Britain and the USA, very well supported in the concert halls, of the music of Sibelius, which gave us enthusiasts a slight acquaintance with some of the names in a remote mythology which inspired many of his compositions. Finland was much associated outside Scandinavia with his name, and the Finns tended to regard this with mild amusement, because they regarded themselves as living unnoticed on the edge of European society.

I was introduced to Sointu Kiviranta, a woman who helped me to understand much about Finland and with whom I have stayed mainly in written contact. She spoke of the pretentious trade in certain Helsinki shops where expensive artifacts, and their reproductions, have always been on display as 'ancient Finnish'. Many were actually examples of Viking culture and there was no surviving native tradition of the epoque being presented.

The Finns had been a very backward tribe during the period when nordic civilisation began to be established. Now, as a nation-state established only in the 20th century, they were all the more determined to develop a new cultural identity. Managing their own affairs without interference for the first time, they had expressed this in the originality and flamboyance of their architecture, as well as in their advanced ideas about life and society. So even before 1940, their country rapidly took on the aspect of the most outwardly modern in Europe.

Finland's geography explains its isolation over centuries. A country with a surface area larger than Italy's and with its lakes covering an area half the size of Scotland; but with a small population whose ancestors had arrived from Asia at a different time from other migrants to Europe, and with a language which was utterly remote from their neighbours', except the Lapps to the north and the Estonians across the Baltic Sea. By type, they were not a very tall race, but remarkably pale-skinned and with high cheek-bones.

Those early commercial travellers, the Vikings, established sufficient control over Finland's coasts for trading purposes, but were more interested in mating with Finnish women than in settling down. Consequently, the blood was gradually mixed with that of the taller, blonde Scandinavians whilst the Finnish language remained remarkably free from foreign influence, except for a few trading terms.

The Swedes eventually colonised the sparsely-populated coastal areas of south-west Finland, controlling the whole country until it was through war taken-over by the Russians in 1809. The Swedish language continued to remain dominant in official matters into the 19th-century whilst Finnish was not widely used in the schools or in a written form generally.

Of great consequence were the efforts of academic writers, Elias Lonnrot and others, to trace Finland's pre-history through their folk poems, which went back at least 2,500 years but had no written version. These had a range and imagery which makes an interesting comparison with Homer, and they also contain a reference to renewal through a virgin birth. They were published in their final version (1849) as the *Kalevala*, the land of heroes, so that the Finns were able to discover the beauty of their language and folk literature, encouraging a sense of national consciousness.

Citizens of Swedish origin remained in the country, felt no seriously divided loyalty and lived harmoniously with the rest. Jan Sibelius came from such a family and when he attended the first Finnish grammar school, had a struggle to master that language, but was encouraged in this by the fascination of the *Kalevala*.

Those south-western areas were the most developed economically, but the Finns' historic homelands were further east, the vast lake areas as far as Karelia. Into the bleak forest regions further north some of them ventured, and that gave rise to a pioneer tradition not so different from that in the U.S.A. The mineral wealth there was being exploited even before independence by which time the Finns were very advanced in technical knowledge and skills. Progress had subsequently been very impressive, and was only held-up by disastrous participation in the second world war, and the loss of much of historic Karelia to the USSR.

When I first arrived, television was insignificant and even radio was heard at restricted times; people seemed correspondingly more self-reliant and, despite their comfortable homes and town life, liked to living close to lake and forest. With so many lakes, possessing an island was not restricted to the rich but was a unique kind of opportunity to feel separated from the human society. I enjoyed hospitality at week-ends in summer houses on two small islands.

Finns are thought to be an unusually introspective race, given to the silences of the north. They do not place as much value on *small talk* as we do, and some of them even think they should study its virtues for the purposes of travel abroad. As small talk should hardly be confused with the art of conversation, it was for me a point in their favour. There is an exceptional interest in amateur dramatics, as well as sports, throughout the country, and I was introduced into a circle of people who liked to enjoy evenings of music-making, which meant there was much to talk about.

At first I imagined that the Finns walked about to strains of Sibelius in their heads, but that was not necessarily the case. They might as well be hearing Oskar Merikanto (1868-1924), opera composer but also a miniaturist whose 200 songs would have been very close to Finnish hearts, and to the idiom of their folk music. Apart from Sibelius, Selim Palmgren (1878-1951) would probably then have been the best known abroad for piano works, and his Second Piano Concerto (*The River*) which might have deserved comparable attention to those of Tchaikovsky.

With their long, sad winters and longing for the sun, those Finns would also have been looking-out to the warmth, languages and songs of the Mediterranean. What I remember foremost is Sointu singing *Anna*, a popular song of that time, in delightfully sunny, relaxed tempo, after a rendering of Richard Strauss' exquisite *Serenade* which gains from an intimate lounge setting.

Helsinki, like Brussels, is a bilingual city, and those that can benefit from this feature are greatly favoured, even if many do not appreciate this: because they are familiar with two utterly different language groups, one loosely described as 'Asiatic'[1]. This makes for linguistic skill and flexibility; in addition, Swedish provides a bridge to the Indo-European languages, and many Finns are as a result among Europe's finest multi-linguists. Sointu does not consider herself unusual for being able to sing, as an amateur, in at least 8 languages.

Conversely, those monolingual Finns often feel hemmed-in psychologically and have much difficulty with pronouncing European languages, with vocabularies separated by the millennia of human existence. They lack at least two voiced consonants, and have to concentrate to distinguish a G from a C and a P from a B. Their highly inflected language, in which every vowel is pronounced, adapts well to music and has given their folk style very distinctive features. A typical melody runs along a small range of pitches, and therefore with correspondingly more note repetition, having also a very simple, insistent rhythm.

The following extract from the *Kalevala* relates to an episode like the *Oedipus* fate theme, with the outburst of the wayward hero Kullervo at the death of a sister whom he has unknowingly seduced. Even to our unfamiliar ears, the repetition and heavy alliteration suggest a fierce expression:

Voi poloinen paiviani
Voipa kurja kummiani
voi kun pi'in sisarueni
turmelin emoni tuoman.
Voi isoni
Voi emoni . . .

That was set to music with piano accompaniment by Sibelius but is better known as a movement in his first, exceptionally large-scale work, the *Kullervo Symphony* of 1892. It was a time, often spent away from home in Helsinki, when the 27-year-old Sibelius could not keep his wayward nature in check, and he confessed to his wife the vices of which alcoholism was a symptom. He was probably suffering then from manic depression, though I have not seen the term written, and out of his personal crisis could have come an empathy with the Kullervo figure, a blundering warrior. This episodic symphony based on runes 32-35 of the *Kalevala* had made Sibelius famous through its Helsinki premiere.

Success did not prevent him withholding the work from publication, a ban which lasted for the rest of his life. The harsh treatment of a composition which had caused an unprecedented stir in Finland, partly on patriotic grounds, must have come from a dissatisfaction with its 'rambling' symphonic structure. Three years later, he decided to take one extended legend and divide it into four very short, cohesive works. His imagination here was fired by another failed (in our eyes) hero of the *Kalevala*, Lemminkainen, a reckless, almost mindless hunter and seducer of women. In his adventures with the *Maidens of Saari*, the theme of two-sided infidelity enables Sibelius to structure the developing conflict around two melodies often played simultaneously, a pointer to his growing mastery of polyphony. *Lemminkainen in Tuonela* (the land of the dead, corresponding to the Greek Hades), is remarkable for its sombre orchestral harmonies, depicting an episode unusual even for mythology. The hero is killed, then his bones are put together by his mother and he is resurrected. Sibelius' orchestral piece about the *Swan of Tuonela*, with its sad cor anglais melody which could be related to eternity, is among his most loved, though theories about its describing a swan come up against the fact that the work was originally written as an overture for an abandoned opera without swans.

Lemminkainen's abduction of a maiden is celebrated in a famous painting by Gallen-Kallela, a student colleague of Sibelius remembered still for his *Kalevala* illustrations. That text also excited much interest abroad, especially its insistent alliteration and assonance. It was a German translation that attracted the attention of American poet, Henry Longfellow, who wrote the Red Indian sage, *Hiawatha*, in respectful imitation[2].

The Kalevala continued to inspire Sibelius at various stages of his life, and nowhere moreso than in the legend of the origin of the world, *Luonnotar*, a work rarely performed until recently because very few sopranos could deal comfortably with its formidable vocal leaps alongside unearthly chromatic melody. It stands unique in his work, though many composers could not have resisted exploiting further such an enthralling sound.

There has sometimes been speculation about very talented persons who were born out of their times and who could not therefore achieve their deserved status. The converse would apply to Sibelius. If exceptional claims are made for his genius, they gain support because he was born when Finland's destiny most needed him. His musical development parallelled the growth of national consciousness.

Finland's quaint status as a Grand Duchy under the Russian Tsar did at least give it some degree of autonomy, which was however revoked by the Tsar's governor-general in 1899, with Russian quickly being installed as the official language. That provoked the great struggle for independence, and Sibelius had already been drawn into the movement, contributing the *Karelia* suite, *Finlandia*, and a sequence of *Historical Scenes*, heroic or celebratory, all for orchestra. Two of *Karelia*'s movements have unusually stressed rhythms, which have added to their popularity, one quite banal, the other part of a distinguished *intermezzo*. *Finlandia*'s snarling brass was thought to symbolise the tyrants, and its patriotism also has an undisguised defiance, though it arrived much too late to become the national anthem[3].

His orchestral works have strong impressionistic qualities, ranging from extended tone poems to brief character sketches, from *Pohjola's Daughter* which describes a hero's failure to complete Herculean tasks, to the exquisite feminacy of two movements in the *Swanwhite* music. With a few instrumental brush-strokes and subtle tonal changes, he can suggest a sunrise, water, a deserted strand, a flight of birds, chattering maidens, or magic. There are arresting harp passages often representing the *kantele*, Karelia's traditional stringed instrument on which the folk poems had been accompanied.

*Tapiola*, a description of the high forests of the *Kalevala*, is extraordinarily inventive within a structure based entirely on one theme, a masterpiece. Conductor Colin Davis spoke of its being *almost totally static and obsessed with the same notes*; *there's a hypnotic element* . . .

Many of his songs including some of the best need to be heard in their orchestral forms[3]. *Autumn Evening* is an impassioned *scena*, with very advanced harmonies but an occasional melodic line which we recognise as elusively Scandinavian. *On the veranda by the harbour* was in 1903 remarkable for its chromaticism which anticipated the style of *Luonnotar* ten years later. *The First Kiss* describes a girl's awakening until one chilling chord denotes Death as a hostile witness. Nearly 100 songs range from the short, ironic *Romeo* to the dramatic *Jubal* and *Black Roses*, and the ultra-Romantic *Was it a dream?* Most were written in his native Swedish, especially for the verses of Finland's best-known poet, Runeberg. He voices his country-men's regret at the passing of the warmer seasons and the sadder aspects of man's relation to nature. It is such themes which inspire so much of Sibelius's program music.

Two Finnish-language miniatures have greatness in their simplicity. Sibelius did not use folk material but each of these consists of a disarmingly beautiful melody with the note-repetition typical of the Finnish idiom: *To Evening* and *Drift-wood*. He had to learn to fashion his music to the special requirements of that language, its inflections and rich vowel-sounds, and did so mainly in his choral and patriotic settings.

Sibelius' early tone poem *En Saga*, revised by 1902, opens in an atmosphere remote from the 19th century or any human world we recognise: swirling middle strings, discordant wood-winds, then a taut, fast string ostinato which accompanies the major theme. This advances at a slower but pronounced pace, though brought to a fierce climax by the brass. The second theme shoots out from three repeated notes, then two new four-note rhythms leads eventually to a primitive dance. The excitement is maintained with the interweaving of thematic fragments given rich tone colour by the divided sections of the orchestra.

This work lasting nearly 20 minutes has a sense of growth and persistent motion sustained by short, repetitious figures, except for an eerie wood-wind interlude. The rhythms have an unusually prominent thematic role as well as giving the work immediate sensuous appeal.

The symphony (after *Kullervo* but numbered one) which appeared in 1899 sounds more traditional than *En Saga*, with broad melodies and leisurely developments, but the opening clarinet theme, which returns to play a decisive role in the finale, would be a curiosity in the recognised Western sym-phony, giving rise to speculation that the Russians of the previous generation, such as Borodin and Tchaikovsky, may have been an influence.

The Second Symphony (1902) is a seminal work of his early maturity. It makes a stark departure from the traditional first-movement form: pregnant fragments of themes merge in a development of increasing power, then gradually disintegrate. After a pizzicato opening of measured pace, the slow movement becomes an illustration of Sibelius' comment that his orchestral writing was *carved in Finnish granite*. A serene melody, with a nine-times repeated note, forms the *trio* section which offsets a furious *scherzo*. Reminiscent in structure and excitement of Beethoven's 5th Symphony, this surges into the finale where two powerful themes in heroic style enjoy the richest of Romantic flings.

By that time, Sibelius was aware of the dangers of becoming too popular, the artistic kiss of death. In self-mockery, he implied that he was not in the entertainment business, offering not cocktails but a glass of water. To its first audience in 1907, his 3rd Symphony must have confounded all expectations, but disarmingly, opening with what sounds like a sea shanty, and the nearest in his symphonies to a Finnish folk melody.[4] Yet it was more classical in feeling with a tendency to gently insistent rhythms, and main themes which are subtly related. There are also suggestions of chorale and pastoral dance, perhaps a return home to the village; but there is remarkable clarity of texture in this orchestral chamber music.

Though it moved consciously away from the grand statements of the earlier symphonies, nothing could have anticipated the 4th (1911), which to some listeners was not so much a glass of water as a slap in the face, an incomprehensible lurch into modernity. It was the most disconcerting of his compositions, harmony sometimes dispensed with, terse phrases replacing warm melody, which the more effectively surfaces briefly in the lake-land coolness of the slow movement. It may be interpreted as an invocation of the austere beauty of the Finnish landscape; but nature has no end and neither has this symphony. There is a mystical feeling throughout, supported by enigmatic key movements; because the work tailed-off without ceremony, some people did not know when to start clapping, and left without doing so. At that premiere, Sibelius had been the conductor and he was hurt. Yet others soon concluded that it was the composer's finest work.

There was a long delay before the 5th Symphony (1923) which had a more familiar sound, a partial return to the language of the 2nd but more terse. It is a tour de force of blazing brass and fierce, swirling rhythms, the finale being dominated by one of the most compelling ostinatos in all symphonic music.

Its companion piece, in time of composition only, was the 6th, as distant in sound and feeling as could be expected in one composer. Its restraint was emphasised by gentle modal language, but it gradually gained critical esteem for its progress towards a polyphonic style which also reflected Sibelius's admiration for the music of Palestrina and of the 16th century. Today it is seen as an important step towards the achievement of the 7th Symphony.

The magic of *En Saga*, the mysticism of *Luonnotar*, the winter of the 4th Symphony, the winds tearing through the forests of *Tapiola* . . . Sibelius' mastery of symphonic expression was taking him into unexplored territory where he was establishing a series of definitive landmarks.

He was aiming for the perfectly concise, cohesive symphony. In the 7th, completed before *Tapiola*, he is impelled to merge the movements into one. If Mozart's last symphony deserved the title *Jupiter*, this one might be called *Olympian*, inevitable, impassioned, then quickening to a wonderfully relaxed interlude before driving to a mounting tension of glowing harmonies, a finality to which the silence that follows seems a part and a resolution. Critical acclaim fixed it as a work which would set the shape for 20th century symphonic development.

By 1935, a New York Philharmonic survey revealed that Sibelius had become for their concert-goers the most popular of all composers, reflecting the exceptional attention always to *Finlandia, En Saga, The Swan of Tuonela*, the Violin Concerto, and the 2nd and 5th Symphonies. That is explained by their personalities and melodic appeal, which spans characteristics of both 19th and 20th century styles: from one violin tune spread-out lovingly over fully $2\frac{1}{2}$ minutes in the concerto's slow movement, to the First Symphony's ten-stroke drum rhythm and a portentous major theme in the 4th Symphony consisting of five notes.

Certain other composers were to take the path of the single-movement symphony; Sibelius's clearly influenced two fine American symphonies, Samuel Barber's first, and Roy Harris' 3rd, both dating from the following decade. The last substantial work was the very extensive incidental music to the *Tempest* (1926), covering in masterly fashion a wide expressive range and the psychological complexities of Shakespeare's play.

Some critics eventually decided the time had arrived for a revision of Sibelius' reputation. Were the 3rd and 6th Symphonies water-colours after his oil paintings, and had Sibelius added too much water? They asked if he had been over-rated by, for example, the influential Englishmen, writer Cecil Gray and conductor Thomas Beecham. They speculated on whether he was completely dried-up and why such a 'serious' composer had written so much inferior salon music.

He attempted to advance from *Tapiola* and the 7th Symphony. His 8th had been promised for 1933 but only the first movement was ready from what was intended to be a long work. Sometimes he was quoted as being optimistic about its completion, but he never explained. One close friend said he could never discuss it, like a mother who had suffered a stillbirth. Perhaps it would be discovered after his death.

The last quarter-century of his life is referred to as the *silence of Jarvenpaa*, the public and international curiosity about his more tranquil life with wife and family only being gratified by spasmodic anecdotes concerning distinguished visitors and their enquiries about his continued composing.

He was troubled by the unending correspondence and questions from well-wishers, so that eventually the bulk was almost too much for his permanent secretary, Santeri Levas, to handle. This man eventually wrote his recollections of the later Sibelius who was specially anxious that his international prominence should not impede the success of younger Finnish composers. He also feared that modern music was becoming 'mathematical' and lacking emotional content, but one very active composer is most highly praised. In 1945, Sibelius thought Shostakovitch's latest symphony, the 7th, was his greatest to date. At a time when Finnish soldiers were helping the Germans to besiege Leningrad, and Sointu was witnessing as a very young army nurse horrifying deaths in Karelia, he had been able to hear recent music on Russian radio. One heartening fact was that before and after the war, according to Levas, he had most cordial relations with Soviet composers despite his being a firm anti-communist.

By the time I visited Jarvenpaa, visitors were totally excluded and he was still living as a nonagenarian with his wife in the home he acquired as a result of a state pension granted when he achieved fame as a relatively young composer. It was this question of the 8th Symphony and any other withheld compositions which intrigued me at that time.

It was two years later that he died, soon to be followed by his wife, a life-long companion. Their home became a national shrine, but no secret hoards of music were to be found and it was eventually assumed he had burnt all traces of the new symphony; his wife had spoken of a dreadful rage and *a big bonfire*.

Some countries in the musical world, but not the Latin ones, had placed an unprecedented importance upon his work within his own lifetime. He did not want to be considered the new Beethoven. Had the burden of reputation been too much for him? He was given to severe self-criticism and with hindsight we can infer some kind of explanation. He had obviously moved into new areas of self-expression and at some point he had found progress impossible . . . he must have felt he had nothing new to say. Whatever the reasons, they belong to the integrity of genius.

It is regrettable that many genuinely inferior composers have not followed his example.

# 23   *Kismet — Fate*

Ah, Moon of my delight who know'st no wane,
The Moon of Heav'n is rising once again:
How oft hereafter rising shall she look
Through this same Garden after me – in vain.

How many of us when young found in extracts from this great poem by Omar Khayyam in translation something of the essence of poetry? Add to this the even more widely loved stories from the *1,001 Nights*, and what other associations can we English-speaking peoples make with the Middle East of the 12th century?

Our awareness is so sketchy that the epoque finds us specially open to the lure of fantasy. Encyclopaedias will tell us that Omar Khayyam died some 40 years before Genghis Khan was born – we've all heard of him – and that in the following century Genghis' followers destroyed the most distinguished city of near-Asia, Baghdad, along with about one million of its citizens.

For pure entertainment, perhaps the less we know of history, the better, so why not transport old Omar to Baghdad and place him in a tale from the *Arabian Nights* with no care for the anomalies? Would Omar have been quite suitable as adviser to the Caliph of Baghdad, the Muslims' religious head? As a (to us) notable agnostic, certainly not; but his subversive views may have been unknown alongside his fame as an astronomer, and he did pay obeisance to prevailing beliefs by taking the pilgrimage to Mecca.

American dramatist Edward Knoblock was to take due poetic licence with a lively story for a new kind of stage spectacular, the 1911 New York production, *Kismet*. Oscar Asche brought it to London for the first of his big successes.

With so many great composers dying in the years just before and after 1900, the opportunities for using their compositions after 50 years without restraint of copyright encouraged several musicals to appear, mainly in the USA. Robert Wright and George Forrest had credit for bringing some quality to the Americanisation of European operetta from the late-1930s and their *Song of Norway,* a genial presentation of Eduard Grieg and his music, was a commercial success. By substituting humour for sentiment, they may in *Kismet* (1953) have created a more durable musical.

If mock-oriental music were required, who better than a Russian composer conjuring the exotic flavour of the Asian parts of the Russian Empire in the 19th century? For a spectacular musical version four decades later, 42 sections of the music score were arranged from Alexander Borodin's compositions, and several of these became popular songs of the mid-1950s.

In any circumstances, many people object on principle to the vulgarisation of classic material for commercial reasons rather than judge by intention and the quality of the finished product. One question for Borodin enthusiasts is whether they would like the muscular opening of his Second Symphony served up as a slick dissertation on *Fate*: 'Then Fate's a thing without a head, a puzzle never understood . . . ' The *Nocturne* from the Second String Quartet was reworked as a leisurely operatic quartet, 'And this is my beloved'. The *scherzo* was transformed into slow 3–4 time for *Baubles, Bangles and Beads.* The *Polovtsian Dances* from the opera *Prince Igor* were to give local colour, with several arrangements and most of the vigorous rhythms being modified. The *Dance of the Female Slaves* provided the theme that became the show-stopping duet, *Stranger in Paradise.*

One of the best-known *Polovtsian* choral sections follows on wildly from what we in the West might take for a very exciting 'Arab' dance. The youthful Zubbediya performs it, most appetising but formidable, and introduced as one of several candidates to become the Caliph's bride. Her name sounds like that of one of Genghis' most feared generals; who knows what subtleties have been written into the script?

The leading character is a beggar and self-styled Poet who calls himself Hajj. Though seemingly a Godless sophisticate like Omar, he would surely not have earned that title through a pilgrimage to Mecca; his activities lie more in the direction of training his daughter to steal purses. Calling Omar Khayyam a *tenth-rate poet laureate* does not commend his literary taste, though by taking a line out of context: *The moving finger writes, and having writ moves on* he glibly asserts that it is a statement of the obvious.

Hajj can juggle with words and sells them at a suitably low price. Confident, exceptionally quick-witted but with enough time to dispense thought-laden platitudes, he bandies reparti with ruthless men who have the power to sever his limbs instantly. His life hangs upon a word. He is as cunning as a commercial traveller and as slippery as a solicitor, but with a common touch which today would earn him a much easier living on the air.

In pantomime tradition, the robber chief, Jawal, seeks a long-lost son, and by making an outrageous promise to find the son within one day, Hajj has at least delayed his own death. He has even talked the father into giving him a purse of 100 gold pieces as advanced payment. In a Baghdad market scene, he uses this to purchase four female slaves ostensibly to look after his daughter, but they are impounded when he is arrested for possessing the stolen gold. So both he and the robber are brought together for punishment, and Jawal recognises the chief justice, the Wazir, as his son.

Both the Wazir and his delectably sophisticated wife, Lalume, are most impressed, he by the apparent miracle, whilst she is tingling with desire for Hajj. He will be asked to use his mystical powers in the service of the Wazir, who wants to marry-off to the young Caliph a repellent trio of knife-wielding ladies. They perform a ritual dance which would make any male fearful for his virility.

The Wazir's intrigues end with his execution, and Hajj, promoted to Emir, will eventually depart with the widow Lalume to a restful oasis. Would Hajj enjoy a settled existence or fret for a life of fraud? His liaison with Lalume is a diverting addition but of course lacks the romance of First Love. Fortunately, as in many Arabic stories of this kind, the local ruler has a habit of stalking his city incognito. The young Caliph has no evil intent and his rapturous meeting with Hajj's daughter Marsineh enables her to move in three easy stages from rags to riches.

Even if these two are cardboard characters, three others can be brought to life, and an effective 'comic opera' team exists:

tenor and soprano, mature baritone and deep-ranging mezzo, and the corrupt justice as a buffo role, with his storming patter-song, *Was I Wazir?*

Hajj is the dynamo that keeps the plot moving and he was made more genial than in the 1911 version when he was not above the occasional murder, a *sturdy beggar* as one theatre critic at the time called him. His song *Fate* might suit a bass, but needs a fine resonance on the higher notes. The elaborate burlesque number, *Gesticulate*, includes the *scherzo* from the First Symphony to this rhythm:

Should Scheherazade undulate her body,
That can be expressed if you gesticulate.

Marsineh rises above the sounds of a bazaar to sing her delicate jewel song, and is well served with two love duets. Lalume is an inventive musical comedy role, such as in the scene where she turns her charm onto Hajj whilst giving her husband cursory stabs of jaded flattery. Her skill in parody and her vocal range are challenged in two contrasting songs. As her introduction, there is a satirical travelogue, *Not since Nineveh*, with preposterous references to the trumpet at Jericho, 'hot' Gomorrah, and not omitting that wall-writing at Babylon, one hundred miles down the Tigris from Baghdad. The second song, *Bored*, is one of the most distinctive additions to the score, long sustained passages, sensuous swoops into the lower register. She also has a tongue-in-cheek duet with Hajj, an oriental send-up on the nature of virtue, with much reference to *Rahadlakum* (Turkish Delight), and jazz trumpet backing.

The mock-philosophic tone of the play is well sustained in the lesser-known songs such as *The sands of time* and *The olive tree*, with Borodin's attractively spun-out melodies deserving respectful treatment.

The musical played at London's vast Stoll Theatre for nearly two years from 1955. Its appeal is apparent in a subsequent recording with international opera singers, Regina Resnik, Adele Leigh and Robert Merrill. It is still tackled by some of the more confident amateur operatic societies and the rich score enables producers to select for effective stage shows without overstraining their resources.

M.G.M. made *Kismet* into a superior musical, directed by Vincente Minelli, well sung with sparkling dance sequences and orchestral score, but the Wazir was deprived of a singing role and Omar not presented as a poet, so that much of the humour is lost.

I have now seen two amateur productions of *Kismet*. The first one, by a group of London university graduates, had exploited the innovative talents of the performers in an enjoyable romp. The Petts Wood (Kent) production succeeded in keeping close to the original; plot, dialogue and musical treatment are intended to be slightly *over the top*, with that precarious balance sustained throughout.

A persistent difficulty is likely to be transferring what was a Hollywood-type spectacular to the small stage. A faithful West-End return could work well because revivals of successful musicals from the mid-20th century are in fashion, for their tunes and vitality, and because of the prevalent nostalgia in theatreland for the lyrical and escapist.

A Composer on top of the World.

1938, *Frau Luna* at the theatre which was to survive the war.

*Frau Luna*
TOP: On the Moon, Women dance . . . and rule.
BOTTOM: 1899, Berlin 'street festivities'.

## 24 *Berliners on the Moon*

I n the 1890s, there was much speculation and rumour about air travel. Berlin engineer Otto Lilienthal made numerous flights in wings until he met his death in 1896, and the achievements of Graf Zeppelin were a talking-point years before the first aeroplane took-off. One amateur balloonist was Heinrich Bolton-Baeckers who successfully indulged his fantasies in written form through his partnership, not unlike that between Gilbert and Sullivan, with composer Paul Lincke. As librettist, he wrote a farce about Venus enjoying a Berlin night-out, though the plot closely parallels that of *Orpheus in the Underworld*. It was a good run-in for, two years later, *Frau Luna* (1899) in which Lincke modestly intended to represent the go-ahead spirit and lively rhythms of Berlin, but which was destined to become the prototype Berlin street-opera. It is also a mock-epic of imagination and desire, dream and reality which lends itself to constant adaptation and innovation.

The second version of this work I saw at the Neu Köllner Oper, a theatre group in a West Berlin suburb who specialise in converting an interesting range of mainly traditional works into very distinctive cabaret-musicals. For this production, they employed nine instrumentalists and nine singers of who one, Regina Anhamm, typified their range of skills. She gave a disciplined performance as a robot for one hour, breaking her silence only for Stentorian bouts of trombone-playing, before bursting out at the start of the second act to play the title-role as a lecherous lunar hostess alternating between operatic and night-club singing. Much fun can be derived from the most basic of stage props, one large, decrepit balloon and a club bar for the respective acts.

Neu Köllner Oper[1] have a keen, discriminating West Berlin audience, full houses in a small functional theatre, ingenuity in presentation whilst retaining the spirit of their originals. From conversations I had with some of those concerned at creative level, they feel they have nothing to gain artistically from seeing classic operetta productions further east, the rivalry of a dedicated, under-funded ensemble towards a lavishly state-financed institution.

My first acquaintance with the authentic *Frau Luna* had taken place the year previously in 1989, after I had passed through the tiresome formalities of the Berlin Wall at Friedrichstrasse Station, to the Metropol theatre opposite. This, with two nearby opera houses, were the prestigious musical venues of the capital of the (East) German Democratic Republic.

Even so, I was surprised by the excellence of a show which represented an unfamiliar style of entertainment raised to a miniature art-form, and by my vague acquaintance with three of the tunes. Two of these, charmingly balletic, had formed part of the *Glow-worm Idyll*[2] as performed around Europe by the renowned ballerina, Pavlova, somewhat before my time.

In *Frau Luna*, they are sung when the curtain rises on a Berlin street by a chorus for schoolgirls, looking very decorative in blue uniforms, not blue jeans but blue-and-white striped dresses and straw boaters; for this is the year 1899, with Kaiser Wilhelm and his grandmother Queen Victoria trying to rule the world.

We meet an officer in splendid white uniform, with spiked helmet and a gleaming new car which must have impressed a trendy actress in flowing gown and large feathered hat. Then there is a community policeman who cannot say where the moon goes in the daytime but who is friendly enough to use a key thrown to him from a balcony window by a winsome woman.

One of those fine tall columns that used to grace the boulevards of Europe's capitals with details of theatre and other cultural events observes the mundane goings-on from some 30 minutes before lighting-up like the Brighton decorations, then wobbling and hovering. At that moment, the Man in the Moon appears in the sky, beckoning and calling in a deep voice for Fritz Steppke to fulfil his destiny. So it is that he and two thoroughly prosaic friends undertake a lunar journey, propelled not by an absurd balloon, as in the original legend, but in the best rocketry that 1899 technology can provide. To their dismay, at the last moment they are joined by Steppke's landlady for no good reason except that she has to dominate every situation in which she finds herself. We shall call her the Berlin *Hausfrau*, though she is not quite a *Frau*, nor, as we soon learn, quite a *Jungfrau* (virgin).

The rocket in space appears to shoot right across the theatre and cinematic effects illustrate the moon journey with pre-1945 film shots, so avoiding space-age clichés, and with an orchestral reprise to entertain the audience whilst there is a 10-minute scene-change before Act II.

Neither space nor language cause problems in operetta but the early interchanges between the Berliners and their lunar hosts, though coherent, are alternately barbed or stunningly commonplace. At the lunar court, certain characters bear resemblances to some we have already seen in the Berlin street. Theophil, the hectoring foreman of the moon-polishing gang, looks like the amorous policeman: Prince Shooting-star flips around the galaxy in a stream-lined car: the woman who directs the lunar choir could be the schoolmistress in fancy dress.

More disconcertingly, old assumptions are challenged: why do we characterise the moon as a man? Females feature prominently in the lunar government which is enlightened enough to have separate ministries for women, love and the arts. The palace guards in red and black uniform have pretty faces and nubile bodies. Yet lunar songs have a similar imagery to ours:

> Softly, silently, like a thief in darkest night,
> With the old, seductive tunes, Love comes stealing in.

Suspense mounts as we are told of the moon's legendary sovereign, Frau Luna, who finally appears in awesome splendour, a shower of primary colours and a grand operatic *scena*. She has a presence not unlike Turandot's, and for the only occasion in the story, time seems to stand still as she holds forth imperiously at the top of the vocal scale. This lunar variant of *coloratura* may sound comical to human ears, but once the assembly have been bewitched, she lapses into a more 'popular' style. There are suggestions that she could commit acts of promiscuity in public that our 19th century monarchs only performed in private.

It is clear that any resemblance to Turandot is purely external, and she is no ice maiden. Yet it might be misleading to see her as an early advocate of the permissive society, as we understand it; she would draw a line at 'decadence'. Whereas Europe's youth today are free to wallow in self-pity and listen to sad music, she is insistent that young people must never give way to depression. She spells this out seductively but firmly in feet-tapping rhythms:

Get your act together, keep your head up high.

Aerobics for the masses as a substitute for sexual pleasure? Whatever her prescriptions, there is no disguising she is an authoritarian hedonist. Cheerfulness is demanded, and also what seems like a *Bacchanal* except that the men are not much involved.

This might help to explain a phenomenon which has perhaps been exercising the imaginations of the less innocent among the audience; the lunar males seem middle-aged and unattractive, with absurd bouffant hair-styles. By contrast, the young women are barely clothed and addicted to energetic dancing; but it is the mature ones who are bearing their bosoms. They display a remarkable variety of erotica, phallic symbols and fetiches.

So what are we to infer about this remote civilisation? Has a long period of sexual deprivation induced this artless sublimation? If so, it is a neat contrast to a situation in the following Lincke-Bolton Baeckers work, *Lysistrata*, where wives organise a sexual strike against war.

The visitors are not competent even in their own terms to deal with the media hype suddenly laid-on, except that the Berlin tailor introduces himself as a *clothing engineer*. Court intrigue is quickly apparent, and when jealousy turns to horse-play, the *Hausfrau* terrifies the assembly with the Berlin accent and makes more impression with her umbrella than Chamberlain could forty years later in Munich.

Frau Luna of course does not see these unseemly activities, but has departed with Steppke, to whom she has taken a fancy. Throughout, he is subjected to a variety of irresistible forces, human and otherwise, and his astonishing naivety extends to sexual matters. He is as far as possible from being an adventurer in the manner of Aeneas, Theseus or Turandot's lover: for him, no song of triumph, no *Nessum dorma*. Propelled into an enormous bed, he declines the voluptuous feast offered as if he were the virginal Parsifal.[3] He is suffering culture shock, has a conscience about his Berlin fiancée and fails to gratify the lady.

As if to save him from embarrassment, the sweet music evaporates and the vision shatters, precipitating unpredictably dramatic events. Supernatural forces are in command as the four Berliners find themselves heading earthwards in their space-ship.

Then the rocket's controls develop errors in the fourth dimension. They reach earth, but ninety years later, landing in front of an unattractive, long white wall, and an assembling of young men in unfamiliar green uniforms, whose only obvious advantage is that they speak German fluently. They describe themselves as frontier guards, but after clearing the intruders from suspicion of being what they call 'N.A.T.O. spies', seem to accept their fantastic story. The four have returned to some kind of Berlin, but it is not their own. They are formally welcomed and invited to join-in the celebrations of the fortieth anniversary of the German Democratic Republic.

The explanations which follow concerning a Germany split into two are as curious as anything they have heard on the moon. The fate of their nation and the cold war are intimidating, and they wish themselves back in the relative sanity of Wilhelmine Germany. One might infer that people prefer the conventions and peculiarities of their own societies than being exposed to the whims of exotic courtiers, lunar princesses, frontier restrictions or politicians with strange obsessions.

Wish-fulfilment appears to operate because the human voyagers are finally returned to their 1899 environment, where nothing has changed. Were the adventures nothing more than a dream of Fritz Steppke? If so, there is some mystery about how Count Zeppelin heard of his prowess and offered him the job he desires above all.

The moment for general celebration is at hand. Steppke's future prospects justify immediate marriage and the ensemble throw everything into a stirring chorus of *Berliner Luft* (Berlin Air), good enough to be heard often among the world's most famous marches.

■ ■ ■

Musical presentations of moon visits date back as far as Haydn, and Daniel Auber composed an opera about a Venus journey on a bronze horse. Later contributions were attributed to the influence of fantasy writer, Jules Verne, who was intrigued by humanity's inclination to attribute our characteristics and problems to the moon and its supposed influence. In the 1870s, Verne had tried to address himself seriously to the problems of space travel, but he also liked musical versions of his farces and had been known to complain if he found them insufficiently eccentric. He might well have approved of this story.

*Frau Luna* has an imaginative, gently satirical plot, and makes very effective play with the ironies and interplay between hope and resignation, the ideal and the common-place, and how man is sustained by and suffers from his dreams. The lyrics extend to the earth's beauty, the evening, the stars and the search for love. Paul Lincke, but not Bolters-Baeckers, lived until the end of the 1945 war:

Our beautiful world must one day have an end.

Lincke's style originates in a popular idiom, but can lend itself to operatic treatment. It has what the Berliners call *Witz und Spritz*, wit and effervescence, bouncy rhythms, catchy tunes easily sung. Its directness goes with a disrespectful approach to serious topics, saucy female attire and high-kick dancing. The well-tried formula of introduction and main theme (chorus or refrain) is followed closely in Lincke's song-making except that the first part is generally up-graded in melodic interest, and he does not want to follow a slow-sad, fast-joyful pattern. A sequence of cheerful melodies as suggested by Frau Luna could quickly become boring, and he cleverly alternates the main stress between opposite ends of the bar, so contrasting two swinging rhythms, as in *Keep your head up high*, which lies somewhere between a *can-can* and a *goose-step*. The result has been a diverting succession of melodies, in turn street-wise, naive, declamatory, ironic, passionate and sentimental. *Frau Luna* contains about forty themes, a generous number compared with modern musicals.

*Once it was predicted* is in bustling speech-song that we hear often in the Brecht-Weill *Three-penny Opera* of thirty years later, and *It's betrayed in your eyes* is close in feeling to the songs Lehar later wrote for Richard Tauber to sing. The symbolism of the plot is caught in the theme-song which translates literally as *Castles on the Moon*, but means *Castles in the Air*, and the 1911 London production underlined the fantasy element by using that title. The song is occasionally heard on British radio as a slow orchestral waltz, not ironic but with a sentimental flavour.

The two characters that typify petty oppressiveness are linked by memories of a youthful indiscretion, and by the *Hausfrau*'s momentary lapse from her Puritan stance. The song, *O, Theophil*, incongruously child-like, has an introduction which should be declaimed as high melodrama. When she sings nostalgically of how she had been seduced for the one and only time in Berlin's Tiergarten, and by a moon-dweller, some very deep, frustrated notes turn romance into farce.

To the pure everything is pure. This is on one level a parable about the 'grass in the next field' and futile searches for the 'seventh heaven'. The disarming gestures of the female moon-dwellers might represent the innocence of the Garden of Eden, or a futuristic age of permissiveness. There's a tasteful suggestiveness which presents in the best light the city's reputation for dramatising the delights of sex.

The dance troupe in *Frau Luna* is given a more than decorative role within the action. The Berlin stage has a great tradition of satirical cabaret and colourful travesties of the military spirit, so visitors from abroad are knocked-back when the female corps de ballet stretch their young limbs as the shock troops of the cat-walk. This device is rarely seen used nowadays so that its impact is the more striking, especially when a cast of 80 and a brass band jump-on to the ramp together and give-out what sound like Berlin street songs. Nimble footwork prevents broken legs as they file through in two columns which cross.

The essential spirit of the work has passed-down through the city's generations, and a revival conscientiously preserves this. It also seizes the option of employing the intervening social or political changes to maximum comic effect in plot and dialogue. This capacity for topical adaptation is a special advantage which operetta can have as a genre, compared with opera where, for example, altering the lyrics could be most problematic, and changing the plot is taboo. Satire has to be sharp and relevant; the rapport across the footlights becomes untimately the measure of success.

The Metropol put so much importance on this that they have never made money through commercial recordings. To take the music home, one might have to obtain a quite different interpretation by another company. The only recording I could obtain in 1992, despite including operatic singers, was a Bavarian attempt to interpret it as a pantomime, so that it was hardly worth playing to English friends. Perhaps because they were not concerned with a stage production, they simply ignored the need for the kind of 'serious' treatment such as we give to G. & S. Other recordings of old favourites might make trendy arrangements, such as flattening-out the rhythms and dispensing with trained singers. That is less acceptable than merely using certain melodies as popular dance-songs, which at one time had been inevitable.

Visiting a communist state used to be, for me, an interesting chance to walk through a looking-glass and take a different perspective on life's values. That could be extended to sharing jokes about the cold war in a theatre. The Berlin Wall episode in Act III was amusingly contrived, an innovation within the 1987 production and now a historical curiosity. Following the political changes by the year 1990, that scene was removed, but the overall version is good enough to last for a second decade.

One cold war joke, however, was retained for some time. In the pre-1990 script, one traveller emerges from the rocket to announce proudly to the Lunatics: *Ich bin ein Berliner*. This reference to John Kennedy's 1963 speech used to get a big laugh, because it was thought to be pretentious. Now that at least half of the audience comes from West Berlin, ridiculing a U.S. president is less fashionable. A reference to east German refugees seeking payments as soon as they arrived in west Germany replaced it in 1990 as the most lively joke.

■  ■  ■

Paul Lincke learned the theatre and cabaret trade by producing in many places, including seasons at Paris' Folies-bergère. One evening as he was about to conduct there, a woman entered the orchestral pit and slapped his face, which the audience thought an excellent opening for a musical farce. It was in fact his wife, come from Germany to investigate his *vie Parisienne*, en route to a divorce.

No such diversions appear to have attended his appearance in 1912 at the London Coliseum *with his Viennese orchestra of 42*.

That was the year after conducting *Frau Luna* at London's Scala theatre in an English version where Hampstead Heath is the take-off point for a balloon onto which a Mrs Bloggins jumps, only to be confronted by a lunar queen who wants to make love to all three of her English companions. Perhaps because of the production, *Castles in the Air* was only a modest success, but a few of Lincke's melodies were heard frequently at dances in Britain for half a century.

Lincke cut a handsome elegant figure, down to his white conducting gloves, and up to his Kaiser Wilhelm moustache. From one photographic pose, he might have been amused that he could look like a physically more perfect specimen of the Kaiser.[4]

He adapted Viennese operetta to a cheeky Berlin model so successfully that other talented composers quickly followed, such as Walter Kollo, rather more sentimental in style, whose *Wedding Night in Paradise* has recently been revived at the Metropol with his grandson, René, in the lead. Viktor Holländer composed many revues and his son, Friedrich, continued in Berlin style with the excellent music for the film, *Blue Angel*, and the seemingly eternal *Falling in love again* sung by Marlene Dietrich.

Born among Berlin's waterways in 1866, Lincke composed with the city's songs in his ears, and his entertainments bore such suggestive titles as the *Mastersingers of Berlin* and the *Amazons of the River Spree*. The royalties were unprecedented in Berlin as he proceeded to compose over twenty stageable works, with music which was often a natural for the Berlin's little 'barrel-organ', the *Drehorgel*. A facility for turning-out popular songs so regularly induced him to set-up his own publishing company which still operates. He was at the height of his popularity still in 1914 and his escapist melodies helped to lighten the load of millions of German soldiers facing death.

As Lincke was an 'Aryan', the Nazis after 1933 were keen to exploit his reputation, but he only produced one final operetta during the war, before dying in 1946. He had been, certainly in spirit, the Offenbach of Berlin, but whatever the qualities of his other revues, farces and operettas, *Frau Luna* is the work which even those friendly rivals, the Saxons and the Rhinelanders, are daring enough to perform in the 1990s, when Munich saw it played by the visiting Berliners.

# 25  *Metropol*

**B**erlin has two city centres, east and west of the Tiergarten. To the east running north-south lies Friedrichstrasse, pre-war the entertainment centre which had given Berlin its international reputation, but which like many famous London streets, is not comparably broad. The government buildings lay to its west but the capital's classic splendour was on the other side near where it is intersected just south of its railway station by the spacious Unter den Linden. From that point eastward as far as Berlin's major cathedral had become the Prussian state's show-centre, including the 1745 opera house, and culminating with the neo-classical buildings of architect Karl Schinkel (1781–1841). Just south of the Unter den Linden is Behrenstrasse which housed the Metropol, one of several musical theatres of the Friedrichstrasse area.

In 1945, nearly everything was a mass of rubble, except the station, and from 1961 the Berlin Wall ran west of that station, and across the Friedrichstrasse south of Behrenstrasse at an intersection called Checkpoint Charlie. By chance, the former leisure area therefore fell into the eastern part of the city, no longer a bustling thoroughfare, and was only gradually built-up again. Near the station was the theatre where Bertolt Brecht had first produced his Three-penny Opera and where in the 1950s, he established the Berliner Ensemble.

By the 1980s, the buildings of the Unter den Linden had been miraculously restored to their historic forms, including the State Opera, whilst a new company, the Komische Oper, had been established on the site of the old Metropol theatre. Within a few minutes' walk of the station, East Berlin had two opera houses, its restored concert hall, the Berliner Ensemble, an operetta, a new, very large variety theatre and some small cabaret spots. An impressive cultural centre by any standards, with non-music theatres, famous museums and three cathedrals in the district.

The Metropol theatre had been opened in 1898, and in highly competitive conditions established itself during the 1920s as Berlin's leading operetta venue, with the Berlin works of Lincke and Walter Kollo, new internationally performed ones by Fall, Lehar and Kalman, as well as the 'golden' Viennese operettas. The soprano Fritzi Massary and tenor Richard Tauber were among the very distinguished artistes, though as Jews, they and many others were barred from 1933 when a decline began inevitably to set-in.

Just after the fall of Berlin, the Soviet military commander gave an historic order that within months, the city was to reopen its opera. The only theatre standing, right alongside the Friedrichstrasse station, was the Admirals Palast, former home of variety, Tiller girls and operetta. It had kept smiling through the depression, the Nazi period, the bombs, and under military occupation for some years would house an opera company and certain historic political gatherings.

The bombed-out Metropol operetta moved to a cinema further out in East Berlin, then eventually took-over the vacated Palast, imposing its own name. This theatre had been built in 1911 for a 3,000 audience, was neither traditionally ornate nor functionally modern, but by the 1980s, with reduced capacity, it was as the Germans say, *gemütlich*, comfortable and welcoming.

Musical visitors from Britain and elsewhere to Vienna will make for the Volksoper, and the Metropol offers productions of comparable style and artistry, but though Berlin is one of the best cities in Europe for entertainment, it is not a recognised 'holiday venue' and the publicity is correspondingly much less. Each has facilities for which there is no precise equivalent in the West. As ensembles, they have the range of skills and flexibility to perform in repertory up to six operettas or musicals in any one week, with at least twice that number available in any period to be seen. The resources required for such a regime are of major operatic scale and would therefore be prohibitive for most theatres in west Europe; the Metropol even operates with duplicate casts, so increasing the demands for versatility. One should not be surprised to see a leading male singer in a travesty role, or the second lead soprano in the *Merry Widow* doing the splits with les girls at Maxims. When she is not padded-up as the *Hausfrau* in *Frau Luna*, perhaps twice a month, Maria Malle may be a slinky night-club hostess in *Hello, Dolly*, a loud dance-band soloist in *Sugar*, give a *soirée intime* of Kurt Weill songs, or sing elsewhere in cabaret Germany's popular film music. Leading Metropol artistes have also contributed much over the years to east German radio and TV.

One of these, soprano Maria Alexander, has recorded since the 1960s a large repertoire, from Mozart to musicals. She enabled me to see her collection of archive material, and gave a valuable insight into some of the productions, such as her singing Cecily (1974) in the East German musical based on Oscar Wilde's *Importance of being Earnest*.

I became aware of my ignorance, and in the West generally, about very interesting developments over many years in eastern Europe's music theatre. Surely a version of a great English comedy in German should have been reported at home, with enquiries as to whether it would have merited a production in translation.

A Berliner remembered with great pleasure, when a schoolgirl, that musical in its original production. She had kept a recording of excerpts, 40 minutes in all, and loaned it for me to bring back to London. The music by Gerd Natchinski is witty and distinctive, one generation on from the *Three-penny Opera*, and in a mocking spirit. It was spiced with rhythms, such as the Black Bottom and Charleston, from the 1920s in which this German version of the play was set.

Embellishments of the original story were to compensate for loss of dialogue but otherwise add to the fun. Finding a socially acceptable excuse for philandering was no longer to be exclusive to two male characters. Girls should be allowed similar pretexts, hence the broader significance of the title, *Mein Freund Bunbury*.

The not-too-young Mr Worthing had acquired £12,000, of course by dubious means, deposited in the Bank of England. Lady Bracknell is duly impressed, though not with all aspects of Mr Worthing's strategy:

'On Mondays, Wednesdays and Fridays I am Jeremias.
On Tuesdays, Thursdays and Saturdays, I am John.
On Sundays, John Jeremias Bunbury.'

Bunburyist Cecily gives herself a laudible alibi by attending the Salvation Army, where we hear an appropriate chorale; but it is a cover for lewd (?) dancing in a night club where *Horror and Sex* is the latest 'hit' and *Piccadilly* a chorus worthy of a dance routine. *Sunshine Girl* has an agreeable Caribbean flavour, and one couple seem to be contemplating tangoing round the world. A welcome change from American localities.

*Bunbury's* potential has been recognised in the decision to schedule its return to the Metropol probably in 1995. It has a satirical bite which has been lacking in the kind of musicals seen recently on the London stage, and as an adaptation of one of the wittiest of all English plays, it would create much interest in London.

The Metropol company have produced most of the finest operettas composed over more than a century. Subject to permission over copyright, without prohibitive charges, musically interesting modern works also have their place. Authentic German versions of *Funny Girl*, *West Side Story*, and *My Fair Lady* have been critically acclaimed. The musical *Sugar*, based on the American film, *Some like it hot*, had been in the repertoire for years, but was recently replaced by the *Wizard of Oz*. This marked a return to one of their specialities, children's musicals, in an exciting new decor but not far from the spirit of the classic American film.

In England, we may recall two songs which were well-known out of their context. *O, my Papa* came from the show, *Fireworks*, and *I'm only a wandering vagabond* from *The Cousin who appeared from nowhere*. Both musicals with strong period appeal have been given stylish productions in recent years.

New initiatives were encouraged between the 1950s and 1980s, with premieres in a wide variety of styles. These included a *Bolero* on a theme of revolution composed by Spanish war veteran, Eberhardt Schmidt, a *Casanova*, an Indian epic and musicals from Russia and Rumania. There was cross-fertilisation with eastern Europe's musical heritage and operetta theatres, events of which we in western Europe heard nothing.

Until 1989, the Metropol company had been able to draw on Berlin's tradition of sophisticated musical theatre, and the talents of the whole of the German Democratic Republic. Following the political change-over, poverty seriously affected theatre attendances, but the Metropol was one of the first to recover, especially as West Berlin had no comparable ensemble. Its policy in face of uncertainties concerning financing and the future was to maintain its high standards and total artistic integrity in a new, commercialised environment. Its new owner is the democratic Berlin Senate which has taken note of the Metropol's unique function and continued support where some other large theatres have come under financial threat.

Specialist operetta-musical theatres flourished in Dresden and Leipzig under the communist system, as well as in Russia, the Ukraine, Poland and Hungary, to mention just those countries further east whose theatres I have visited. A Munich theatre critic recently deplored the lack of comparable specialist institutions in the whole of west or southern Germany: one might add, the whole of western Europe. It must be said, though, that scores of west German towns have retained their professional music theatres, combining opera and operetta in one building.

The desirability of music repertory ensembles, to complement those devoted to opera, is appreciated in enlightened western European circles, but no-one can be sure where the necessary subsidies would come from. One important movement in that direction has been in England where the National Theatre has produced several 20th century musicals very successfully. In these ventures, commercial interests may therefore hold back until the box office performance is demonstrated.

Sadly, it is only government or communal enterprise which could have the foresight and the will to give a needed stimulus to the theatre of quality. If this seems to echo Bernard Shaw's comments a century ago, the difference is that the commercial theatre now experiences serious decline.

Yet there is an extraneous factor which causes anxiety about the Metropol's future or at least its future location. By the accident of history, the theatre is now sitting on a gold-mine, the development area immediately east of the old Berlin Wall. The real estate value of central East Berlin is colossal, and powerful financiers are considering every ingenious device to get their hands on the treasure. From 1990 onwards, there was

Dream and Reality. 1910 poster, and the Metropol bombed-out to a cinema in the Soviet sector (1945-55).

*Metropol*
TOP: *Beggar Student*: a Polish Trio
BOTTOM: *Orpheus in the Underworld*: Hell is boring company.

no shortage of proposals for changes affecting the Metropol, and fortunately, the Senate has treated these with scepticism; but there is a lingering fear that money interests will persist until they get the political decisions they want.

*Madame Favart*: Treachery accuses Innocence.

# 26　*Shakespeare as Melodrama*

The term melodrama has come to be associated with crudely-peformed, excessively sentimental plays often dating from the popular 'Victorian' theatre. Yet its pure meaning relates to what was a very desirable form of play-with-song and orchestral accompaniment. In recent times, this conception has become much too costly to be widely used, though it should work very well, such as when being adapted by the BBC for radio.

Examples have been briefly mentioned in this book, works from Beethoven to Grieg and Delius, but a perhaps unique opportunity occurred in London (1994) to assess the original effectiveness of a distinguished composition in its dramatic setting. Sibelius had prepared the incidental music to Shakespeare's *Tempest* for a Copenhagen theatre in 1926, but it has since been heard only in orchestral suites or isolated excerpts. This London concert performance was therefore an historic music event, given with the assistance of the Gothenburg orchestra, a chamber choir and an impressive array of singers and actors.

Of the better-known excerpts, the opening description of a storm, fragments of elemental sound, an orchestral *tour de force* using whole-tone scales and without any developments, is as impressive as one might hope from the man who had just composed *Tapiola*. Of the character pieces, *Prospero* suggests a dignified, enlightened despot, but the portrait of a *Miranda* some way from maturing to womanhood has always been considered by the critics as insipid music, though it has a soft, yielding quality which fits well immediately after the scene in which she proposes marriage to Ferdinand. For that idyllic love, Sibelius employs early 18th century pastiche in the *Entr'acte*, and much later in the *Dance of the Naiads*, more solemn than a Haydn minuet. The *Berceuse*, familiar in an orchestral suite, is just recognisable in the arrangement for harmonium and harp with which Miranda is lulled to sleep. The *Humoresque* is associated with those feckless brothers,

Stephano and Trinculo, a dance which might mock a folksy style but would not be too strenuous for those inebriates, though appropriately it meets-up with some chastening chords.

Except for a gentle *Intermezzo* accompanying Alonso's grief when he believes that his son Ferdinand has been drowned, Prospero's enemies from Milan are given no music. The opposition are rendered harmless by the spirit Ariel to an accompaniment of the exotic *Dance of the Shapes*. The three remaining malcontents are well-served with music as, fired only by Dutch courage, they sing a merry-go-round three-some, a *Canon*, which takes on a more gleeful spirit than their characters suggest. Stephano has a four-square sailors' song whilst the freakish Caliban dances to a thumping melody of savage tones, in an elusive key.

Sibelius was clearly attracted to this play by the prospect of invoking the subterranean forces at the command of Prospero. Two disparate circumstances are curiously linked when Ariel plays the Milanese visitors to sleep on the flute whilst his own recollections of suffering are sketched in the tortured harmonies of the *Oak Tree* movement. The *Chorus of the Winds*, seemingly benign at first with its harp sounds, merges into a serene wood-wind passage which has introduced the noble Ferdinand, until there is a sudden darkening of mood when Ariel proceeds to discharge his punitive duties and conjures-up sinister images. Ariel's songs are constrained by other spirits until he is finally granted freedom when he breaks loose in the fourth one, *Where the bee sucks*, with a tempo favoured by Sibelius, the bolero. In the other fine solo aria, we just have time to savour Juno's seductive but fleeting song, closer to the world of Romantic opera.

The impassioned string writing of Sibelius' much-discussed *Andante Festivo* (1922) is echoed in the *Epilogue* (*largo*) when Prospero breaks his magic staff and goes into contemplative retirement. This is preceded by the final march which has some of the panache and phrasing of the better-known *Cortège* in Rimsky-Korsakov's *Golden Cockerel*.

There are of course several passages best heard in, or only in their stage context, including the *Rainbow*, with its threatening atmosphere, the thoroughly bucolic *Harvesters*, a setting-loose of guard dogs, and the sharp orchestral phrases depicting

Ariel's instant transferences. The spoken text lasts fewer than 15 minutes, giving a useful sketch of the plot.

As a by-product of the work which went into this partial reconstruction, a commercial recording was effected, but despite the voices and harmonium, many enthusiasts may prefer the orchestral suites, with their astonishing use of the less familiar instruments, giving the work a powerful symphonic feeling.

Considering the quality of the descriptive skills that Sibelius put into this final stage work, one wonders what he might have been capable of creating in this vein during his seemingly inactive period of the 1930s. What could he have made of the supernatural within the Faust-Mephistopheles relation, or of *King Lear*'s scene on the heath for which Verdi, after much deliberation, had decided against composing from fear of his own sanity?

# *Appendix*

A pianoforte has 51 notes, in the proportion of seven white to five black. Playing all the notes from left to right in succession runs through the chromatic scale in ascending levels of pitch, one semitone distance between each sound. If they are struck equally, no note sounds more important than any other.

Each black note is spaced between two white ones. If we play all the white notes in ascending order, one note is more prominent, having a kind of gravitational pull in relation to the others, and is called the key-note. The one in the centre of the key-board is called the middle C, the next to the right, D, then E, F, G, A, B and C (an octave higher than middle C). Played in sequence, they form the diatonic scale of C major. The most remarkable aspect of this relates to their pitch frequencies:

C,260 D,292½ E,325 F,357½ G,390 A,433 B,487½ C,520
(These figures which are averages vary proportionally with atmospheric conditions and are therefore not often stated in textbooks.)

We tend to regard the two Cs as the 'same note' played at one octave distance; the one frequency must be double the other. G one octave higher has a frequency of 780. Middle G has a close arithmetical relation to the Cs above and below, 2:3:4, and C, E, G, C have the proportions of 4:5:6:8.

In that scale, G also exercises a pull on nearby notes, less than C's but sufficient for it to be called the dominant note in the key of C; and E has a lesser pull on D and F. It is logical that when C, E, G, C are played simultaneously (a so-called common chord), they sound perfectly harmonious, concordant. C, E, G form a major triad; because there is a black note between each of them, they are separated by two semitones (one whole tone). Their affinity is such that playing them without other notes intervening, as in the phrase *Blue Danube so blue* inevitably sounds cheerful.

In relation to melody-making in the Romantic period, a chromatic movement (eg between adjacent notes not in the same key) was to be increasingly common, and Liszt experimented with chromatic scales, which have no 'gravitational pull', which we precisely call tonality, or sense of key. To use a note outside the key is to make the tonality uncertain, even if only for a moment; to use several of these notes in melody could destroy any sense of key or tonality. A chromatic chord in isolation can be very emotive.

In the key of C major, we assume that a 'closed' melody is an enjoyable sequence of notes completed on C, whereas if it ends on another note, it is called 'open'. The melodic progress along this intelligible sequence of notes may be compared to walking along a path. A, B, D or F are slight deviations, but using a black note is to leave the track, and creates a sense of uncertainty. Finally settling at a C or the major triad in C is a fulfilment, called in music a cadence.

Most of our listening is casual, not concentrated, so we often prefer melodies which remain assuringly on course. 'Light' music is a term often associated with melodies comfortably near the key-note, and easy to assimilate, and most from the time of Mozart to the Beatles have been. Melody which strays far or long from its key-note is said to be 'difficult' but if we have the concentration to follow it along strange paths, that may also be rewarding.

Only in relation to C major, all the black notes are called accidentals. They are not situated between B and C or E and F; the one between D and E is called a sharpened D or a flattened E, D sharp or E flat. And similarly, for the other black notes. If an accidental is introduced into a melody in any key, it may be as a move towards another key.

Each of the 12 differently named notes has its own diatonic scale, with the same arithmetic relationship between notes. Since G is the dominant in the key of C, its key has the same notes except that the seventh one, F, has to be sharpened. Since D is the dominant one in the key of G, its key has the same notes except that its seventh one, C, has to be sharpened. And so forth.

In the key of G, the common chord of G, B, D, G (played simultaneously) has frequencies of 360, 450, 540, 720, proportionally 4, 5, 6, 8. And likewise for other keys.

Harmony is the playing of different notes together, and the more remote the arithmetic relation of frequencies, the more discordant a combination of two notes would be, such as C and D, or moreso, C and C sharp.

B and F are specially remote, arithmetically and in sound. A melodic movement from B to F or F to B is a space of three tones, a tritone, which was banned by the Church for centuries as the 'Devil's interval' (*diabolus in musica*). Exceptionally few tunes make that movement and its anguished feeling can be heard in the leap of 'Maria' in Bernstein's song of that title. Liszt used the interval in his *Dante Sonata* repeatedly to illustrate Hell, and Sibelius for other purposes in his 4th Symphony.

Key changes (modulations) between closely related keys were favoured in the classical period, such as C to G or G to D, but the Romantics began to make bigger tonal leaps in order to heighten the dramatic and emotive effects.

The diatonic minor scales all have their third note (the mediant) flattened, so, in the key of C, the minor triad consists of C, E flat and G. In the key of A, the minor triad is therefore A, C, E, so that A minor is related closely to C major. That modulation was therefore commonly used.

The effect of moving from minor to major key can be specially uplifting, and symphonies did that frequently for a triumphant conclusion. Classical music (eg Haydn's) is mainly in the major, but the Romantics tended to use the minor keys increasingly, especially to express the sadder emotions. Yet there is no uniformity about this; composers such as Prokofief and Gershwin could employ the minor keys in a humorous, joyful or stimulating manner.

# Notes

## 1. Classical and Romantic Composers

1. See Appendix.

## 2. The Nature of Romantic Melody

1. See Appendix.
2. Modes and other key systems:

    Using only the piano's white keys, if one composes a melody with D, E, F, or G as the key-note, the effect will be unfamiliar, and these four keys, and others, are called modes. (One based on A is close to A minor.)

    These modal scales had been discarded in sophisticated European composition, but are very important in folk music or in some non-European civilisations. They were common in Church music to the 17th century, some sounding very austere, therefore suitable for worship. The diatonic major, essentially European, was becoming popular but the Church at first thought it too light and wordly. By the classical period, it was dominating.

    In the 20th century there has been more experimenting with the modal systems. Much English folk music was centred on D, the so-called Dorian mode (named after the Greek system), which was often used by Vaughan Williams and others.

    Medieval music typically consists of simple modal melody, one note played at a time (monody), such as in plain-song. By the 16th century, two or more melodies could be played simultaneously, leading to the great age of polyphony in the work of Palestrina and others. A familiar example is the canon where one melody is sung by groups starting-off at different times.

    Gradually, single melody supported by chords, that is, HARMONY, rose to ascendancy. It has been a unique feature of European civilisation which it has served to the greatest effect, and as a feature of our musical language is widely admired now by non-European societies.

It is a big irony that much popular European music produced today lacks the emotive effects of rich harmonies, and has subordinated melody to rhythm, to which it often denies the immense advantages of change and acceleration.

Chromatic scales have come into prominence during the 20th century. The whole-tone scale divides the octave among six equi-distant notes. It also sounds and feels remarkably different from the diatonic scales, and its greatest exponent has been Claude Debussy, such as in his opera, *Pelléas & Mélisande*.

One of the pentatonic scales is located purely on the five black notes of the piano. It therefore has two 'leaps' of three semitones, and is often used to suggest 'Chinese' melody. The words *I've got rhythm* (Gershwin) use four of these in rising sequence. The *Promenade* theme in Mussorgsky's *Pictures at an Exhibition* employs all five.

## 3. G.B. Shaw as London Music Critic

1. *Leitmotive* is German plural for *Leitmotiv*, in English, 'motif(s)'. This is a theme representing a person, locality, object or concept, which Wagner often wove into the orchestral text. Berlioz had even earlier employed *une idée fixe*, such as representing the 'loved one' in the *Symphonie fantastique* (1830).
2. Shaw often writes of the *life force*, the irresistible urge for creativity in its many forms.
3. A chord of the 9th, 11th or 13th, for example in the key of C, would include respectively the D, F or A from the octave above.
4. *Rataplan* imitates a drum beat, and was therefore related to recruiting songs, as in Verdi's *Forza del Destino* and many other operas and operettas.
5. *Mignon* has a fine overture, using a compelling *mazurka* rhythm from the opera's well-known coloratura aria. In *Hamlet*, Ophelia's 'mad scene' starts with an elegant instrumental phrase which I would have taken for Liszt. The

second part of her song uses the beatiful Swedish folk-song, *Neckanspolska*; from Elsinore Castle, the Swedish coastline should be visible.

## 4. A Dissenting Critic

1. For example, Brahms thought in purely musical terms; to alter the orchestration of his symphonies would be unthinkable. Yet no-one was more conscious of the 'philosophical' nature of such compositions, a matter of *life and death* compared with the days of Haydn when composing was fun, *a joke*.

## 7. 1866 And All That

1. Offenbach's *Vie Parisienne* had the theme of rich foreign visitors, including a most flamboyant Brazilian dancing-away a fortune, and being exploited by younger Parisians living on their wits.
2. For the B.B.C.'s admirable 1968 adaptation of *Nana*, the music for two of Schneider's characterisations would have been most suitable, and the martial *Grand Duchess* won out over the sensuous *Belle Hélène*; Nana did plan her seductions with military precision and enjoyed applying disciplinary measures to her men.
3. There was an excess of royal blood in Germany. At that time, it was fashionable for German princes to be proposed for foreign monarchies. This prince came from a devout Catholic branch of the Hohenzollern family and for this reason might have been quite acceptable. According to historian A.J.P. Tayor, Bismarck could not be accused of provocation.

## 8. The Appeal of Viennese Operetta

1. Jeanne Dubarry follows her heart in the operetta, and references to her being guillotined after 1789 for squandering the nation's wealth would not be appropriate.
2. *I give my heart* was the title of a British film with Evelyn Laye singing.

## 9. A Man of Many Parts

1. By 1893, the activities of 'ladies of the night' in the foyer and promenade at the Empire had reached the point where legislation against the theatre was under consideration. Winston Churchill wrote to the 'Westminster Gazette' in favour of 'freedom', then in his own words led a 'riot' at the Empire on the evening of 3 November with other Sandhurst cadets.
2. A 1994 Berlin production of Offenbach's 'medieval' farce, *Croquefer* (in German, *Ritter Eisenfrass*), revives the tradition. A dumb, one-armed, one-eyed, stiff-legged warrior named *Strike 'em dead* stumbles around the auditorium carrying a high signal-box on his back, pulling strings for sign-posts to pop-up with 'relevant' messages. The sight of his long-lost daughter of course brings back his singing voice. See also chapter 24, note 1.
3. Film versions of *Mlle Nitouche* were made with Raimu and Fernandel.

## 10. A Parisian Comedy

1. Italian Francesco Cilea's opera, *Adriana Lecouvreur* (1902), followed this version and gave the heroine much warmly lyrical music.
2. Refer also to chapter 7. As the trend-setter for Parisian 'spectaculars' over three decades, Meyerbeer's operatic style rarely escaped parody in Offenbach's large works, or even in slighter ones such as *Croquefer*. The genial Meyerbeer is said always to have attended and enjoyed these jokes, habitually on the night after an Offenbach premiere.

## 12. After 'Carmen': Massenet & Chabrier

1. To appreciate common attitudes towards Berlioz in his lifetime, listen to the elongated or continuous melodies, the anguished harmonies, the wood-wind colouring in various passages of his masterpiece, *Les nuit's d'été* (Summer nights), in a version for female voice and orchestra. Then contrast

with a sparkling, extrovert overture by Hérold, such as the well-known *Zampa*, or by Auber.

2. It reached London in 1904 under the title *Salome*, and was located in Ethiopia to satisfy the censor's wish that the story should be distanced from its Biblical association. The appearance of Richard Strauss' *Salome*, based on Oscar Wilde's lurid play, one year later was pure coincidence, and the contrasts in treatment of the plot are striking. Where Wilde's Salome reacts to John the Baptist's rejection of her sexual advances by willing his death, Massenet's Salome destroys herself for love when her mother Hérodiade has him killed.

3. The other well-known (successful) seductresses in Romantic opera are Dalilah and Carmen. None from Italy? What does that suggest?

4. Manon's opening theme in the finale is remarkably like the popular slow waltz, *Fascination*. The only surprising fact is that the perpetrator remained undiscovered for decades: Ravel, under a pseudonym.

5. Massenet was inspired to compose *Thais* by the allegedly beautiful American singer, Sybil Sanderson, who died tragically in 1903. Scot Mary Garden performed the role over 22 years, and her acting ability can be seen in a silent film version.

6. Athanael's motif can be detected in the first five notes of the popular chanson, *La vie en rose*.

7. The writer has seen 8 Massenet operas in London in recent years, and concert performances of 3 others, including the British premiere of *Ariane* by the London-based Massenet Society.

8. See chapter 3, note 3.

9. Opera North have current productions of *L'Etoile* and *Le roi malgré lui*, and Chabrier was well represented at the 1994 Edinburgh Festival for the centenary of his death.


## 13. National Music

1. For his opera *Turandot*, Weber composed a 'Chinese' theme, using a pentatonic scale. It intrigued Paul Hindemith, who selected it, altering one note to make it more

spicy, for his *Symphonic Metamorphosis on Themes by Weber*, a work that is a humorous fusion of Romantic melody and modern orchestral sounds.

2. A performance by Leopold Stokowski is among several compelling ones which have been retained on disc as classics.

3. Smetana composed some *Czech Dances*, but they are scarcely performed in Britain. He preceded Dvorak, and his 'folk' dances in the *Bartered Bride* are famous, whilst the national element is important in his symphonic poems and some operas.

4. His *Second Rhapsody* consists of mainly student tunes written for the University of Uppsala, an interesting parallel with Brahms' *Academic Festival Overture* written for Breslau University.

5. A Hungarian nursery tune sounding like *Twinkle, twinkle, little star* (rather than *Baa, baa, blacksheep*) was used in a set of variations which serve as a very entertaining commentary on Romantic piano concertos, especially on the style of Liszt and Brahms. The composer, Erno Dohnanyi.

## 14. Before the American Invasion

1. See also the opening references in the chapter on *Kismet*.

2. The Players theatre club, recently housed in a modern building under London's Charing Cross station, offers all the year round professional entertainment. This is based on the Victorian music hall, its songs, costumes, staging and other traditions including masters of ceremony and reparti, with impromptu comments from the well-primed club members in the audience, at least 20 separate shows each year, and a Xmas pantomime. The year is assumed to be 1899, and Queen Victoria is always toasted. In the intervals, popular music of the period is played in warm, orchestral versions, always including J. Strauss' *Souvenirs of Covent Garden*.

3. One of its bars contains an interesting display of theatre posters from the opening years until the 1920s. The theatre has been the home of opera, now the E.N.O., since 1968, eventually thereby fulfilling its destiny.

4. Many of these songs are still kept alive at week-end 'barn dances'. These perform the formation dance, so named, a 32-bar routine which can therefore take-in most popular songs but concentrates on those loved from the late 19th and early 20th centuries. The barn dance has completed a century of popularity, now mainly for family groups.

5. *Chu Chin Chow* was made into a black-and-white Hollywood musical of the early 1930s, not the best way to be handed down to posterity. The film had two interesting links with stage history, George Robey playing Ali Baba, along with famous German actor, Fritz Kortner, as Abu Hassan.

6. The original 1917 recording by the Daly's theatre company and orchestra was transferred to an L.P.

7. In piano rag-time, the left hand constantly repeats a steady beat whilst the right hand plays strongly syncopated rhythm (placing the stress in the 'wrong' time.) So syncopation became associated with jazz, though composers such as Beethoven used it very extensively.

8. Milhaud celebrated it with a fine balletic composition, *La création du monde*, a companion-piece to *Boeuf sur le toit* (Ox on the roof), with its Brazilian dance rhythms.

## 16. Edward Elgar, Germany and the 1914–18 War

1. Strauss and Richter had urged Elgar to compose an opera, but only decades later in 1932 did he start work. His preference had been Ben Jonson's (1572–1637) *Devil is an Ass*, though impresario Barry Jackson had suggested the same man's *Silent Woman*, based around an elderly man's hatred of noise. Coincidentally, that work had been adapted by Stefan Zweig, then in February 1933, Elgar heard that Strauss had written *Die Schweigsame Frau*. Elgar pressed on with the *Devil*, giving it a Spanish flavour as *The Spanish Lady*, and substantial sections such as the final love duet and several dances, exist unorchestrated. Elgar had ambitious plans for it, a lengthy work, even an English *Meistersinger*. Jackson comments ('Music and Letters', Jan 1943) that if completed, it would have been among the half-dozen of the world's greatest comedy-operas.

In 1994, a version for an orchestra of no more than 25 players was prepared from the sketches by Elgar scholar, Percy Young, for a Cambridge production. An indication of Elgar's feeling for the stage are the large number of exquisite songs he wrote for *Starlight Express*. This was a play sympathetic to childhood aspirations, produced in 1915, and the music has greatly justified its being recorded some 60 years later. Imagine my pleasure when, sometime in the 1980s, I heard that *Starlight Express* was to appear again in London's West End, and my disappointment when I discovered the title was being used by Lloyd-Webber for a roller-skating spectacular.

2. 'For English ears, Elgar's music is much too emotional and not free from vulgarity . . . the orchestral works are . . . lively in colour, but pompous in style, and of a too deliberate nobility of expression.'

   These words were written by English music professor Edward Dent for an edition of Adler's 'Handbuch der Musikgeschichte'. They brought a furious protest given rapid press release in February 1931 and signed by numerous celebrities including William Walton and John Ireland.

3. See chapter 4, note 1.

4. As a result, many of these interpretations have been transferred to modern recordings. His least-known *Pomp and Circumstance March*, number 5, is played very fast and business-like, as if by an impatient father. It could serve as the ceremonial march of a light infantry regiment.

## 17. The English Music Renaissance

1. Decades later, television might have been the ideal medium for this work.

2. The aristocratic Arthur Bliss once attended a Moscow music festival in the company of the Soviet leadership. On his return, he praised them for their interest and made uncomplimentary remarks about the negative attitude of members of the British government. That was on television at the height of the *cold war*.

## 18. Ralph Vaughan Williams as Writer on Music

1. The main theme has no special distinction, and is quickly embellished. The work's decorative features would not have appealed to R.V.W. Beethoven dedicated it to a lady, but it is a miniature among his sonatas.
2. The *Eroica* melody's first four notes are on the key-note and the dominant, most assertive, followed by a set of variations suggesting the character of the hero.

   The *Judex* is magnificent in its devotional context, but R.V.W. might have later reached a similar conclusion to Shaw's. (See chapter 3)
3. Both themes rise with deliberate stride and are immensely impressive. The *Ancient Romans* has a feeling of supernatural power, but the *Antartica*'s is entirely characteristic of R.V.W. It originated in a film sequence showing the wearisome march of explorers across a frozen landscape.
4. The comment was laconic, but in the 1920s, it might have seemed more controversial. Liszt's reputation as a showman has gradually subsided, but that was surely a significant part of what R.V.W. disliked in the man. On the other hand, respect for Brahms was implicit in his philosophy, and he did not feel the need to prove his greatness.

## 19. Bartok and Transylvania

1. Asymmetrical rhythms. Try dancing to some, preferably in the safety of your home.
2. The microcosm features importantly in Bartok's imagery.
3. Apart from the Shostakovitch send-up referred to in chapter 21, there is a broad melody from Budapest operetta, whilst the finale contains an obvious similarity to a popular dance number, *Tico-tico*. These themes presumably symbolise city life.

## 21. Russian Melody, Romanticism & Soviet Policy

1. Leon Bakst (1866–1924) was the first great set designer for the Ballets Russes, adding immense visual impact to a

sequence of world-famed productions. Themes included Cleopatra and Scheherazade whilst he favoured Greek classics: Daphnis & Cloe, Narcissus & Echo.

2. It found its way within a few years into a song for a Walt Disney film, *Snow White and the Seven Dwarfs*, rhythm unchanged, but some simplification of the melody.

3. The *Adagio* became the signature tune of BBC TV's *Onedin Line* serial. Less noticed but very affective, even subliminally so, was the wealth of incidental music used, especially during sea voyages and in moments of drama. It consisted of emotive passages composed by late-Romantics, Mahler, Sibelius, Respighi and several others after 1890 and mostly 20th century, decades after the action in the drama.

There were some intriguing aspects to this. The music was never allowed to become intrusive, so what proportion of viewers were conscious of its impact?

## 22. Finland and Sibelius

1. The Finns were so called by Latin writers who noted their migration to their present homelands, *Suomi*, in the first century A.D. Their language is of the Finno-Ugric linguistic group originating in the Urals area, and distantly related to *Magyar* (Hungarian). The Hungarians arrived in central Europe during the 9th century and are not related to the Huns.

2. Samuel Coleridge-Taylor (1875–1912) composed the cantata, *Hiawatha*.

3. 50 years too late. Friedrich Pacius, a Helsinki music professor born in Hamburg, composed the Finnish anthem, which was also used by the Estonians. *Finlandia* became the anthem of the provisional African state of Biafra during the Nigerian civil war.

4. In this direction, Sibelius' five Xmas songs (opus 1) are a curiosity and very appealing.

## 24. Berliners on the Moon

1. Established in 1988, they have among others, already adapted the *Beggar's Opera*: *Don Quixote on Amanthea* (to a

libretto by Charles Favart): Stravinsky's *Soldier's Tale*: the *Emperor of Atlantis* (music by concentration-camp victim, Victor Ullman): *In Taberna* (medieval songs): *The Proud City* (by Swedish folk-composer, Carl Bellman): *Hit Parade of 1912*: the *False Fifties* (a send-up of the Adenauer period): *Aurora* (music by E.T.A. Hoffman): two pastiches for the Mozart bicentenary, and Offenbach's *Ritter Eisenfrass*.

2. Classic F.M. Radio used an alternative title, the *Gavotte Pavlova*. In *Frau Luna*, it is an interpellation from Lincke's classical operetta, *Lysistrata* (1902). The two melodies were recorded by the Mills' Brothers around 1950, and one phrase found its way into a 'pop' success of 1975, the *Bohemian Rhapsody*. Several *Frau Luna* melodies added to the zany atmosphere as background music to the re-issued version of Charles Chaplin's short classic, *The Cure*.

3. In an earlier version, Frau Luna led Fritz into an enchanted garden, but if the music has a brief hint of Wagner, it is *Tannhäuser* rather than *Parsifal*.

4. The Kaiser had a withered arm, perhaps disastrously for the world, because his military posturing may have been a way of compensating.